OCS Study
MMS 2004-067

Sperm Whale Seismic Study in the Gulf of Mexico

Annual Report: Year 2

U.S. Department of the Interior
Minerals Management Service
Gulf of Mexico OCS Region

OCS Study
MMS 2004-067

Sperm Whale Seismic Study in the Gulf of Mexico

Annual Report: Year 2

Authors

Ann E. Jochens
Douglas C. Biggs

Prepared under MMS Contract
1435-01-02-CA-85186
by
Texas A&M University
Department of Oceanography
College Station, Texas 77843-3146

Published by

U.S. Department of the Interior
Minerals Management Service
Gulf of Mexico OCS Region

New Orleans
September 2004

DISCLAIMER

This report was prepared under contract between the Minerals Management Service (MMS) and the Texas A&M Research Foundation. This report has been technically reviewed by the MMS, and it has been approved for publication. Approval does not signify that the contents necessarily reflect the views and policies of the MMS, nor does mention of trade names or commercial products constitute endorsement or recommendation for use. It is, however, exempt from review and compliance with the MMS editorial standards.

REPORT AVAILABILITY

Extra copies of the report may be obtained from the Public Information Office (Mail Stop 5034) at the following address:

U.S. Department of the Interior
Minerals Management Service
Gulf of Mexico OCS Region
Public Information Office (MS 5034)
1201 Elmwood Park Boulevard
New Orleans, Louisiana 70123-2394

Telephone: (504) 736-2619 or
1-800-200-GULF

CITATION

Suggested citation:

ABOUT THE COVER

The cover art shows an example of different mark types that can be found on flukes of sperm whales. The unique characteristics of individual flukes, including overall shape and different mark types, allow the photographic identification of individual sperm whales. The degree of fluke marking on a sperm whale may vary between areas depending on factors such as predation levels. The presence or absence of two types of marks, holes and missing portions, as shown in the figure, can be used to investigate differences in markings between the regions such as the northern Gulf of Mexico, the Sea of Cortez, and the South East Pacific. [Photo taken by Nathalie Jaquet for SWSS]

ACKNOWLEDGMENTS

This report would not have been possible without the contributions of a large number of people. Each principal investigator (PI) of the Sperm Whale Seismic Study (SWSS) contributed ideas to and authorship of portions of the text, and many participated in the cruises and in data reduction and processing. The principal investigators, their affiliations, and their tasks are:

Ann E. Jochens	TAMU	Program Manager, Co-PI for habitat characterization
Douglas C. Biggs	TAMU	Project Scientist, PI for habitat characterization
Dan Engelhaupt	UDurham	PI for genetic analyses
Jonathan Gordon	Ecologic[1]	Co-PI for Photo-ID and mesoscale survey
Matthew K. Howard	TAMU	Data Manager
Nathalie Jaquet	TAMUG	Co-PI for Photo-ID and mesoscale survey
Mark Johnson	WHOI	Co-PI for D-tag/CEE study
Robert L. Leben	CU	Co-PI for habitat characterization
Bruce Mate	OSU	PI for S-tag whale tagging and tracking
Patrick Miller	WHOI[2]	Co-PI for D-tag/CEE study
Joel Ortega-Ortiz	OSU	Co-PI for S-tag study
Aaron Thode	SIO	PI for 3-D Passive Acoustic Tracking study
Peter Tyack	WHOI	PI for D-tag/CEE study
Bernd Würsig	TAMUG	Co-PI for Photo-ID and mesoscale survey

For habitat characterization, Steve DiMarco, Amanda Olson, and John Wormuth of TAMU contributed to the authorship of this report, as well as to processing/analysis of data sets. Leila Belabbassi assisted with preparation of the report. Natacha Aguilar de Soto, Matt Grund, Valeria Teloni, Maria Elena Quero, Amy Beier, and John Diebold (on the spar buoy) contributed to the authorship of the D-tag/controlled exposure experiment (CEE) data collection section. We appreciate the contributions of Dr. Chuanmin Hu, Executive Director of the Institute for Marine Remote Sensing at the College of Marine Science of the University of South Florida, for providing ocean color images and ideas.

To all who participated on the three SWSS cruises we extend our great appreciation for making the 2003 field program a great success. In particular, thanks to the whale survey and habitat characterization cruise science team: Ricardo Antunes (Whale Museum, Madeira, Portugal), Steve Berkowitz (Coastal Carolina University, South Carolina), Doug Biggs (TAMU College Station), Paul Clark (TAMU, College Station), Dan Engelhaupt (Durham University, UK), Mike Fredericks (TAMU, College Station), Jonathan Gordon (Ecologic Ltd., UK), Thomas Gordon (Vanishing Point, Plymouth, UK), Bill Green (TAMU, Galveston), Nathalie Jaquet (TAMU Galveston), Erin LaBrecque (New Hampshire), Jamie McKee (SAIC, Shalimar, FL), Sonia Mendes (Aberdeen University, UK), Andrey Mishonov (Moscow University for Geodesy & Cartography, RU), Simon Mustoe (Applied Ecology Solutions, Pty Ltd., Melbourne, AU), Amanda Olson (TAMU, College Station), Will Rayment (Otago University, Dunedin, NZ), Christoph Richter (Queens University, Kingston, ONT, Canada), Mark Tasker (Joint Nature Conservation Cttee, Aberdeen, UK), Sarah Tsoflias (MMS Environmental Sciences), Jonathan Vallarta (Heriot-Watt University, Edinburgh, UK), Eddie Webb (TAMU, College Station), Trudi Webster (New Zealand), R.J. Wilson (TAMU, College Station), and John Wormuth (TAMU College Station).

Thanks to the D-tag/CEE science team assembled by WHOI for D-tag/CEE work aboard R/V *Maurice Ewing*: Natacha Aguilar de Soto, Dee Allen, Amy Beier, Alessandro Bocconcelli, Irene

---

[1] also at the University of St. Andrews, UK
[2] presently at the University of St. Andrews, UK

Briga, Kara Buckstaff, Dan Engelhaupt (Durham Univ. UK), Matt Grund, Mark Johnson (WHOI), Patrick Miller (U. of St. Andrews), Anna Nousek, Michela Podesta, Todd Pusser, Maria Elena Quero, Sue Rocca, Kenneth Alex Shorter, Valeria Teloni, Suzanne Yin. Thanks also to the LDEO staff on the *Ewing:* Emily Chapp, John Diebold, Ethan Gold, and Chris Leidhold.

Thanks to the D-tag/CEE science team on the M/V *Kondor Explorer*: Craig Douglas (SEAMAP Inc.), Terry Ketler (IEN), Joal Newcomb (EARS buoy team, Naval Research Laboratory), Doug Nowacek (WHOI), Carol Roden (MMS New Orleans), Sandy Sawyer (Fairfield Industries), Jim Showalter (EARS buoy team, NRL), and Aaron Thode (SIO). Special thanks Terry Ketler (IEN) for braving life aboard both the *Ewing* and *Kondor* in the interests of making a video for MMS.

Thanks to the S-tag cruise science team: Trent Apple (Texas), Marty Bohn (TAMU GERG), Dan Engelhaupt (Durham University, UK), Willie Flemings (TAMU GERG), Bill Green (TAMU Galveston), Ladd Irvine (OSU Newport), Ann Jochens (TAMU College Station), Terry Ketler (IEN San Francisco), Anurag Kumar (OSU), Rhoni Lahn (OSU), Bill Lang (MMS New Orleans), Dan Lewer (OSU Newport), Bruce Mate (OSU Newport), Mary Lou Mate (OSU Newport), Bruce Miller (OSU), Elizabeth Mitchell (TAMU College Station), Tom Norris (SAIC), Laura Opsommer (OSU), Joel Ortega-Ortiz (OSU Newport), Alicia Salazar (TAMU College Station), Sarah Tsoflias (MMS New Orleans), Eddie Webb (TAMU College Station), Andrew Wigton (ExxonMobil), Elizabeth Zele (OSU), and Elizabeth Zúñiga (OSU Newport).

Without the hard work of the ships' masters and crew, the science teams would not have been able to complete their tasks successfully and safely. So we extend sincere thanks to Captain Dana O. Dyer III and the crew of the *R/V Gyre*, Captain James E. O'Loughlin and the crew of the *Ewing*, and to the Captain and crew of the *Kondor Explorer* for jobs well done. The dedicated shore-based efforts of Desmond Rolf, Sandy Green, and Bill Green of the *Gyre* TAMU Marine Operations went above and beyond the call of duty and contributed to the success of the study. We also thank Dr. Norman Guinasso and Mr. John Walpert of TAMU GERG for their assistance with preparing the 38-kHz ADCP, and Mr. Tomas Follett of OSU for facilitating delivery of S-tag whale location information to SWSS scientists during their cruises.

The use of a seismic source vessel, which was crucial for conducting the CEEs, would not have been possible without the contribution of the seismic source and vessel, *M/V Kondor Explorer* by the Industry Research Funders Coalition (IRFC), consisting of BP Corporation, ExxonMobil Exploration Company, Shell Exploration & Production Company, ConocoPhillips, Chevron-Texaco Exploration & Production Company, and the International Association of Geophysical Contractors (IAGC) on behalf of its members. SWSS scientists extend thanks to Chip Gill and Alastair Fenwick of IAGC, as well as all members of IRFC, for their enthusiastic work in support of SWSS. On behalf of IAGC, we would like to thank Finn Arne Aas of Seabird Management AS; Jeff Cleland, Phil Fontana, and Nicola Quinn of Veritas DGC; Robert Walker, Richard Jenkins, and Hans-Peter Waldner of Petroleum Geo-Services; Mark Baisa of Thales GeoSolutions, as well as their donation of the SkyFix DGPS; Ian Rogers of WesternGeco, as well as the loan of a Fast Rescue Craft for the cruise.

The enthusiastic and timely support of Dr. William Lang, the MMS Project Officer, is greatly appreciated, as is his participation on the S-tag cruise. We also greatly appreciate the cruise participation and thoughtful support of Sarah Tsoflias and Carol Roden of MMS. Thanks also to Dr. Robert Gisiner of ONR and Dr. Alexander Shor of NSF for their contributions, both in support of tag development and in supporting the use of the *R/V Ewing* in field year 2003.

Finally, any program as large and complex as this one needs the help of many in the administration of the project. We thank Stacie Arms of TAMUG, Carol Delancey of OSU, Tracie Robertson and Martha Tackett of TAMRF, and Mary Jane Tucci of WHOI for their many efforts in support of SWSS.

TABLE OF CONTENTS

PAGE

List of Figures ix

List of Tables xiii

Acronyms xv

1. Executive Summary 1
    1.1 Introduction 1
    1.2 Field Measurements 1
    1.3 Technical Summary 2

2. Introduction 3
    2.1 Program Participants 3
    2.2 Program Activities for Year 2 4
    2.3 Report Organization 5

3. Data Collection Cruises 7
    3.1 Whale Survey and Habitat Characterization Cruise 2003 7
    3.2 D-tag Cruise 2003 34
    3.3 S-tag Cruise 2003 55
    3.4 3-D Passive Acoustic Tracking During D-tag Cruise 2003 78

4. Technical Summary 85
    4.1 Status Report on Satellite-Monitored Radio Tag 85
    4.2 Molecular Ecology of Sperm Whales (*Physeter macrocephalus*) in the
         Northern Gulf of Mexico 86
    4.3 Studies Report on SWSS Records with the Digital Sound Recording Tag 87
    4.4 Sperm Whale Abundance, Habitat Use, and Aspects of Social Organization
         in the Northern Gulf of Mexico 90
    4.5 Tracking Sperm Whale (*Physeter macrocephalus*) Dive Profiles Using a
         Towed Passive Acoustic Array 104
    4.6 Habitat Characterization: Eddy Forced Variations in On-margin and Off-
         margin Summertime Circulation Along the 1000-m Isobath of the Northern
         Gulf of Mexico, 2002-2003 109
    4.7 Habitat Characterization: Upper-Ocean Current Observations During
         Summer: 2002 and 2003 Central Slopes of the Northern Gulf of Mexico 131
    4.8 Habitat Characterization: Midwater Trawling Program 133
    4.9 Habitat Characterization: 38-kHz ADCP Investigation of Deep Scattering
         Layers 135

5. Literature Cited 141

Appendix: D-tag/CEE Mitigation Protocol 145

LIST OF FIGURES

FIGURE | PAGE

3.1.1. Ship track for SWSS 2003 WSHC cruise aboard R/V *Gyre* 31 May – 20 June 2003.. 8

3.1.2. Locations of visual sightings of sperm whales on the SWSS 2003 WSHC cruise in May/June 2003 superimposed over the daytime cruise track 10

3.1.3. Locations of CTD and XBT stations on SWSS 2003 WSHC cruise.................... 15

3.1.4. Locations of chlorophyll samples on the SWSS 2003 WSHC cruise................. 15

3.1.5. Visual sightings of toothed whales and delphiniids on the SWSS 2003 WSHC cruise 22

3.1.6. Acoustic detections of sperm whales on SWSS 2003 WSHC cruise superimposed on the cruise track occupied while towing the hydrophone arrays 28

3.1.7. Locations of biopsy samples on SWSS 2003 WSHC cruise............................. 28

3.1.8. Locations of IKMT collections on SWSS 2003 WSHC cruise......................... 30

3.1.9. Histioteuthid squid and fang-tooth blackfish from IKMT collections near 94°W. 32

3.1.10. Plot of backscatter intensity from the 38 kHz ADCP.................................... 33

3.2.1. D-tag cruise track of R/V *Maurice Ewing* for SWSS 2003 and locations of XBT drops. 37

3.2.2. Locations of D-tag deployments and skin samples superimposed over the cruise track 44

3.2.3. Dimensions of the airgun array towed by the *Kondor*................................... 45

3.2.4. Source vessel *Kondor* in relation to the observation vessel *Ewing* while the *Kondor* airguns were active... 45

3.2.5 Track of the *Kondor* and spar buoy during the calibration run on 15 June 2003.. 54

3.3.1. Cruise track for SWSS 2003 S-tag cruise, R/V *Gyre* 03G07, conducted 26 June – 14 July 2003.. 57

3.3.2. Sea surface height fields for the period 26 June through 13 July 2003 during the SWSS 2003 S-tag cruise... 59

3.3.3. Locations of XBT and CTD stations, superimposed on the cruise track, taken during SWSS 2003 S-tag cruise 61

3.3.4. Potential temperature-salinity diagrams for the five CTD stations taken during the SWSS 2003 S-tag cruise... 62

3.3.5. Cruise track and locations of chlorophyll stations taken during the SWSS 2003 S-tag cruise 64

3.3.6. SWSS 2003 S-tag cruise track with the track during the visual survey effort superimposed.. 66

3.3.7. Cruise track line and locations of sightings of sperm whales recorded during the SWSS 2003 S-tag cruise... 67

3.3.8. Sightings of cetaceans, other than sperm whales, recorded during the SWSS 2003 S-tag cruise 69

3.3.9. Histogram of qualitative scores from acoustic listening periods....................... 72

3.3.10. Acoustic contacts during the SWSS 2003 S-tag cruise 73

3.3.11. Locations of the 15 successful tag attachments during the SWSS 2003 S-tag cruise 75

3.3.12. Locations of biopsy samples for whales tagged in 2003 and 2002 and of the sloughed skin sample 77

3.4.1. Example of autonomous flash-memory recorder deployed from *Kondor* and *Ewing* 79

3.4.2. Flash memory recorder and depth logger attached at the end of a 100-m polypro rope... 79

ix

LIST OF FIGURES
(continued)

FIGURE		PAGE
3.4.3.	Examples of data collected from autonomous recorder on June 18	82
3.4.4.	Plot of arrival angles detected on SEAMAP array, using elements 2 and 3 (11-m spacing), between 11:30 AM and midnight CDT on 18 June 2003	83
4.4.1.	The Gulf of Mexico with study area outlined	91
4.4.2.	Survey track lines designed using the Distance Program and realized track lines during SWSS 2003 WSHC cruise	92
4.4.3.	Number of sperm whales photo-identified each year; data set used for abundance estimates	94
4.4.4.	Mean resighting distances (in nm) for identified individuals over a time span up to 9 years	95
4.4.5.	Small-scale movements of groups of sperm whales in different areas of the northern Gulf of Mexico.	96
4.4.6.	Root-mean square displacements for 8 groups that were followed for 8 to 12 hours	97
4.4.7.	Estimated group sizes for groups that were followed >7 hours in June 2003	98
4.4.8.	Example of 2 mark types used to investigate differences in markings between regions	99
4.4.9.	Length distribution for groups of female and immature sperm whales in the northern Gulf of Mexico and in the Sea of Cortez	102
4.4.10.	Plot of photographic and acoustic body length measurements of Gulf of Mexico sperm whales	103
4.5.1.	Deployment geometry of towed passive acoustic range-depth tracking system	105
4.5.2.	A spectrogram display illustrating the measurements required for range-depth tracking	106
4.5.3.	Example of automated estimates of relative arrival times of the surface echoes relative to the direct paths and the relative arrival times of the sounds on two different hydrophones using data from 19 June 2003	107
4.5.4.	Example of range-depth tracking even in the presence of hydrophone clipping. .	108
4.6.1.	SSH field for 10 May 2002	110
4.6.2.	Comparison of SSH conditions along the northern margin of the Gulf of Mexico in May 2002 and May 2003	111
4.6.3.	Comparison of SSH conditions along the northern margin of the Gulf of Mexico in June 2002 and June 2003	112
4.6.4.	Comparison of monthly composite SeaWiFS imagery and SSH conditions for June 2002 and June 2003	113
4.6.5.	Chlorophyll fluorescence versus salinity for June 2002 S-tag cruise on *Gyre*.	114
4.6.6.	Comparison of monthly composite SeaWiFS imagery and SSH conditions for June 2002 and October 2002	115
4.6.7.	Comparison of monthly composite SeaWiFS imagery and SSH conditions for July 2002 and August 2002	116
4.6.8.	Chlorophyll fluorescence versus salinity for September 2002 D-tag cruise on *Gyre*	117
4.6.9.	SSH conditions in May 2003, showing separation of LC Eddy "Sargassum."	118
4.6.10.	SeaWiFS composite for 18-24 May 2003, confirming separation of LC Eddy "Sargassum."	119
4.6.11.	CTD profile from 11 June 2003 shows subsurface evidence for Subtropical Underwater	120

LIST OF FIGURES
(continued)

FIGURE		PAGE
4.6.12.	Relation of SSH to 15°C depths from XBT drops in early June 2003	121
4.6.13.	Relation of SSH to 15°C depths from XBT drops in mid-June 2003	122
4.6.14.	Synopsis of 15°C depths, determined during SWSS 2003 WSHC cruise on *Gyre*, plotted versus longitude	123
4.6.15.	Summary plot of location of XBT stations occupied by R/V *Gyre* and R/V *Ewing* in June and July 2003, superimposed on SSH conditions for mid-June 2003	124
4.6.16.	Sperm whale sightings superimposed on 15°C depth during SWSS 2003 WSHC cruise on *Gyre*	125
4.6.17.	At the northern edge of LCE "Sargassum," the SWSS 2003 WSHC cruise encountered a sharp surface front on 16 June 2003	126
4.6.18.	Chlorophyll fluorescence versus salinity on SWSS 2003 WSHC cruise on *Gyre*	127
4.6.19.	Chlorophyll fluorescence versus salinity on SWSS 2003 S-tag cruise on *Gyre*	128
4.6.20.	Relation of SSH to 15°C depths from XBT drops made on the July 2003 S-tag cruise on *Gyre*	129
4.6.21.	Comparison of monthly composite SeaWiFs imagery and SSH conditions for June 2003 and April 2003	130
4.7.1.	Sea surface height anomaly field for 11 June 2003 with currents at 41 m from the 38-kHz ADCP superimposed	132
4.8.1.	The relationship between meters of wire out and depth of the trawl for five tows representing different wind and current conditions	134
4.8.2.	The volume filtered in the targeted depth interval as a percentage of the total volume filtered for each trawl	135
4.9.1.	Relative backscatter counts shown for Gulf of Mexico slope region and for the deep basin region	137
4.9.2.	Relative backscatter counts recorded by the 38-kHz ADCP for the 100, 600, and 700 m depth bins for the SWSS 2003 WSHC cruise	138

LIST OF TABLES

TABLE		PAGE
3.0	Cruises Conducted in 2002 and 2003 for and Related to the Sperm Whale Seismic Study	7
3.1.1	Science Personnel for SWSS 2003 WSHC Cruise Aboard the R/V *Gyre*	9
3.1.2	Summary of CTD Stations on SWSS 2003 WSHC Cruise	12
3.1.3	Summary of XBT Stations on SWSS 2003 WSHC Cruise	12
3.1.4	Chlorophyll Stations on SWSS 2003 WSHC Cruise	16
3.1.5	Synopsis of Nautical Miles and Hours of Effort Status	20
3.1.6	Nautical Miles and Hours of Effort for Each Effort Status by Sea State	20
3.1.7	Locations of Sightings of Toothed Whales and Delphiniids on SWSS 2003 WSHC Cruise	21
3.1.8	Synopsis of Fluke-Out Sequences for Photo-ID	24
3.1.9	Tissue Collection/Genetic Typing Samples Collected During SWSS 2003 WSHC Cruise	29
3.1.10	Summary of IKMT and MOCNESS Tows Taken on SWSS 2003 WSHC Cruise	31
3.2.1	The SWSS 2003 D-tag Cruise: D-tag/CEE Science Team on R/V *Maurice Ewing*	35
3.2.2	The SWSS 2003 D-tag Cruise: LDEO Science Team on R/V *Maurice Ewing*	35
3.2.3	The SWSS 2003 D-tag Cruise: Multi-Purpose Science Team on *M/V Kondor Explorer*	36
3.2.4	Daily Summary of Tagging and CEE Activity During D-tag Cruise	38
3.2.5	Location, Date, Time, and Depth of the 15°C Isotherm at XBT Stations	41
3.2.6	Summary of D-tag Deployments for SWSS 2003	43
3.2.7	Summary of Visual Effort During SWSS 2003 D-tag Cruise	51
3.2.8	Tissue Collection/Genetic Typing Samples Collected During 2003 D-tag Fieldwork	52
3.3.1	Science Personnel for SWSS 2003 S-tag Cruise Aboard the R/V *Gyre*	56
3.3.2	Summary of Hydrographic Stations on SWSS 2003 S-tag Cruise	60
3.3.3	Chlorophyll Stations for the SWSS 2003 S-tag Cruise	62
3.3.4	Visual Survey Effort by Day on the SWSS 2003 S-tag Cruise	66
3.3.5	Sightings of Cetaceans Other Than Sperm Whales	67
3.3.6	Locations of Sightings of Cetaceans, Other Than Sperm Whales, Recorded During the SWSS 2003 S-tag Cruise	68
3.3.7	Locations of Deployments of Sperm Whale Tags During SWSS 2003 S-tag Cruise	74
3.3.8	Tissue Collection/Genetic Typing Samples Collected During the SWSS 2003 S-tag Cruise	76
4.4.1	Percentage of Individuals Having Holes and/or Missing Portions in Their Flukes	100
4.4.2	Proportion of 1st Year Calves and Large Mature Males in the Northern Gulf of Mexico Versus the Sea of Cortez	101
4.8.1	Results of Z Tests of All Combinations of Displacement Volumes (DV) for All Trawls	134
4.9.1	Occurrence of Scattering Below the Main DSL (> 650 m) Out of the Number of Possible Days in Water Less Than or Greater Than 1000 Meters for Each Cruise While Over the Slope and Deep Basin	136
4.9.2	Occurrence of Scattering Below the Main DSL (> 650 m) Out of the Number of Possible Days When in Cyclonic, Anticyclonic, Boundary, or No Feature in the Four Hydrographic Regions	138

ACRONYMS

ADCP	Acoustic Doppler current profiler
AGU	American Geophysical Union
AIM	Acoustic Integration Model
CCAR	Colorado Center for Astrodynamics Research, University of Colorado
CDT	Central Daylight Time
CEE	controlled exposure experiment
CHL	chlorophyll
CMS	Cetacean Monitoring System
CPA	closest point of approach
CTD	conductivity-temperature-depth sensor
CU	University of Colorado
DGPS	Differential Global Positioning System
DGoMB	Deepwater Gulf of Mexico Benthic Habitats Program
DNA	deoxyribose nucleic acid
DSL	Deep Scattering Layer
D-tag	Digital-recording acoustic tag (also DTAG)
DV	displacement volume
EARS	Environmental Acoustic Recording System
GERG	Geochemical and Environmental Research Group at TAMU
GIS	Geographical Information System
GPS	Global Positioning System
GulfCet	Gulf of Mexico Cetacean Study
IAGC	International Association of Geophysical Contractors
IEN	Interactive Educational Network
IFAW	International Fund for Animal Welfare
IKMT	Isaacs-Kidd Midwater Trawl
IMaRS	Institute for Marine Remote Sensing
IPI	inter pulse interval
IRFC	Industry Research Funders Coalition
ITM	Information Transfer Meeting
LC	Loop Current
LCE	Loop Current eddy
LDEO	Lamont Dougherty Earth Observatory
MCS	middle continental slope
MMS	Minerals Management Service, U.S. Department of the Interior
MOCNESS	Multiple Opening-Closing Net and Environmental Sampling System
MRC	Mississippi River Canyon
MRD	Mississippi River Delta
mtDNA	mitochondrial DNA
M/V	Marine Vessel
NASA	National Aeronautics and Space Administration
NATO	North Atlantic Treaty Organization
NMEA	National Marine Electronic Association, standard protocol for GPS receivers to transmit data
NMFS	National Marine Fisheries Service (now NOAA Fisheries)
NOAA	National Oceanic and Atmospheric Administration
NRL	Naval Research Laboratory
NSF	National Science Foundation
ONR	Office of Naval Research
OSU	Oregon State University

ACRONYMS
(continued)

Photo-ID	Photographic-Identification
PI	Principal Investigator
PMEL	Pacific Marine Environmental Laboratory
QA/QC	quality assurance/quality control
RHIB	Rigid-Hulled Inflatable Boat
RL	Received Level
R/V	research vessel
SAIC	Science Applications International Corporation
SeaWiFS	Sea-viewing Wide Field-of-view Sensor
SIO	Scripps Institution of Oceanography
SRB	Science Review Board
SSH	Sea surface height
S-tag	Satellite-tracked radio tag
SWAMP	Sperm Whale Acoustic Monitoring Program
SWSS	Sperm Whale Seismic Study
TAMU	Texas A&M University
TAMUG	Texas A&M University-Galveston
TAMRF	Texas A&M Research Foundation
TDTR	Time Depth and Temperature Recorder
UD	University of Durham, UK
USF	University of South Florida
UTC	Universal Coordinated Time
VHF	Very High Frequency
WHOI	Woods Hole Oceanographic Institution
WSE	Warm Slope Eddy
WSHC	Sperm Whale Survey and Habitat Characterization
XBT	expendable bathythermograph probe

1 EXECUTIVE SUMMARY

1.1   Introduction

This is the second annual report of the Sperm Whale Seismic Study (SWSS). SWSS is a multi-institutional, interdisciplinary study supported by the Minerals Management Service (MMS) of the U.S. Department of the Interior under Cooperative Agreement 1435-01-02-CA-85186 for *Cooperative Research on Sperm Whales and their Response to Seismic Exploration in the Gulf of Mexico* through the Texas A&M Research Foundation. Under SWSS, scientists from Ecologic, Oregon State University (OSU), Scripps Institution of Oceanography (SIO), Texas A&M University (TAMU), Texas A&M University-Galveston (TAMUG), University of Colorado (CU), University of Durham (UD), and Woods Hole Oceanographic Institution (WHOI) develop and implement scientific research plans in coordination with MMS, the Office of Naval Research (ONR), National Science Foundation (NSF), and Industry Research Funders Coalition (IRFC).

The principal study tasks and associated institutions are: Satellite-tracked radio tags (S-tags) by OSU; Digital-recording acoustic tags (D-tags) and Controlled Exposure Experiments (CEEs) by WHOI; Habitat characterization by TAMU; Photo-identification and mesoscale population studies by Ecologic and TAMUG; Biopsy/genetic analyses by UD; 3-D passive acoustic tracking by SIO; Program management by TAMU; and Data management by TAMU. Terry Ketler of Interactive Educational Network (IEN) is preparing video documentation of the SWSS field efforts during summer 2003. Additionally, a five-member Science Review Board (SRB) was established in year 2 to provide review and comments on the draft Synthesis Report. The program objectives and task goals are set out in the first annual report (Jochens and Biggs 2003).

1.2   Field Measurements

The 2003 field work consisted of two cruises in late May/early June 2003 and one cruise in June/July 2003. Remote sensing images of sea surface height, ocean color, and sea surface temperature were obtained before and during the cruises and provided to the interested scientists on the ships. All activities associated with sperm whales were conducted pursuant to approved permits from NOAA Fisheries (formerly the National Marine Fisheries Service or NMFS).

The D-tag/CEE cruise was conducted from the science vessel R/V *Maurice Ewing* working in coordination with the seismic source vessel M/V *Kondor Explorer*. The D-tag/CEE cruise on the *Ewing* departed Gulfport, MS, on 3 June and ended in Galveston, TX, on 24 June 2003. The main area for the study was around the 1000-m isobath between 91° and 87°W in the northern Gulf of Mexico. The *Kondor* rendezvoused with *Ewing* on 9 June and CEE work ended 22 June 2003. A stringent mitigation protocol was used to assure that no marine mammal or turtle would be exposed to sound levels about 180 dB re 1 µPa RMS. A total of 11 D-tags were deployed for 80.5 hours of on-animal data collection; seven of the tags provided sloughed skin samples for use in genetic analyses. Three CEEs were conducted with 2 tags out during one test and 1 tag out on two others. An additional CEE with tags on two sperm whales was begun but then curtailed during ramp-up due to mitigation. Both tags also detached shortly after the curtailment. Rough weather and scarcity of whales resulted in seven lost days for CEE work. Preliminary estimates of received levels during the CEEs ranged from 145-155 dB. Additionally, 376 hours of high-quality sperm whale recordings were collected, 4,430 fixes were made on 810 different surfacings of sperm whales, 13 high-quality photo-ID shots were taken, and 19 good-quality XBT profiles were collected. Additionally, experimental passive acoustic monitoring was conducted from *Ewing* and *Kondor*, video of the work efforts was taken, and, under a non-SWSS project, airgun calibration tests were performed using an EARS buoy.

1

Concurrently with the D-tag cruise, a sperm whale survey and habitat characterization (WSHC) cruise was conducted aboard the R/V *Gyre*. The WSHC cruise surveyed for sperm whales along the middle continental slope of the northern Gulf of Mexico between 94.75°W and 86.75°W in water depths ranging from 500 m to 1430 m. It departed Galveston, TX, on 30 May 2003 and returned on 21 June 2003. Over 360 hours of acoustical monitoring with tandem two-hydrophone arrays and over 200 hours of visual search with BigEye binoculars were completed. Photo-identification and photogrammetry, conducted from two rigid-hulled inflatable boats, resulted in collection of 152 photo-ID sequences, with 79 different sperm whale individuals identified, of which 57 were individuals not previously identified. Ten biopsy and three sloughed skin samples were collected for genetic analyses. Near-surface water was pumped from 3.5 m to log surface temperature, salinity, and fluorescence once per minute. Filtered water samples were analyzed for chlorophyll to calibrate the fluorescence data. Ocean current velocity in the upper 300 m and upper 900 m was monitored continuously with RD Instruments hull-mounted 153 kHz ADCP and 38 kHz ADCP, respectively. To profile temperature in the upper 760 m, 89 XBTs were dropped. Eight CTD casts were made to determine the temperature-salinity structure of the water. Nighttime activities on the cruise included midwater trawling and plankton sampling. Twenty-five oblique tows were made using an Isaacs-Kidd Midwater Trawl (IKMT) with mouth opening of 14.7 m^2. An 8-net collection with depth-stratified tows was made using a Multiple Opening-Closing Net and Environmental Sensing System (MOCNESS) with mouth opening of 1 m^2. The collections were rich in groups such as hatchet fishes, myctophids, viperfish, large decapod crustaceans, and euphausiids. Small-size individuals of cephalopods also were present.

The S-tag cruise conducted from 26 June through 14 July 2003 aboard the R/V *Gyre*. The cruise left Galveston, TX, but, due to Hurricane Claudette, ended earlier than planned in Pascagoula, MS. Field work consisted of tagging sperm whales with satellite-tracked radio tags, associated video work, photo-ID, and biopsy sampling. In addition to tagging activities, surveys for sperm whales were conducted using visual observations and passive acoustics. Samples were collected for habitat characterization. Videotape was taken for MMS use. Fifteen sperm whales were tagged with S-tags and 15 biopsy/skin samples were obtained. In water depths > ~700 m, the acoustic team monitored for vocalizing sperm whales for over 260 hours using tandem two-hydrophone arrays. Visual observers searched the sea surface with BigEye binoculars for over 130 hours during daylight to locate sperm whales that were at the surface. Additionally, 5 CTD stations were made, 48 XBTs provided profiles of temperature in the upper 760 m, and 75 samples were filtered and analyzed for chlorophyll content. Ocean current velocity in the upper 300 m and 900 m was monitored continuously with hull-mounted 153 kHz and 38 kHz ADCPs. Near-surface water from the ship's hull depth of 3.5 m was pumped continuously to log surface temperature, salinity, and chlorophyll fluorescence once per minute.

1.3   Technical Summary

On 19-21 November 2003, the SWSS Workshop and Planning Meeting was held at the Shell Westhollow Technology Center in Houston, TX. Attendees came from the scientific community (SWSS, EARS, AIM, airgun calibration, and other project scientists), the federal government (including MMS, NSF, ONR, and NOAA), the Marine Mammal Commission, the geophysical contractor and oil & gas industries, and the SWSS Science Review Board. Written summaries of the SWSS presentations are given in this report. These include the status of the S-tag and D-tag/CEE tasks; discussion of the molecular ecology of sperm whales in the northern Gulf of Mexico; preliminary results on sperm whale abundance, habitat use, and aspects of social organization in the northern Gulf of Mexico; summary on tracking sperm whale dive profiles using a towed passive acoustic array; and preliminary results on habitat characterization including descriptions of eddy forced variations in on-margin and off-margin summertime circulation along the 1000-m isobath of the northern Gulf of Mexico, upper-ocean current observations during summer over the central slopes of the northern Gulf of Mexico, the midwater trawling program, and 38-kHz ADCP investigation of deep scattering layers.

2 INTRODUCTION

The first annual report for the Sperm Whale Seismic Study (SWSS) detailed the program objectives, tasks, and participants, the data collection and processing for the S-tag and D-tag cruises in year 1, and the methods for data collection and quality assurance/quality control (QA/QC), as well as presenting preliminary technical discussions (Jochens and Biggs 2003). This report focuses on the data collection and analysis efforts during year 2 of the study.

2.1   Program Participants

SWSS is a multi-institutional, interdisciplinary study supported by the Minerals Management Service (MMS) of the U.S. Department of the Interior under Cooperative Agreement 1435-01-02-CA-85186 for *Cooperative Research on Sperm Whales and their Response to Seismic Exploration in the Gulf of Mexico*. Additional support for SWSS activities is provided by the Office of Naval Research (ONR), the National Science Foundation (NSF), and the Industry Research Funders Coalition (IRFC), which is a coalition of the International Association of Geophysical Contractors (IAGC) and five oil and gas exploration and production companies.

ONR supports tag development. NSF provided year 2 support through grant support to Lamont Dougherty Earth Observatory (LDEO) for use of the R/V *Maurice Ewing* in D-tag work for SWSS 2003. Coordinated efforts with LDEO to calibrate academic and industry air-gun arrays also were planned and conducted. For the 2003 field year, the IRFC contributed the seismic source vessel, M/V *Kondor Explorer*, and its crew used in the Controlled Exposure Experiments (CEEs) of the D-tag cruise. The seismic source vessel is a critical contribution to the D-tag effort because it allows controlled exposure experiments with sound from airguns. IRFC also provided support for calibration tests with *Kondor* airguns of the Environmental Acoustic Recording System (EARS) buoy that is part of a separate MMS-sponsored study.

The principal academic SWSS scientists conducting the study are

> Ecologic: Jonathan Gordon (also at the University of St. Andrews, UK)
> Oregon State University (OSU): Bruce Mate and Joel Ortega-Ortiz
> Scripps Institution of Oceanography (SIO): Aaron Thode
> Texas A&M University (TAMU): Ann Jochens (SWSS Program Manager), Douglas Biggs, Matthew Howard, and John Wormuth
> Texas A&M University-Galveston (TAMUG): Bernd Würsig and Nathalie Jaquet
> University of Colorado (CU): Robert Leben
> University of Durham (UD): Daniel Engelhaupt
> Woods Hole Oceanographic Institution (WHOI): Peter Tyack, Mark Johnson, and Patrick Miller (now at the University of St. Andrews, UK)

The principal study tasks and associated institutions are: Satellite-tracked radio tags (S-tags) by OSU; Digital-recording acoustic tags (D-tags) and CEEs by WHOI; Habitat characterization by TAMU; Photo-identification and mesoscale population studies by Ecologic and TAMUG; Biopsy/genetic analyses by UD; 3-D passive acoustic tracking by SIO; Program management by TAMU; and Data management by TAMU. All activities associated with marine mammals are conducted pursuant to approved permits from NOAA Fisheries. Additionally, Terry Ketler of Interactive Educational Network (IEN) is preparing video documentation of the SWSS field efforts during summer 2003.

A SWSS Science Review Board (SRB) was established to provide review and comments on the draft Synthesis Report. The SRB consists of one federal representative (Debra Palka, NOAA), one industry representative (Phil Fontana, Veritas DGC), and three scientific representatives

(Daniel Costa of the University of California-Santa Cruz, Robert Hofman retired from the Marine Mammal Commission, and Doug Wartzok of Florida International University).

2.2   Program Activities for Year 2

The field effort in year 2 consisted of three cruises between May and July 2003. The first two cruises were conducted concurrently in late May and early June. The D-tag/CEE cruise was conducted through the coordination of the work on the science vessel R/V *Ewing* and the seismic source vessel M/V *Kondor*. Concurrently, a sperm whale survey and habitat characterization (WSHC) cruise was conducted aboard the R/V *Gyre*. All three ships worked cooperatively to maximize the results obtained during this part of SWSS. The third cruise was the S-tag cruise in June and July 2003 aboard the R/V *Gyre*. In addition to the S-tag work, it included habitat characterization work. Section 3 discusses each of these three cruises and the data collected.

Two new work tasks were initiated in year 2. Aaron Thode of SIO participated on the D-tag/CEE cruise to conduct experiments on the 3-D passive acoustic tracking of sperm whales. Terry Ketler of IEN was contracted to prepare a short video documenting the year 2 field work effort. He participated in both the D-tag and S-tag cruises to conduct filming and interviews.

A number of presentations on SWSS results were made at scientific conferences and two publications were submitted to and accepted by scientific journals based in part or in whole on SWSS work. The publications were:

1.   "Swimming gaits, passive drag, and buoyancy of diving sperm whales (*Physeter macrocephalus*)" by Patrick J.O. Miller, Mark Johnson, Peter L. Tyack, and Eugene A. Terray, in the *Journal of Experimental Biology*, **207** (11): 1953-1967.

2.   "Tracking sperm whale (*Physeter macrocephalus*) dive profiles using a towed passive acoustic array" by Aaron Thode, in the *Journal of the Acoustical Society of America*, **116** (1), 245-253.

The SWSS-related presentations at science conferences were:

1.   Mate, B.R. Seasonal distribution and habitat characterization of sperm whales in the Gulf of Mexico from Argos satellite-monitored radio tracking. Invited presentation, XV Biennial Conference on the Biology of Marine Mammals, sponsored by The Society for Marine Mammalogy, 14-19 December 2003, Greensboro, NC.

2.   Biggs, D.C., M.K. Howard, A.E. Jochens, S.F. DiMarco, R.R. Leben, and C. Hu. Operational applications of satellite altimetry and ocean color to support studies of sperm whale habitat use in the Gulf of Mexico. AGU Ocean Ocean Sciences Meeting 2004, Portland, OR, Invited presentation, session OS12C (26 January 2004).

3.   Olson, A.M., D.C. Biggs, S.F. DiMarco, and J.H. Wormuth. 38 kHz ADCP investigation of Gulf of Mexico deep scattering layers. AGU Ocean Sciences Meeting 2004, Portland, OR, Poster presentation, session OS51E (30 January 2004).

Two other presentations at the AGU Ocean Sciences Meeting 2004 mentioned the SWSS project. Neither presentation keynoted SWSS data, although SWSS data from summers 2002 and 2003 were used along with other historical data to describe the currents and water properties (temperature, salinity, nutrients, oxygen) in the northern Gulf of Mexico. These were:

1.   DiMarco, S.F., A.E. Jochens, N.L. Guinasso, and M.K. Howard. Vertical current structure of the deepwater Gulf of Mexico from shipboard ADCP observations. Invited presentation, 27 January 2004.

2.   Jochens, A.E., M.K. Howard, and S.F. DiMarco. Recent observations of water properties in the Gulf of Mexico. Contributed presentation, 27 January 2004.

A number of SWSS presentations were made at the SWSS Workshop and Planning Meeting held 19-21 November 2003. Summaries of these talks are given in section 4.

2.3   Report Organization

This is the second annual report of SWSS. It reports on the data-gathering efforts; changes in equipment, measurement and analytical methodologies employed; and **preliminary** data analysis and results of the various data types collected. **There are no extensive analyses or syntheses of the information**; such will be provided in the final Synthesis Report at the conclusion of SWSS.

Section 1 of this report is the executive summary. Section 3 details the data acquisition of the tag measurements, visual and acoustic observations, genetic samples, and physical and biological oceanographic data. Section 4 presents brief technical discussions of the data, and, for D-tag, a discussion of changes in methodology for data collection. Other instrumentation and methods for data collection, QA/QC, and analysis were as reported in the first SWSS annual report (Jochens and Biggs 2003). All times are reported in Universal Coordinated Time (UTC) unless stated otherwise. References are provided in Section 5.

3 DATA COLLECTION CRUISES

Section 3 provides an overview of the SWSS data collection activities from April through October 2003. It describes data gathering efforts on the cruises. Information on instrumentation, data collection methods, and data processing procedures are described in Section 4 of Jochens and Biggs (2003) with augmentation given in the subsections below.

Table 3.0 lists the SWSS field cruises conducted from April 2002 through October 2003. Information on cruises in 2002 is reported in Jochens and Biggs (2003). Field cruises conducted in 2003 consisted of, concurrently, a Whale Survey and Habitat Characterization cruise (WSHC) on the R/V *Gyre* and a D-tag/CEE cruise aboard the R/V *Maurice Ewing* and M/V *Kondor Explorer*. These were followed by an S-tag/habitat characterization cruise on the R/V *Gyre*. Also shown in Table 3.0 is an associated cruise, conducted immediately before and after the D-tag/CEE cruise, to calibrate the airgun array from the EARS buoy. Data collection on each SWSS cruise is described below.

Table 3.0

Cruises Conducted in 2002 and 2003 for and Related to the Sperm Whale Seismic Study
(Additional cruises are planned for summer 2004.)

Year	Ship	Cruise	Start Date	End Date
2002	R/V *Gyre*	S-tag	20 June 2002	8 July 2002
2002	R/V *Gyre*	D-tag	19 August 2002	15 September 2002
2002	M/V *Rylan T*	CEE with *Gyre*	29 August 2003	12 September 2002
2003	R/V *Gyre*	Habitat survey	31 May 2002	21 June 2003
2003	R/V *Maurice Ewing*	D-tag	3 June 2003	24 June 2003
2003	M/V *Kondor Explorer*	CEE with *Ewing*	7 June 2003	22 June 2003
2003	M/V *Kondor Explorer*	EARS buoy*	22 June 2003	25 June 2003
2003	R/V *Gyre*	S-tag	26 June 2003	14 July 2003

* EARS is not part of SWSS, but is a sister program supported by MMS and IRFC

3.1 Whale Survey and Habitat Characterization Cruise 2003

The Whale Survey and Habitat Characterization (WSHC) cruise was conducted aboard the R/V *Gyre* (cruise 03G06) from 31 May through 21 June 2003. The cruise left Galveston, TX, late evening on 30 May and returned late evening on 21 June. Field work consisted of a survey for sperm whales along the middle continental slope (MCS) of the northern Gulf of Mexico between 94.75°W and 86.75°W (Figure 3.1.1). An integral part of the survey effort was to gather physical and biological oceanographic data for characterization of the oceanographic habitat in which whales were encountered. Doug Biggs of TAMU was the Field Party Chief and was in charge of the habitat characterization work. Jonathan Gordon of Ecologic and Nathalie Jaquet of TAMUG were in charge of the whale survey activities. Dan Engelhaupt of UD was responsible for collection of tissue samples. Table 3.1.1 lists the cruise participants and their roles. Additional

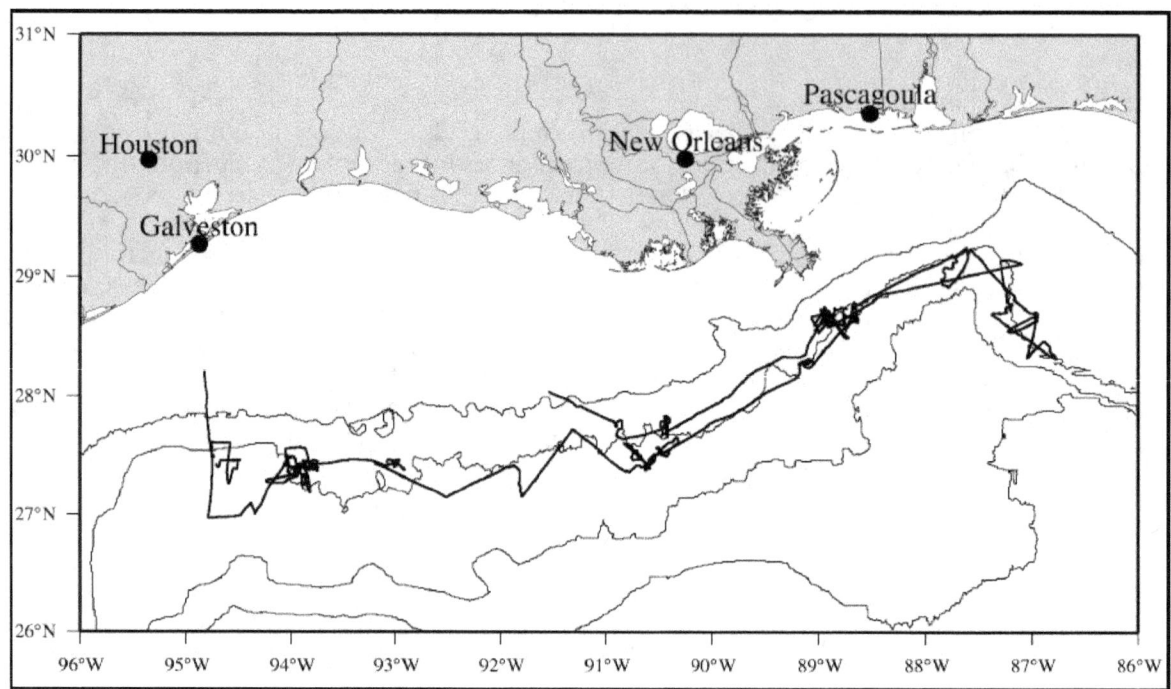

Figure 3.1.1. Ship track for SWSS 2003 WSHC cruise aboard R/V *Gyre* 31 May – 20 June 2003. Locations where sperm whales were followed are evidenced by looping track portions. Contours are shown for the 200, 1000, 2000, and 3000-m isobaths.

information associated with this cruise is in Sections 4.2 (genetic analyses), 4.4 (photo-identification analyses), and 4.6 through 4.9 (habitat characterization).

Previous sperm whale work focused mainly on known areas, such as the Mississippi Canyon and the deepwater region off the Mississippi River delta, frequented by sperm whales. Since the Mississippi Canyon was the focal area for CEE activities by the R/V *Ewing* and M/V *Kondor*, which were operating concurrently with R/V *Gyre*, the WSHC cruise spent little sampling time there. Rather the WSHC search effort was conducted along the upper slope of the Alaminos Canyon in the western Gulf and near deepwater production platforms Diana and Hoover, where sports fishermen had reported seeing sperm whales in summer 2002, as well as in the deepwater canyons close to the Mississippi River delta. The latter area was of special interest since in May 2003 four of the 18 sperm whales that were tagged in 2002 with satellite-monitored tags were transmitting back locations in that region. Updated location information on S-tagged whales was sent by OSU to *Gyre* every 4 days on WSHC. Several of these radio-tagged animals were observed during the three weeks of survey.

Because of good success in locating whales in water depths of 800-1000 m during the SWSS 2002 cruises, most of the visual and acoustic search effort this cruise was centered in the same range. However, water depths between 500 m and 1430 m also were searched.

Both acoustic and visual techniques were used to search for sperm whales as the cruise surveyed the MCS. Matched Ecologic tandem two-hydrophone arrays were towed, one off the port quarter and the other off the starboard quarter of the stern, for over 360 hours. BigEyes were generally

8

Table 3.1.1

Science Personnel for SWSS 2003 WSHC Cruise Aboard the R/V *Gyre*

Description	Personnel	Institution
Field Party Chief	Doug Biggs (Oceanography team leader)	TAMU
Acoustic Team	Ricardo Antunes (Team Leader)	Whale Museum, PT
	Sarah Tsoflias	MMS
	Sonia Mendez	Portugal
	Jon Vallarta	Mexico
Photography,	Nathalie Jaquet (Team Co-Leader)	TAMUG
Photogrammetry,	Jonathan Gordon (Team Co-Leader)	Ecologic Ltd., UK
and Small Boat	Will Rayment	Univ. Otago, NZ
Acoustics	Christoph Richter	Queens Univ., ONT
Visual Team	Erin LaBrecque (Team Leader)	TAMU
	Jamie McKee	SAIC, Shalimar, FL
	Mark Tasker	JNCC*, Aberdeen, UK
	Trudi Webster	New Zealand
	Simon Mustoe	AES*, Melbourne, AU
	Thom Gordon	United Kingdom
Trawling Team	John Wormuth (Team Leader)	TAMU
	Steve Berkowitz	CCU*, South Carolina
	Andrey Mishonov	MUGC*, RU
Biopsy	Dan Engelhaupt	Durham Univ., UK
Oceanography	Amanda Olson	TAMU
TAMU Technicians	Eddie Webb (Electronics Technician)	TAMU
	Paul Clark (Electronics Technician)	TAMU
	Bill Green (Deck Engineer)	TAMU
	Mike Fredericks (Deck Engineer)	TAMU

* JNCC = Joint Nature Conservation Committee; AES = Applied Ecology Solutions, Pty Ltd.;
  CCU = Coastal Carolina Univ.; MUGC = Moscow University for Geodesy & Cartography

manned from 05:50 - 19:30 CDT each day, except during rain squalls or when breeze and sea conditions exceeded Beaufort 4. Total visual search time was over 200 hours. Two rigid-hulled inflatable boats (RHIBs) were deployed when weather and sea conditions allowed for photo-identification and photogrammetry. During the 3 week period of the survey over the MCS, one or both small boats were launched on 18 days. On most of these days, sperm whales were encountered in groups of 3-16 animals. Figure 3.1.2 overlays on the daytime part of the ship track the locations where whales were observed by visual observers. Although most of the whales were seen in water depths between 800 m and 1000 m, they also were heard or seen in water depths both shallower (to 600 m) and deeper (to 1300 m).

9

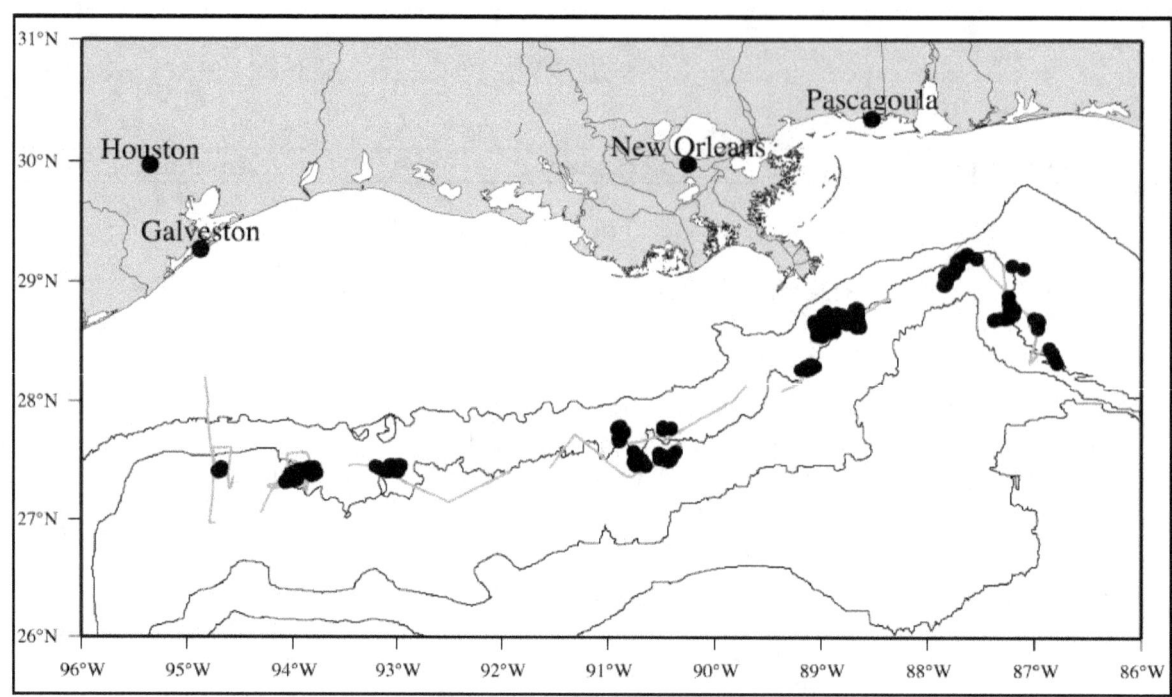

Figure 3.1.2. Locations of visual sightings of sperm whales (dots) on the SWSS 2003 WSHC cruise in May/June 2003 superimposed over the daytime cruise track (light gray line). Contours are shown for the 200, 1000, 2000, and 3000-m isobaths.

Near-surface water was pumped from the ship's hull depth of 3.5 m through SeaBird temperature and conductivity sensors and a Turner Designs Model 10 fluorometer to log surface temperature, salinity, and chlorophyll fluorescence once per minute. Ocean current velocity in the upper 300 m and upper 900 m was monitored continuously with RD Instruments hull-mounted 153 kHz ADCP and 38 kHz ADCP, respectively. At 8 locations, CTD casts were made with a SeaBird Electronics SeaCat internally-recording CTD to record profiles of conductivity (salinity) and temperature with depth. Eighty-nine XBTs were dropped to profile temperature in the upper 760 m. These generally were dropped every 10 nautical miles (18 km), although on days when whales were being followed, XBTs usually were dropped more frequently to obtain finer spatial resolution. Sippican Deep Blue XBTs were dropped during the first ten days of the cruise and Sippican T7 XBTs were used to complete the rest of the survey.

Photo-ID/Photogrammetry and Biopsy/Genetic Typing activities were conducted in accordance with federal permits from NOAA Fisheries to Texas A&M University-Galveston (permit 821-1588-00), and to Dan Engelhaupt/University of Durham (permit 909-1465-02).

Oceanographic Habitat
The habitat characterization work was coordinated by Doug Biggs. The pre-cruise map of sea surface height (SSH) for 28 May 2003 indicated that SSH over the slope and in deepwater was higher than SSH over the shelf. Thus, surface currents over the middle continental slope were expected to flow generally from west to east.

The SSH analysis further indicated that the western edge of a very large deepwater anticyclonic (clockwise circulating) Loop Current eddy (LCE) was located near 27.5°N, 91°W. The LCE was

10

named Eddy Sargassum by the oil and gas industry service company that tracks the Loop Current and its associated eddies. The altimetry indicated this LCE, which had separated from the Loop Current only a few weeks before the ship sailed, had an SSH anomaly of > 40 cm and that to its north there was an area of cyclonic circulation where SSH dipped as low as –20 cm. When combined, these extrema correspond to a gradient of SSH of > 60 cm across a distance of less than 30 nautical miles. Thus, it was expected that very strong surface currents would be encountered as the ship transited the western and northern periphery of this big LCE.

Because the location of this big LCE in the SSH analysis of 28 May showed its northern edge reached mid-slope water depths, it was anticipated that strong clockwise surface currents around the LCE would block Mississippi River water from flowing to the west. From this geometry, it was expected that the clockwise circulation around the LCE would entrain the low salinity, higher chlorophyll shelf water near the mouth of the Mississippi River and transport this "green" water to the east and off the margin into DeSoto Canyon. Subsequent SSH analyses for 8, 15, and 17 June showed this same general geometry, but also showed that from May to June the northern periphery of the LCE was moving increasingly up slope between 91°W and 89°W.

The locations, dates, times, and 15°C isotherm depths of the CTD and XBT stations are given in Tables 3.1.2 and 3.1.3, respectively. Figure 3.1.3 shows a map of the locations. Temperature, salinity, and fluorescence from a depth of ~3.5 m were logged once per minute throughout the cruise. The sample locations are shown in Figure 3.1.4. The locations, dates, and times of the chlorophyll samples are given in Table 3.1.4, with the map of locations given in Figure 3.1.4. These samples are used to calibrate the continuous fluorescence data. ADCP data were collected continuously along the track generally in water depths of about 15 m or more for the 153 kHz ADCP and about 35 m or more for the 38 kHz ADCP.

Data from the flow-through system, XBT drops, CTD stations, and ADCPs confirmed the intensity of the SSH gradient across Eddy Sargassum and its capture of Mississippi River water and eastward transport of that low salinity water. West of 93°W and east of 88.5°W, the surface salinity was generally less than 35 and the water was visibly greenish in color. Chlorophyll fluorescence in this "green" water exceeded 165 mvolts, equivalent to > 0.25 μg chlorophyll·L^{-1}. In many locations along the track between 93°W and 88.5°W, surface salinity was greater than 36. Here, the water was azure blue in color and chlorophyll fluorescence was generally < 130 mvolts, equivalent to < 0.15 μg chlorophyll·L^{-1}. The exception, however, was where the surface current exceeded 2 knots in the periphery of Eddy Sargassum. In these areas, chlorophyll fluorescence reached 185 mvolts, or about 0.3 μg chlorophyll·L^{-1} and so was roughly double the maximum of 0.15 μg chlorophyll·L^{-1} found within Eddy Sargassum.

Whales were heard and/or seen both in green water and in blue water environments. Many of the encounters with whales were at or near the high velocity periphery of this big LCE. Other concentrations of whales were found in the areas of cyclonic circulation at 93-94°W along the upper reaches of Alaminos Canyon and at 87-88°W near the head of DeSoto Canyon.

<u>Visual Survey and Monitoring</u>
A visual observation station was established on the flying bridge. It consisted of two stand-mounted 25x BigEye binoculars and a data entry station. At least three observers maintained a continuous watch during daylight hours, generally 05:50–19:30 CDT, while the ship surveyed or tracked whales in water depths greater than 500 m. A rolling two-hour watch system was implemented. This provided the observers with sufficient breaks to maintain motivation and vigilance while ensuring that an appreciation of the whales' general behavior and activity patterns was preserved and transferred within the bridge team as it gradually changed over the day. During "busy periods", for example when members of a large group were being tracked, "resting" observers would be drafted in to provide assistance.

11

Table 3.1.2

Summary of CTD Stations on SWSS 2003 WSHC Cruise

Station	Date (mm/dd/yyyy)	Time (UTC)	Longitude (°W)	Latitude (°N)	15°C Depth (m)
CTD-01	05/31/2003	20:30	-94.753	27.505	218
CTD-02	06/03/2003	05:46	-93.818	27.186	194
CTD-03	06/04/2003	06:36	-93.936	27.344	203
CTD-04	06/10/2003	02:56	-90.470	27.470	225
CTD-05	06/11/2003	05:13	-88.924	28.414	242
CTD-06	06/13/2003	05:53	-87.667	29.048	166
CTD-07	06/14/2003	02:41	-86.945	28.685	168
CTD-08	06/16/2003	06:47	-88.741	28.486	282

Table 3.1.3

Summary of XBT Stations on SWSS 2003 WSHC Cruise

Station	Date (mm/dd/yyyy)	Time (UTC)	Longitude (°W)	Latitude (°N)	15°C Depth (m)
XBT-1	06/01/2003	15:55	-94.582	27.595	216
XBT-2	06/01/2003	17:41	-94.747	27.601	240
XBT-3	06/01/2003	19:22	-94.750	27.443	241
XBT-4	06/01/2003	21:00	-94.755	27.276	249
XBT-5	06/01/2003	22:38	-94.769	27.109	258
XBT-6	06/01/2003	23:58	-94.788	26.977	245
XBT-7	06/02/2003	02:16	-94.546	26.981	236
XBT-8	06/02/2003	05:59	-94.398	27.080	229
XBT-9	06/02/2003	11:57	-94.246	27.163	223
XBT-10	06/02/2003	14:08	-94.150	27.306	224
XBT-11	06/02/2003	16:26	-94.039	27.424	206
XBT-12	06/03/2003	00:16	-93.893	27.426	202
XBT-13	06/03/2003	02:16	-93.828	27.277	223
XBT-14	06/03/2003	13:32	-93.975	27.386	208
XBT-15	06/03/2003	16:08	-94.036	27.557	178
XBT-16	06/03/2003	18:07	-93.860	27.542	176
XBT-17	06/04/2003	21:48	-93.745	27.377	213
XBT-18	06/05/2003	09:24	-93.601	27.440	200
XBT-19	06/05/2003	11:34	-93.401	27.468	213
XBT-20	06/05/2003	13:51	-93.189	27.446	205
XBT-21	06/05/2003	18:35	-93.027	27.457	191
XBT-22	06/06/2003	13:16	-92.868	27.297	199

Table 3.1.3

Summary of XBT Stations on SWSS 2003 WSHC Cruise (continued)

Station	Date (mm/dd/yyyy)	Time (UTC)	Longitude (°W)	Latitude (°N)	15°C Depth (m)
XBT-23	06/06/2003	15:11	-92.699	27.227	210
XBT-24	06/06/2003	17:10	-92.531	27.148	218
XBT-25	06/06/2003	19:21	-92.340	27.225	237
XBT-26	06/06/2003	21:20	-92.178	27.297	248
XBT-27	06/06/2003	23:36	-92.002	27.369	252
XBT-28	06/07/2003	02:14	-91.824	27.379	241
XBT-29	06/07/2003	05:09	-91.810	27.214	245
XBT-30	06/07/2003	09:08	-91.656	27.313	228
XBT-31	06/07/2003	10:52	-91.541	27.445	223
XBT-32	06/07/2003	12:38	-91.430	27.579	194
XBT-33	06/07/2003	14:33	-91.309	27.718	195
XBT-34	06/07/2003	17:34	-91.158	27.614	203
XBT-35	06/07/2003	19:28	-91.012	27.502	216
XBT-36	06/07/2003	21:30	-90.865	27.391	229
XBT-37	06/08/2003	00:28	-90.657	27.403	227
XBT-38	06/08/2003	17:24	-90.671	27.466	221
XBT-39	06/09/2003	02:06	-90.601	27.585	211
XBT-40	06/09/2003	13:27	-90.444	27.576	252
XBT-41	06/09/2003	20:57	-90.489	27.518	242
XBT-42	06/10/2003	05:03	-90.275	27.615	274
XBT-43	06/10/2003	06:11	-90.112	27.706	298
XBT-44	06/10/2003	07:25	-89.943	27.801	309
XBT-45	06/10/2003	08:25	-89.768	27.863	323
XBT-46	06/10/2003	09:27	-89.599	27.965	326
XBT-47	06/10/2003	10:43	-89.387	28.079	320
XBT-48	06/10/2003	11:49	-89.200	28.165	326
XBT-49	06/10/2003	16:00	-89.046	28.289	321
XBT-50	06/11/2003	08:32	-88.795	28.545	227
XBT-51	06/11/2003	10:06	-88.642	28.651	212
XBT-52	06/12/2003	06:04	-88.558	28.810	192
XBT-53	06/12/2003	07:21	-88.376	28.897	195
XBT-54	06/12/2003	08:35	-88.204	28.979	177
XBT-55	06/12/2003	09:57	-88.003	29.067	174
XBT-56	06/12/2003	11:04	-87.827	29.137	189
XBT-57	06/12/2003	12:55	-87.654	29.214	173
XBT-58	06/13/2003	12:54	-87.480	29.144	162
XBT-59	06/13/2003	14:57	-87.360	29.014	157
XBT-60	06/13/2003	16:52	-87.228	28.890	169
XBT-61	06/13/2003	19:54	-87.098	28.761	163
XBT-62	06/13/2003	21:58	-86.959	28.683	172
XBT-63	06/14/2003	13:55	-86.991	28.500	152
XBT-64	06/14/2003	15:53	-87.052	28.336	155

13

Table 3.1.3

Summary of XBT Stations on SWSS 2003 WSHC Cruise (continued)

Station	Date (mm/dd/yyyy)	Time (UTC)	Longitude (°W)	Latitude (°N)	15°C Depth (m)
XBT-65	06/14/2003	19:21	-86.901	28.457	161
XBT-66	06/14/2003	23:24	-86.776	28.317	164
XBT-67	06/15/2003	07:09	-87.169	28.553	165
XBT-68	06/15/2003	10:06	-87.336	28.662	189
XBT-69	06/15/2003	23:45	-87.237	29.142	178
XBT-70	06/16/2003	05:32	-87.615	29.008	198
XBT-71	06/16/2003	06:47	-87.804	28.969	206
XBT-72	06/16/2003	22:27	-88.935	28.734	213
XBT-73	06/17/2003	15:50	-88.960	28.580	256
XBT-74	06/17/2003	19:00	-89.055	28.639	253
XBT-75	06/19/2003	04:11	-89.073	28.476	267
XBT-76	06/19/2003	05:58	-89.184	28.330	283
XBT-77	06/19/2003	07:30	-89.373	28.315	271
XBT-78	06/19/2003	09:12	-89.543	28.231	260
XBT-79	06/19/2003	10:47	-89.699	28.134	273
XBT-80	06/19/2003	12:19	-89.827	28.007	259
XBT-81	06/19/2003	14:52	-89.990	27.921	241
XBT-82	06/19/2003	17:08	-90.157	27.841	216
XBT-83	06/19/2003	19:10	-90.323	27.752	250
XBT-84	06/19/2003	21:31	-90.467	27.667	240
XBT-85	06/20/2003	00:49	-90.440	27.794	229
XBT-86	06/20/2003	12:04	-90.620	27.682	228
XBT-87	06/20/2003	15:29	-90.898	27.665	204
XBT-88	06/20/2003	20:56	-90.959	27.798	194
XBT-89	06/20/2003	22:17	-91.130	27.868	178

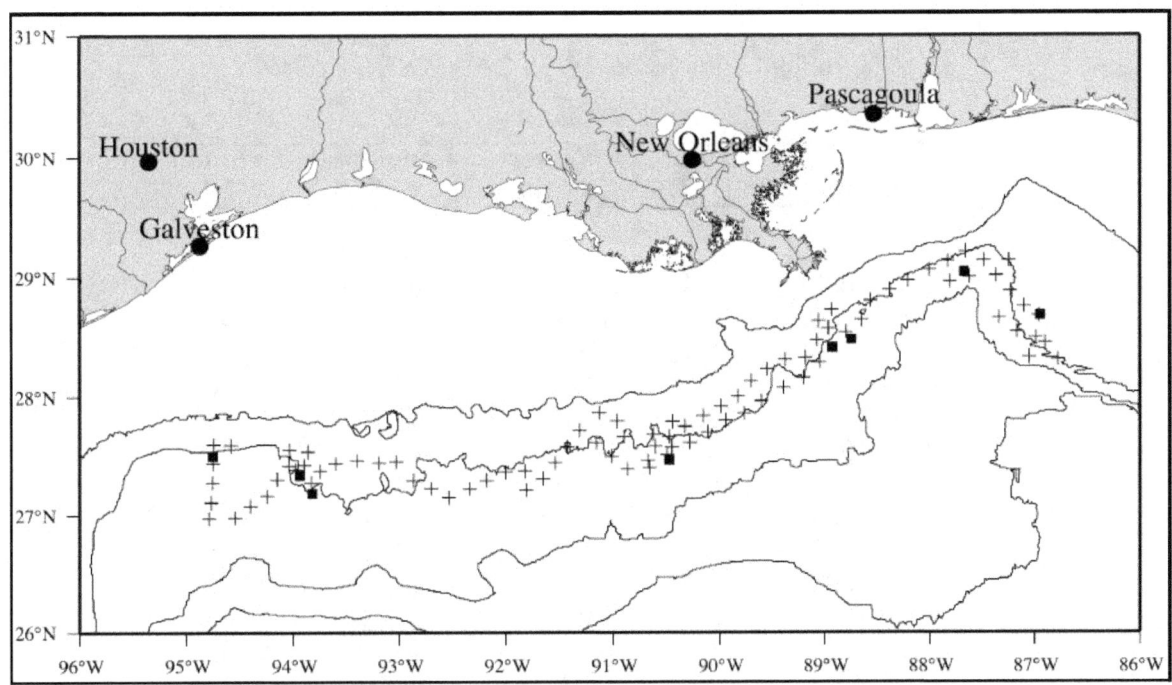

Figure 3.1.3. Locations of CTD (square) and XBT (plus) stations on SWSS 2003 WSHC cruise. Contours are shown for the 200, 1000, 2000, and 3000-m isobaths.

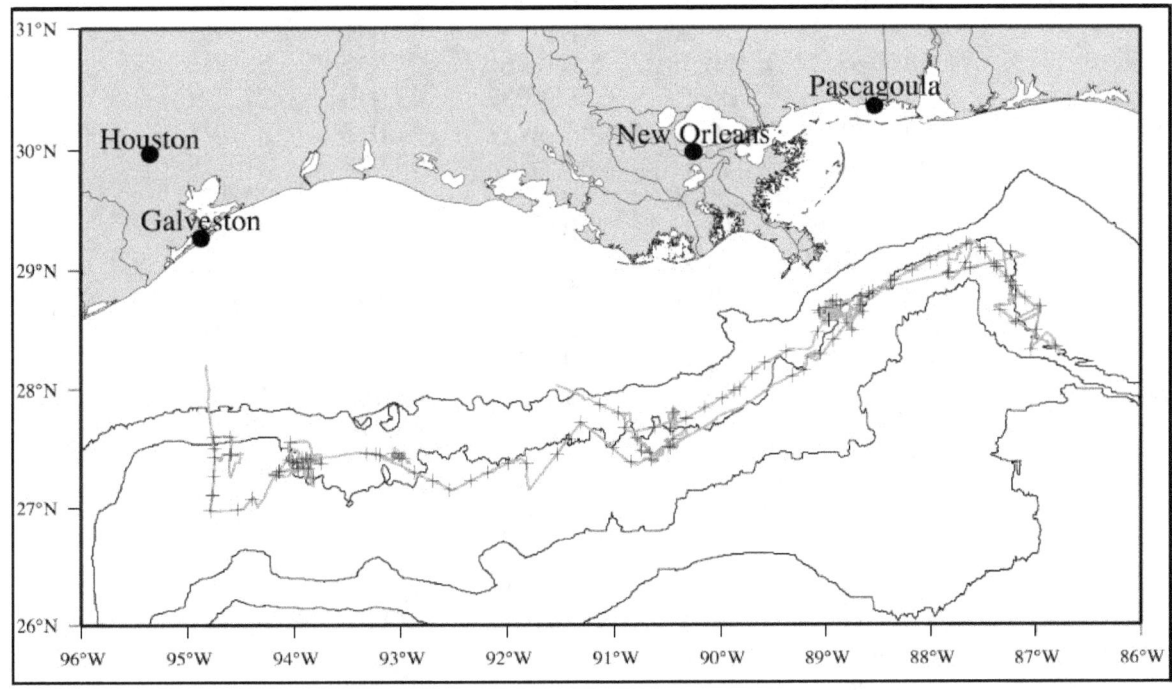

Figure 3.1.4. Locations of chlorophyll samples on the SWSS 2003 WSHC cruise. Contours are shown for the 200, 1000, 2000, and 3000-m isobaths.

Table 3.1.4

Chlorophyll Stations on SWSS 2003 WSHC Cruise

Date (mm/dd/yyyy)	Time (UTC)	Nearest Station	Longitude (°W)	Latitude (°N)
05/31/2003	20:38	CTD-01	-94.750	27.504
06/01/2003	02:32	underway	-94.587	27.455
06/01/2003	07:05	underway	-94.599	27.459
06/01/2003	16:13	XBT-1	-94.599	27.605
06/01/2003	17:51	XBT-2	-94.753	27.600
06/01/2003	19:29	XBT-3	-94.751	27.432
06/01/2003	21:03	XBT-4	-94.755	27.270
06/01/2003	22:38	XBT-5	-94.769	27.108
06/02/2003	00:00	XBT-6	-94.788	26.973
06/02/2003	02:41	XBT-7	-94.531	26.983
06/02/2003	06:01	XBT-8	-94.396	27.081
06/02/2003	13:51	XBT-9	-94.168	27.284
06/02/2003	14:13	XBT-10	-94.145	27.312
06/02/2003	16:15	XBT-11	-94.051	27.411
06/02/2003	22:16	low salinity	-93.959	27.332
06/03/2003	00:16	XBT-12	-93.891	27.424
06/03/2003	04:10	XBT-13	-93.824	27.261
06/03/2003	10:08	underway	-93.873	27.332
06/03/2003	13:32	XBT-14	-93.977	27.387
06/03/2003	16:06	XBT-15	-94.041	27.556
06/03/2003	20:58	XBT-16	-93.852	27.404
06/04/2003	06:19	CTD-03	-93.916	27.350
06/04/2003	16:02	underway	-94.015	27.393
06/04/2003	17:35	underway	-93.923	27.421
06/04/2003	21:48	XBT-17	-93.745	27.377
06/05/2003	12:23	XBT-19	-93.324	27.463
06/05/2003	13:21	underway	-93.235	27.458
06/05/2003	13:48	XBT-20	-93.194	27.448
06/05/2003	17:41	underway	-93.067	27.462
06/05/2003	18:13	XBT-21	-93.046	27.464
06/06/2003	00:30	underway	-92.981	27.419
06/06/2003	05:14	CTD	-93.014	27.439
06/06/2003	13:13	XBT-22	-92.871	27.298
06/06/2003	15:09	XBT-23	-92.701	27.228
06/06/2003	17:02	XBT-24	-92.540	27.153
06/06/2003	19:22	XBT-25	-92.337	27.227
06/06/2003	21:20	XBT-26	-92.179	27.297
06/06/2003	23:46	XBT-27	-91.988	27.377
06/07/2003	02:14	XBT-28	-91.823	27.378
06/07/2003	10:58	XBT-31	-91.535	27.453
06/07/2003	12:39	XBT-32	-91.429	27.579

16

Table 3.1.4

Chlorophyll Stations on SWSS 2003 WSHC Cruise (continued)

Date (mm/dd/yyyy)	Time (UTC)	Nearest Station	Longitude (°W)	Latitude (°N)
06/07/2003	14:32	XBT-33	-91.312	27.718
06/07/2003	19:27	XBT-35	-91.015	27.504
06/07/2003	21:33	XBT-36	-90.844	27.388
06/08/2003	00:28	XBT-37	-90.655	27.403
06/08/2003	15:50	underway	-90.747	27.480
06/08/2003	17:24	XBT-38	-90.671	27.466
06/09/2003	02:07	XBT-39	-90.790	27.585
06/09/2003	13:26	XBT-40	-90.445	27.575
06/09/2003	20:57	XBT-41	-90.488	27.518
06/10/2003	02:55	CTD-04	-90.473	27.506
06/10/2003	11:07	XBT-47	-89.316	28.108
06/10/2003	11:46	XBT-48	-89.203	28.165
06/10/2003	15:55	XBT-49	-89.048	28.292
06/11/2003	04:57	CTD-05	-88.930	28.411
06/11/2003	08:38	XBT-50	-88.793	28.550
06/11/2003	10:06	XBT-51	-88.642	28.650
06/11/2003	13:48	on whales	-88.649	28.776
06/12/2003	05:57	XBT-52	-88.577	28.800
06/12/2003	06:09	rising fluor	-88.545	28.816
06/12/2003	07:23	XBT-53	-88.376	28.897
06/12/2003	07:36	high fluor	-88.341	28.914
06/12/2003	08:48	XBT-54	-88.172	28.994
06/12/2003	09:57	XBT-55	-88.004	29.066
06/12/2003	11:03	XBT-56	-87.826	29.137
06/12/2003	12:53	XBT-57	-87.656	29.212
06/13/2003	00:19	on whales	-87.839	28.972
06/13/2003	05:46	CTD-6	-87.668	29.045
06/13/2003	12:22	S gradient	-87.514	29.177
06/13/2003	12:56	XBT-58	-87.477	29.141
06/13/2003	14:26	S gradient	-87.389	29.037
06/13/2003	14:53	XBT-59	-87.363	29.017
06/13/2003	16:08	S gradient	-87.277	28.938
06/13/2003	16:48	XBT-60	-87.232	28.894
06/13/2003	17:25	S gradient	-87.184	28.856
06/13/2003	19:54	XBT-61	-87.096	28.760
06/13/2003	21:59	XBT-62	-86.958	28.688
06/14/2003	14:03	XBT-63	-86.994	28.489
06/14/2003	16:03	XBT-64	-87.043	28.326
06/14/2003	22:27	near whale	-86.805	28.349
06/15/2003	07:40	XBT-67	-87.186	28.559
06/15/2003	10:02	XBT-68	-87.332	28.659

Table 3.1.4

Chlorophyll Stations on SWSS 2003 WSHC Cruise (continued)

Date (mm/dd/yyyy)	Time (UTC)	Nearest Station	Longitude (°W)	Latitude (°N)
06/15/2003	17:22	on whales	-87.191	28.782
06/15/2003	23:47	XBT-69	-87.233	29.142
06/16/2003	05:31	XBT-70	-87.615	29.007
06/16/2003	06:56	XBT-71	-87.826	28.965
06/16/2003	15:48	underway	-88.664	28.702
06/16/2003	22:24	XBT-72	-88.934	28.732
06/17/2003	06:43	CTD-8	-88.744	28.486
06/17/2003	15:55	XBT-73	-88.965	28.575
06/17/2003	23:12	underway	-88.853	28.705
06/18/2003	13:57	underway	-88.900	28.740
06/18/2003	19:03	XBT-74	-89.056	28.640
06/18/2003	19:32	front	-89.066	28.657
06/18/2003	20:49	near whales	-89.007	28.681
06/19/2003	04:12	XBT-75	-89.075	28.472
06/19/2003	07:30	XBT-77	-89.373	28.315
06/19/2003	9:32	XBT-78	-89.581	28.215
06/19/2003	10:52	XBT-79	-89.707	28.127
06/19/2003	12:17	XBT-80	-89.824	28.009
06/19/2003	13:04	underway	-89.875	27.986
06/19/2003	14:52	XBT-81	-89.990	27.921
06/19/2003	17:08	XBT-82	-90.157	27.841
06/19/2003	19:10	XBT-83	-90.322	27.752
06/19/2003	21:31	XBT-84	-90.467	27.667
06/20/2003	01:03	XBT-85	-90.444	27.805
06/20/2003	12:03	XBT-86	-90.622	27.681
06/20/2003	15:29	XBT-87	-90.903	27.678
06/20/2003	20:56	XBT-88	-90.959	27.799
06/20/2003	22:19	XBT-89	-91.135	27.870

While on watch, observers moved between roles on the flying bridge every 40 minutes. Two observers scanned with BigEye binoculars, hand-held binoculars, and/or by naked eye. The third person, the data recorder, concentrated on the near field using only naked eye and 7x50 binoculars. The data recorder also entered data into the *Logger* program on a laptop computer. *Logger* is a data collection and depiction software program written by Douglas Gillespie and made freely available by the International Fund for Animal Welfare to assist marine conservation projects. The watch order was chosen so that observers with complimentary skills and levels of experience were distributed through the rotation. While tracking sperm whales, the watch rotation was adapted to facilitate the need for at least one extra person on the flying bridge to handle radio communications.

The *Gyre* carried two rigid-hull inflatable boats (RHIBs) for this cruise: RHIB-1 was a 25-foot Zodiac Hurricane powered by an inboard Volvo diesel, and RHIB-2 was an 18-foot Avon Searider powered by a 70 Hp Johnson two stroke outboard. The visual team on *Gyre* worked in different modes depending on whether the acoustic team was tracking sperm whales at sunrise (track mode) and/or a RHIB was deployed. The vessel might be either searching for whales or, once they had been found, tracking them. In "line survey" searching mode, the vessel followed predetermined tracks and the visual team followed survey procedures that matched closely those used by NOAA Fisheries for line transect surveys. When the team was searching for whales but not following predetermined survey tracks or when the RHIBs were launched to search for whales acoustically, visual effort was scored as simply "searching". Another searching mode, termed "hunch", was in place when searching was directed to a predetermined area believed to contain whales (e.g., when searching an area reported to have a satellite tagged whale). While searching, the visual team operated independently from the acoustic team so that data on relative detection efficiencies of visual and acoustic methods could be collected.

Once sperm whales were detected the visual team's primary role became that of tracking the locations and movements of whales and helping the RHIBs to get close to them for photo-ID or biopsy. The locations of all first sightings and final submergences and/or fluke-ups were recorded in *Logger*, along with notes on any behaviors observed by the visual team and/or behaviors reported by RHIB teams. These data also provide detailed information on group movements and distributions.

In track mode the visual and acoustic teams worked closely together. The aim was to amalgamate all information on the location and behavior of whales (visual data, acoustic data from the *Gyre*'s arrays, and acoustic information from the RHIB boats' directional hydrophones) to form a comprehensive view of the whales' movements and behavior. The visual team also requested course and speed changes from the *Gyre* bridge to keep the vessel in a position so its visual coverage of whale groups, which typically spread over several miles, was optimal. The understanding and good humor that the officers on the *Gyre* bridge showed in responding to the numerous requests of the scientists for course changes, while navigating the vessel safely around other shipping and oil rigs, are acknowledged.

Over 200 hours were spent on survey effort during which time the vessel covered over 800 miles. These hours are broken down by effort category in Table 3.1.5. It can be seen that more than half of the entire visual effort was expended in tracking groups of sperm whales. Table 3.1.6 provides a more detailed breakdown showing effort expended in each category for different sea states. Locations of sperm whale sightings during line survey, searching, and tracking modes are summarized in Figure 3.1.2. In Figure 3.1.5 are shown locations of sightings of pilot whale (*Globicephala macrorhynchus*), melon-headed whale (*Peponocephala electra*), pygmy/dwarf sperm whale (*Kogia* sp.), a mixed school of melon-headed whale, rough-toothed dolphin and Fraser's dolphin (*P. electra, Steno bredanensis* and *Lagenodelphis hosei*), unidentified blackfish, and unidentified whale sightings and pantropical spotted dolphins (*Stenella attenuata*), and unidentified dolphins (some schools could not be identified while tracking sperm whales). Table 3.1.7 provides a listing of associated locations.

Sperm whales were sighted in all the major search areas along the continental slope. No whales were found in the Mississippi Canyon this year, but virtually no daytime effort was expended in this area to avoid any possibility of interference with the CEE work of the *Ewing* and *Kondor*.

Use of RHIBs
Use of RHIBs to increase sperm whale detection range: On days when the weather was favorable but sperm whales had not been located either visually or acoustically by the *Gyre*, search efficiency was increased by dispatching one or both of the RHIBs to listen with their stereo dipping hydrophones. Usually RHIBs were launched to acoustically monitor at stations

approximately 3 miles apart. A pair of omni-directional hydrophones (Hi Tech HTI-96-MIN) with amplifier/conditioner in a water proof case was available for each RHIB for this purpose.

Table 3.1.5

Synopsis of Nautical Miles and Hours of Effort Status

Effort Status	Nautical Miles of Trackline	Hours of Effort
Track	363.3	122.2
Line	251.1	49.1
Search	175.7	38.9
Hunch	7.3	1.4
Off effort	18.4	5.0
Total	815.8	216.6

Table 3.1.6

Nautical Miles and Hours of Effort for Each Effort Status by Sea State

Effort Status	Beaufort Sea State	Nautical Miles of Trackline	Hours of Effort
Line	2	102.9	20.2
	3	107.2	20.8
	3.5	26.5	5.0
	4	14.5	3.0
Searching	1	6.8	2.0
	2	108.5	23.1
	3	55.3	11.9
	3.5	3.5	1.3
	4	1.5	0.7
Tracking	1	34.9	13.0
	2	125.4	42.3
	3	142.7	45.0
	3.5	28.0	9.9
	4	32.2	11.9
Hunch	3	7.3	1.4

Note: Sea State 3.5 has white caps just beginning to form, which decreased searching/sighting ability.

Table 3.1.7

Locations of Sightings of Toothed Whales and Delphiniids on SWSS 2003 WSHC Cruise

Species Names	Longitude (°W)	Latitude (°N)
Kogia sp	-90.733	27.545
Melon-Headed Whale	-94.036	27.442
Melon-Headed Whale	-87.039	28.353
Melon-Headed Whale	-86.825	28.379
Mixed Group*	-87.016	28.350
Pilot Whale	-94.732	27.607
Pilot Whale	-92.989	27.433
Pilot Whale	-88.895	28.689
Pilot Whale	-91.053	27.836
Unidentified Blackfish	-91.094	27.568
Unidentified Blackfish	-88.542	28.766
Unidentified Whale	-90.727	27.399
Pantropical Spotted Dolphin	-94.155	27.300
Pantropical Spotted Dolphin	-90.533	27.473
Pantropical Spotted Dolphin	-90.587	27.455
Pantropical Spotted Dolphin	-90.588	27.453
Pantropical Spotted Dolphin	-90.606	27.425
Pantropical Spotted Dolphin	-90.590	27.443
Pantropical Spotted Dolphin	-90.488	27.538
Pantropical Spotted Dolphin	-89.088	28.289
Pantropical Spotted Dolphin	-89.095	28.276
Pantropical Spotted Dolphin	-86.993	28.664
Pantropical Spotted Dolphin	-86.976	28.573
Pantropical Spotted Dolphin	-86.991	28.500
Pantropical Spotted Dolphin	-86.828	28.417
Pantropical Spotted Dolphin	-90.878	27.655
Unidentified Dolphin	-94.050	27.429
Unidentified Dolphin	-90.509	27.519
Unidentified Dolphin	-90.476	27.524
Unidentified Dolphin	-86.957	28.670
Unidentified Dolphin	-86.982	28.547
Unidentified Dolphin	-86.986	28.529
Unidentified Dolphin	-86.997	28.482
Unidentified Dolphin	-86.854	28.440
Unidentified Dolphin	-86.845	28.433
Unidentified Dolphin	-88.433	28.838
Unidentified Dolphin	-88.940	28.735
Unidentified Dolphin	-88.993	28.661
Unidentified Dolphin	-88.974	28.687
Unidentified Dolphin	-89.793	28.041
Unidentified Dolphin	-89.842	27.995
Unidentified Dolphin	-90.407	27.711

*Melon-headed, rough-toothed, Frasier's mixed group

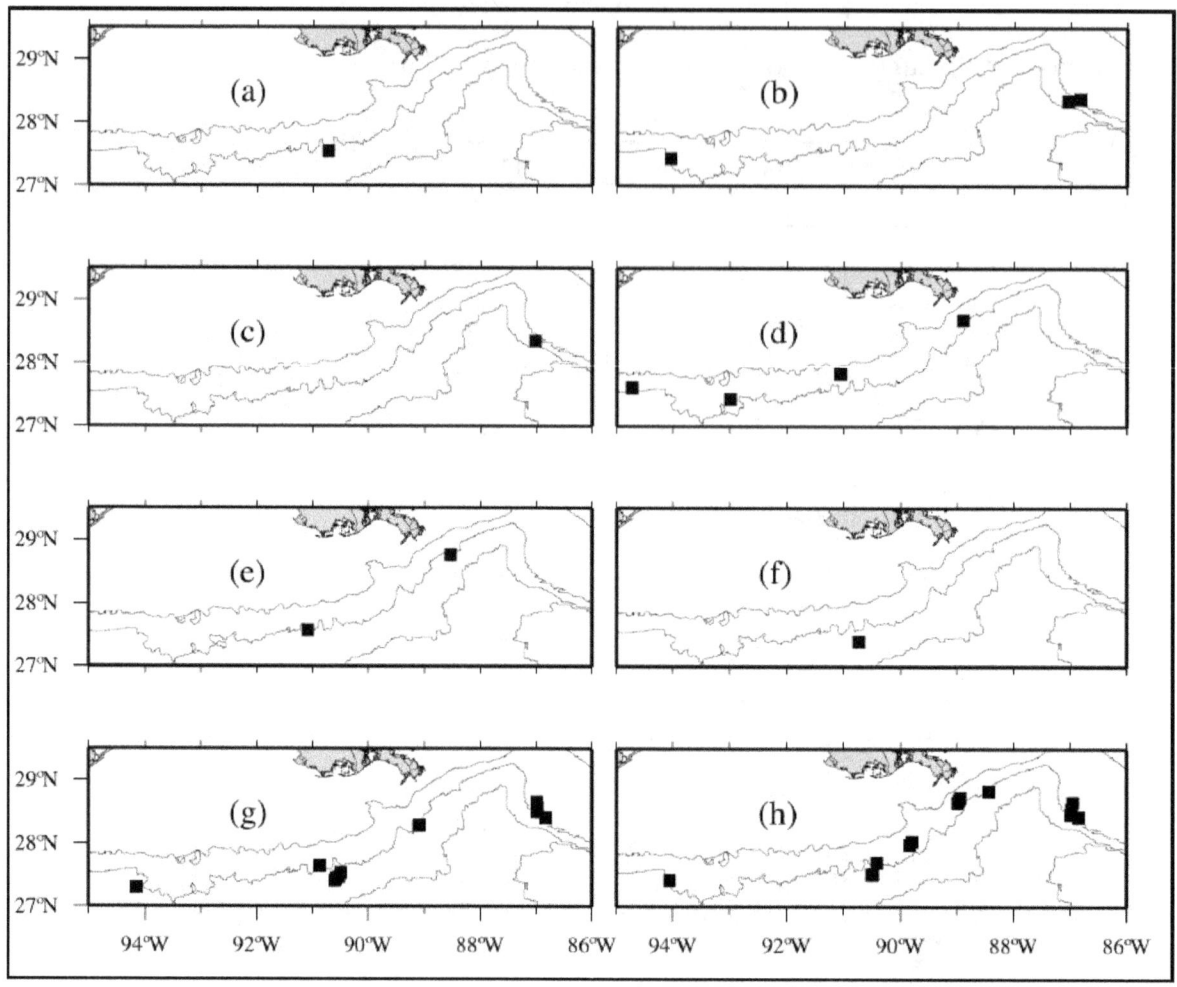

Figure 3.1.5. Visual sightings of toothed whales and delphiniids on the SWSS 2003 WSHC cruise. Shown are (a) *Kogia* sp.; (b) melon-headed whale; (c) melon-headed, rough-toothed, Frasier's mixed group; (d) pilot whale; (e) unidentified blackfish; (f) unidentified whale; (g) pantropical spotted dolphin; (h) unidentified dolphin. Contours are shown for the 200, 1000, 2000, and 3000-m isobaths.

Typically the RHIBs would parallel the course of the *Gyre* about 3 miles abeam and stop to monitor for 5-10 minutes every three miles. Once whales were detected, a directional hydrophone was used to close on the whales and the *Gyre* closed with the RHIB for support. When operated in this mode, the RHIB greatly extended the effective acoustic swath and when in use, RHIBs usually made the first detection of whales. Once, when listening conditions were very favorable, a group of whales were detected at an estimated range of 10 miles.

Out of the 20 days of survey over the MCS during this cruise, sperm whales were seen and/or heard on 18 days, and one or both RHIBs were deployed on 17. On ten of these days, visual contact was made with whales between 6 AM and 8 AM local time. On the other eight days, a RHIB was launched as soon as the weather allowed, and whales were always found by the RHIB away team before the end of the day. On only one occasion, when both RHIBs developed engine problems, could whales not be followed. On another occasion, whales were detected late in the day and not tracked down until approximately 19:45 CDT by which time the declining daylight was not suitable for photo-identification. On the 2 days that whales were neither seen nor heard (1 and 6 June), the science team effectively was weathered out. The sea was too rough for launching even RHIB 2, and the visual team was off effort for part of these days because of heavy rainfall.

It is clear that dispatching one or both of the RHIBs abeam of the *Gyre* significantly increases detection range, and several groups of sperm whales would not have been detected if the RHIBs had not been used in conjunction with the visual and acoustic teams onboard.

Use of RHIBs for photo-identification, recordings and behavioral observations: For photo-ID, the smaller Avon was found to be the preferable RHIB. It was easier to launch and could often be put in the water in weather that precluded the deployment of the larger RHIB 1. It was more responsive and maneuverable. It also was more comfortable as the larger RHIB 2 tended to slam in moderate seas. Weather permitting, RHIB 2 was launched whenever sperm whales were sighted. RHIB 1 was only occasionally launched to increase data collection when the team was with a significantly large or spread out group of whales. The limited times in which both RHIBs were launched was partly because of the practical and weather restrictions mentioned above, but also because only one of the two digital cameras available for photo-ID was really fit for the purpose. Both of the RHIBs were crewed by two and sometimes three members of the scientific party who were experienced in driving small boats close to whales, tracking whales using a directional hydrophone, and taking fluke identification photographs. RHIBs were equipped with palmtop computers (HP 200 XL) in water-proof housings linked to a GPS (Garmin 76) which allowed the detailed track of the boat as well as the position of whales to be recorded accurately.

Photo-Identification
Identification photographs were taken using the digital EOS 1D Canon Camera with a Sigma 100-300 mm telephoto lens, and with the Fuji FinePix with a Tokina 300 mm lens. Ranges to whales were measured using Bushnell 1000 laser range finders. The system based on the Canon EOS1D, which can shoot at 8 frames per second (fps), was ideal. The system based on the Fuji FinePix was restricted by a low frame rate (<2 fps) and also suffered from a software bug that caused it to occasionally freeze up.

Of the 20 days spent surveying, 17 days in total were spent with sperm whales in conjunction with the small boat operations for photo-ID and/or biopsy. Some of these days were unfortunately cut short due to either bad weather (e.g., 2 and 17 June) or because whales were found late in the day (e.g., 3, 14, and 16 June) or both (e.g., 19 June).

The majority of the whale aggregations located this year were rather small (6-10 individuals). Large assemblages of sperm whales (15-20+ individuals) were found only off the Mississippi River delta area on 17 and 18 June. Only one apparently lone animal was encountered (14 June). Total length of this individual was estimated as only 9.8 meters using fluke photogrammetry. Small groups of approximately 3 whales were identified in the western Gulf (3 and 19 June). Analyses of the available photogrammetry data are underway to determine if the individual animals in these groups may have been small males or large immature males. When genetics results from biopsy samples taken 3 June are analyzed, these should add significantly to the final analysis.

A total of 152 photo-identification sequences were taken with up to 24 IDs obtained in a single day (Table 3.1.8). Seventy-nine different sperm whale individuals were identified during this 3 week cruise and 65 of these had images of sufficiently high quality to be used to estimate sperm whale population in the northern Gulf using mark-recapture techniques. Others were represented by images that are good enough to be used for less exacting photo-identification analyses.

23

Table 3.1.8

Synopsis of Fluke-Out Sequences for Photo-ID

Date (mm/dd/yyyy)	# of ID Sequences	# of Animals Determined to be Different Individuals	# of Different Individuals with High Quality Identification Photograph
06/02/2003	1	1	1
06/03/2003	6	3	3
06/04/2003	7	7	4
06/05/2003	8	4	2
06/08/2003	17	5	4
06/09/2003	10	6	6
06/10/2003	13	5	5
06/11/2003	11	7	7
06/12/2003	13	5	5
06/14/2003	3	1	1
06/15/2003	18	8	7
06/16/2003	5	3	2
06/17/2003	9	6	5
06/18/2003	24	16	11
06/19/2003	1	1	1
06/20/2003	6	5	5
Total	**152**	**83**	**69**

At the end of 2002, the sperm whale catalogue for the Gulf of Mexico, which contains images collected over the eight years between 1994 and 2002, contained 96 individuals represented by good quality photo-identification photographs. This three-week survey on which photo-ID was one of several research priorities has made a significant contribution to the catalogue by contributing 57 new individuals (duplicate individuals have already been discounted). The Gulf of Mexico catalogue now stands at a total of 153 individual sperm whales.

Resightings of Satellite Tagged Whales
Five of the 18 whales that were radio-tagged on the SWSS 2002 S-tag cruise were still transmitting their locations on a four-day cycle in mid-May 2003. Four of these radio-tagged whales were located close off the Mississippi River delta. On 18 June, the survey position was less than 5 miles from where one of these tagged animals had transmitted just hours earlier. The group of whales sighted and followed with small boats on 18 June in fact included 3 whales with satellite tags. Photographs of the tag and attachment area were taken for each individual and 2 of the 3 animals could be photo-identified. The third tagged animal, which persistently performed low fluke-up dives, could not be adequately photographed. Other satellite-tagged whales were also seen on other occasions on the cruise, but due to rough weather good photographs could not be obtained.

Length Measurements

To estimate sperm whale total length, which might allow an assessment of population age structure, 87 photo-identification photographs were taken in conjunction with a measurement of the distance to the fluke using a Bushnell Yardage 1000 laser range finder. This method allows fluke width, which can be related to body length, to be determined accurately. Using a polynomial regression derived from whaling data, total length will be calculated for these 87 encounters.

Sperm whale size also can be measured acoustically from click interpulse intervals. Whenever possible, recordings were made at the beginning of the dive of each identified individual using the RHIB acoustic recordings systems.

Several of the groups sighted were thought to be nursery groups, and medium to large calves were sighted on 6 of the 20 days (4, 8, 11, 12, 17, and 18 June). No calves considered to be small or newly born were observed.

Codas were heard whenever whales were engaged in social behavior and these were recorded from the RHIBs as well as from the *Gyre*. Because of the engine and propeller noise radiated by the *Gyre*, codas recordings from the small RHIBs were clearer than those recorded by the Ecologic hydrophone arrays towed from the larger vessel.

Acoustic Monitoring, Detection, and Tracking

For this cruise, two matched two-hydrophone streamer systems, assembled by Ecologic UK Ltd., were the primary survey tool. Each array had hydrophone streamer sections consisting of 2 hydrophone elements (Benthos AQ-4) and respective pre-amplifiers (Magrec) providing 30dB gain and with a 100Hz low cut filter. These were mounted 3 m apart and housed in a ~10 m long polyurethane tube and 400 m of strengthened tow cable with a hair fairing sheath to reduce cable noise. One of these arrays, referred to as the "source array", was equipped with a third element (Benthos AQ-2000) mounted halfway between the other two. This was used as an active element, driven by an amplifier from the ship, to allow the relative spacing of the two streamers to be determined acoustically. The other array, deemed the "linear array", was equipped with a group of six parallel elements (Benthos AQ-4) with 150-cm spacing between them connected to one Magrec preamplifier. This experimental configuration should provide some directionality and increased gain, abeam, to cancel a portion of the ship noise, and this could improve the ability to detect sperm whales acoustically. However, due to technical difficulties this configuration was not extensively tested and did not provide promising results.

Each array was also equipped with depth sensors (Keller PA-9SE-50 50bar 4-20mA sensor) whose readings were displayed on panel meters (Asahi Keiki A5000 display units) installed in the acoustics lab. These units also were linked to one of the labs' computers by means of a RS-232 serial connection. The serial string was read by custom software, developed during the cruise by Ricardo Antunes, and logged within the acoustic *Logger* database. The depth readings of the depth sensors were calibrated using a Time-Depth Recorder (Seabird Electronics Model no. 39), which was attached to the arrays during a trial deployment.

A tandem hydrophone configuration was chosen because, if towed on identical cable lengths, the two arrays should stream alongside each other to form a two dimensional directional array approximately 400 m behind the vessel. It was hoped that this configuration would allow side-to-side ambiguity to be resolved without maneuvering the vessel. The two hydrophones also provided opportunities to explore the use of long baseline linear configurations and of course provided backup if required.

The Ecologic hydrophones were deployed at their maximum cable length. As several turns had to remain on the cable winch drum, the streamers towed approximately 390 m astern of the vessel. Hydrophone depth depends on tow speed and cable length. With all the cable deployed the hydrophone elements towed at an approximate depth of 35 m at ship speed of 5 knots. Tow depth increased to > 100 m when the ship slowed to 2-2.5 knots. During surveys the vessel maintained a speed of 6 knots, which represented a good compromise between reducing noise and covering ground. The arrays were left deployed during small boat operations including boat launch and recovery. When trawling with IKMT, which was usually at night, the arrays were recovered on board.

The primary acoustic monitoring station was established in a dry lab aft of the computer room on the 01 deck. A team of four acoustic monitoring personnel (monitors) provided 24-hour coverage for all of the time that the ship was at sea and off the continental shelf. During different phases of the cruise and depending on the requirements, acoustic monitors either conducted standard survey monitoring, conducted searches for whales, or assisted in tracking groups and locating individuals for photo-ID.

The click detection and display program, *Rainbow Click*, ran continuously during monitoring and the detection records were stored as computer files. *Rainbow Click* software was written by Douglas Gillespie and is made freely available for marine conservation and protection projects by the International Fund for Animal Welfare. The companion *Ishmael* program was run continuously in real-time spectrogram mode and provided valuable assistance in visually detecting cetacean vocalizations. *Ishmael*, written by David Mellinger, is also freely available software with a variety of acoustic detection and display functions.

Hydrophone Search and Survey: When surveying/searching for whales the monitors listened carefully to the hydrophones using stereo headphones for one minute every 15 minutes, and then scored and noted levels of seismics noise and cetacean vocalizations in the *Logger* program. Monitors listened to a training program on the first day of the cruise and compared the way they scored sounds among themselves during the cruise to maintain a consistent scoring system. At other times output from the hydrophone arrays were output on high quality speakers in the acoustic lab. In addition, 20-second acoustic samples were recorded automatically as .wav files every two minutes and continuous recordings were made of interesting noises, including vocalizations from identified cetaceans, click trains from single animals over entire dives, and coda vocalizations from sperm whale social groups.

Animal Tracking: Once acoustic contacts had been made and come abeam if the vessel was operating in survey mode, the role of the acoustic team became to track vocalizing whales to keep the vessel close to them and provide the visual tracking team with information on bearings to vocalizing animals. Other information of use to the visual team were cases when a particular whale stopped clicking. This was usually an indication that it had nearly finished its dive and would soon surface. When whales were encountered at night acoustic monitoring might have to keep the vessel close to whales for extended periods relying entirely on acoustic cues. To achieve this, the acoustic team made use of the tandem arrays running *Rainbow Click* on two different computers. *Rainbow Click* calculates bearings to the sound source (whale) from the arrival delay of clicks between the 2 hydrophone elements of a single array. However, this produces two possible bearings, one on each side of the array. On this project, *Rainbow Click* was run simultaneously on a second monitoring computer to compare time of arrival between the two rear hydrophones in each streamer. This second display provided information to resolve side-to-side bearings, overcoming the limitation associated with the use of only front/back elements. With practice, monitors were able to match patterns of clicks from particular whales on the two displays. In this way the acoustics team could, on most occasions, tell the bearing and direction of sperm whales relative to the array without having the *Gyre* turn and this significantly enhanced their localization and tracking ability.

Multi-Channel Acoustic Recordings: On several occasions, usually after recovering the RHIBs and before trawling, 4-channel recordings were made using 2 elements of each array. Several different array configurations were explored by changing the length of cable of the "linear array". The objective of these recordings was to gather data to be used for development and improvement of sperm whale acoustic location methods for tracking and survey using a wide aperture linear array.

Small Boat Acoustic Monitoring: Each of the RHIB boats carried their own portable acoustic stations, consisting of a pair of Hi-Tech HTI-96-MIN hydrophones with 30 m of cable, an amplifier/conditioner box, a Creative Labs Nomad Jukebox3 recorder, and hand-held directional hydrophone units. On days when the weather was favorable but no whales had been found, one or more of the RHIBs might be dispatched to listen (see "Use of RHIBs" above). The *Gyre* is a relatively noisy vessel, particularly for acoustic research purposes, whereas a stationary RHIB is a very quiet platform. It was clear that the acoustic range from the RHIBs was much greater than that from the *Gyre*.

Acoustically equipped RHIBs also proved to be a most effective method for fine-scale tracking during extended encounters with groups of whales. Monitoring could be performed away from the noise of the *Gyre*, and the small boats could respond and move quickly to localize animals complimenting the continuous tracking that the *Gyre* acoustic team could perform.

Acoustic Tracking Preliminary Results: A total of 956 standard one-minute stations were completed while searching for and tracking whales. Sperm whales were detected at 555 (58%) of these (Figure 3.1.6). Sperm whales were detected acoustically at or near about 25% of the XBT and CTD stations. In addition to monitoring for cetacean vocalizations, the presence of anthropogenic noise was noted. The *Gyre*'s own engine and prop sound masked many sources of anthropogenic noise, but seismic shots were a prominent part of the acoustic environment and were detected during approximately 30% of the listening stations.

Tissue Collection/Genetic Typing
Because biopsy samples are usually taken as whales fluke up, photo-ID images and biopsy samples can be taken efficiently and concurrently. Thus, plans were to do biopsy sampling as much as possible in conjunction with photo-identification work. However, the biopsy work was curtailed when Dan Engelhaupt transferred to the R/V *Ewing* on 9 June 2003 to assist with tasks on the D-tag/CEE SWSS cruise (see Section 3.2).

While Dan Engelhaupt was aboard *Gyre* from 31 May through 8 June, biopsy sampling techniques were combined with photo-ID, photogrammetry, and acoustic data to further understanding of sperm whale social and population structure. A total of thirteen skin samples were collected during the cruise (Table 3.1.9 and Figure 3.1.7). Nine biopsy samples with 9 matching photo-ID fluke photographs were taken of whales west of 90°W. One biopsy sample was collected below the dorsal hump of a whale that was logging at the surface. Three samples of sloughed skin were collected after breaching and socializing events, although no photo-ID shots were collected for these whales. All tissue samples obtained are expected to provide ample material for genetic applications. No significantly large males (whales that appear to be sexually and physically mature based on estimated sizes) were encountered and therefore none were sampled.

Overall, the combination of fluke biopsy sampling (waiting until a whale 'flukes-up' before releasing the dart), photo-ID, photogrammetry, and acoustic recordings of sperm whales proved highly successful. Although fluke sampling is a more difficult method of obtaining a tissue sample, the amount of accompanying information (e.g., a whale's fluke ID) is well worth the additional effort. The genetic information for an individual whale can be used each time a whale

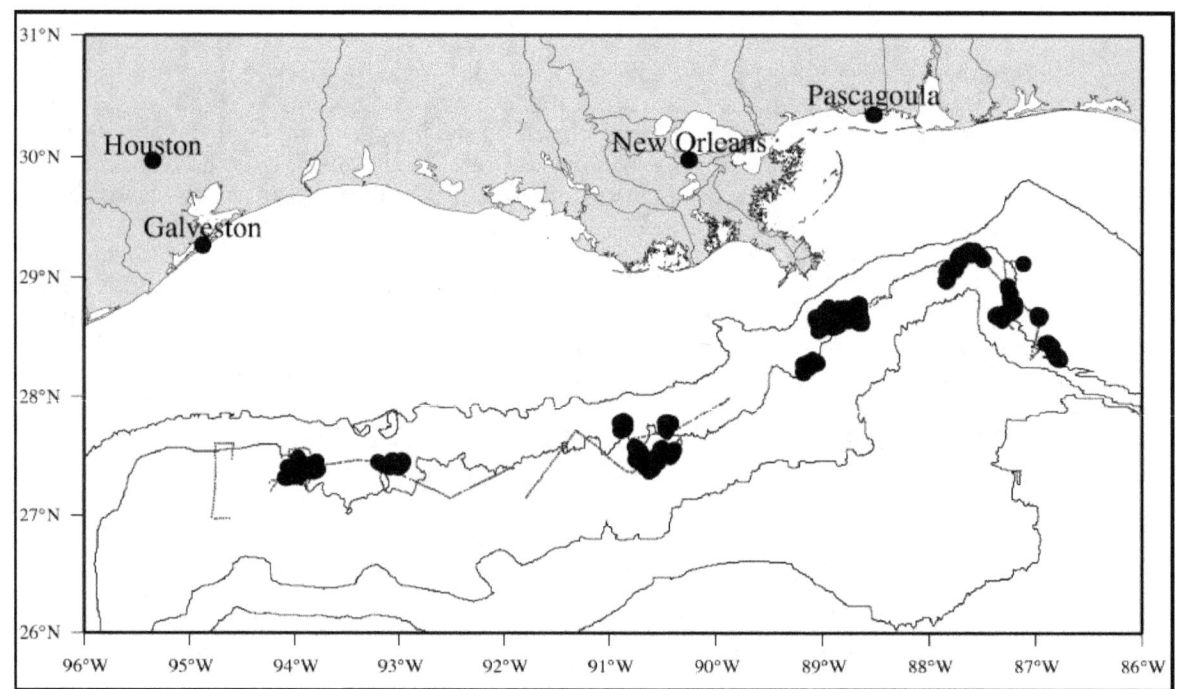

Figure 3.1.6. Acoustic detections of sperm whales (dots) on SWSS 2003 WSHC cruise superimposed on the cruise track occupied while towing the hydrophone arrays (gray line). Contours are shown for the 200, 1000, 2000, and 3000-m isobaths.

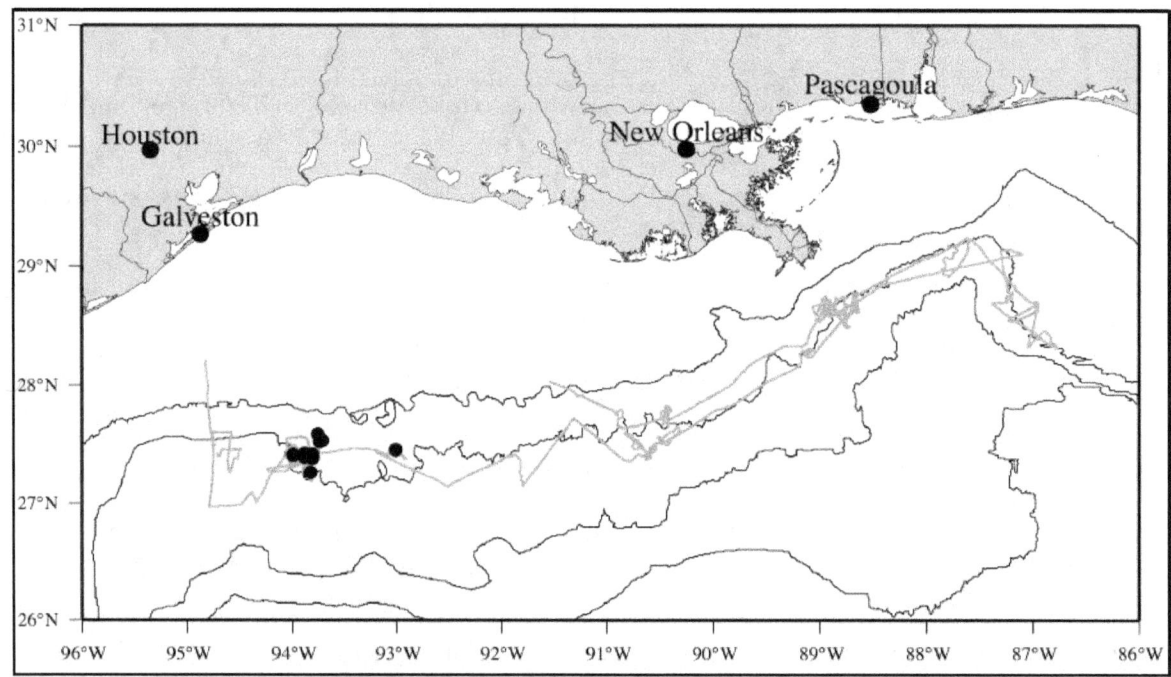

Figure 3.1.7. Locations of biopsy samples on SWSS 2003 WSHC cruise. Contours are shown for the 200, 1000, 2000, and 3000-m isobaths.

Table 3.1.9

Tissue Collection/Genetic Typing Samples Collected During SWSS 2003 WSHC Cruise
(The sample number is coded for the date in dd/mm/yy format and the sequence number.)

Sample #	Tissue Type	Group #	Approx. # whales in the area	Latitude (°N)	Longitude (°W)
030602-01	Biopsy	1	8	27.2654	93.8251
030602-02	Sloughed Skin	1	8	27.3995	93.8852
030602-03	Sloughed Skin	1	8	27.3995	93.8852
030602-04	Biopsy	1	8	27.3995	93.8852
030603-01	Biopsy	2	6	27.3865	93.8111
030604-01	Biopsy	2	6	27.4119	93.8816
030604-02	Biopsy	2	6	27.4228	93.8422
030604-03	Biopsy	2	6	27.4188	93.8091
030605-02	Biopsy	3	8	27.4551	93.0028
030605-03	Sloughed Skin	3	8	27.4109	93.9954
030608-01	Biopsy	4	6	27.5267	93.7363
030608-02	Biopsy	4	6	27.5350	93.7133
030608-03	Biopsy	4	6	27.5916	93.7547

is photo-identified in the future. High levels of communication and coordination between the RHIB's crew, the visual team, the acoustics team, and the *Gyre's* crew lead to good success.

Midwater Trawling and Plankton Sampling
A 15-foot Isaacs-Kidd Midwater Trawl with a mouth opening of 14.7 m^2 was used for oblique tows to sample depths of 0-400 m, 0-600 m and 0-800 m. A General Oceanics flowmeter was suspended in the mouth to measure volume of water filtered. A SeaBird Time, Depth, and Temperature Recorder (TDTR, Model 39) was attached to one of the bridle wires to measure these parameters at 10 second intervals. Meters of wire out and real time were tabulated every 200 m. This allowed an estimate to be made of the amount of wire out needed to reach the targeted depths at which whales are thought to be feeding based on data from D-tagged animals from summer 2002 and from email reports received from R/V *Ewing*.

Twenty-five tows were made at various locations representative of LCE, cyclone, and adjacent slope water along the 800-1000-m isobaths (Figure 3.1.8). Calibration data generated with the first pair of tows allowed the targeted depths to be reached during subsequent tows to within as little as 5 m and as much as 25 m. Typically the first 200 m of wire would be set at a ship speed of 3 knots and with the rest set at speeds up to 4 knots. Wire was paid out at 50 m/min to about 1,000 m short of maximum wire out. Then the winch would be slowed to 30m/min. This turns out to be critical to "get the slack" out of the wire to achieve the desired depth. Sampling time in the interval of interest was maximized by stopping the winch for 10 minute intervals and retrieving wire at 30m/min in the interval. When the top of the interval was reached, the ship was slowed to 3 knots and wire in was increased to 50m/min. One IKMT sample was lost when the

PVC cod end came apart on the ninth trawl. After that use of a cod end was stopped, andthe canvas distal end of the net was tied off instead. Volumes filtered per trawl ranged from 119,000 to 281,000 cubic meters (see Table 3.1.10).

The IKMT collections are rich in groups such as hatchet fishes, myctophids, viperfish, large decapod crustaceans, and euphausiids. The quick look impression is that medium-size to large cephalopods are not in high abundance in the IKMT collections, but small specimens in the 1-2 cm size range are likely to be found when these trawl samples are sorted. The most common medium to large squid in the IKMT collections are histioteuthids and enoploteuthids. The largest histioteuthid taken in an IKMT trawl (Figure 3.1.9) was about 30 cm long. Larger individuals of this family are known to be part of the diet of sperm whales based on squid beaks identified from the stomachs of whales commercially harvested in the 19th and 20th century.

Two of the IKMT samples were sorted at sea into fishes, crustaceans and "everything else". In the lab, the groups sorted from these two and from all the rest of the trawls will be broken down into smaller, more taxonomically defined groups, and for each of these groups the wet volume biomass will be measured as wet displacement volume. Given the recording of the actual maximum depths of the samples as well as temperature from the SeaBird sensor on the net and the time spent in each depth interval, these collections represent the most intensive and best-documented midwater trawl samples ever collected in the Gulf of Mexico.

In addition, a Multiple Opening-Closing Net and Environmental Sampling System (MOCNESS) tow was taken. Its nine nets sampled from 0-800 m, with one sample taken from 0-400 m to be comparable to the 3 shallow IKMTs and one sample taken over each 50 m interval from 400-800 m. So a total of nine samples were collected with that single MOCNESS deployment. The deeper MOCNESS samples collected very little plankton volume.

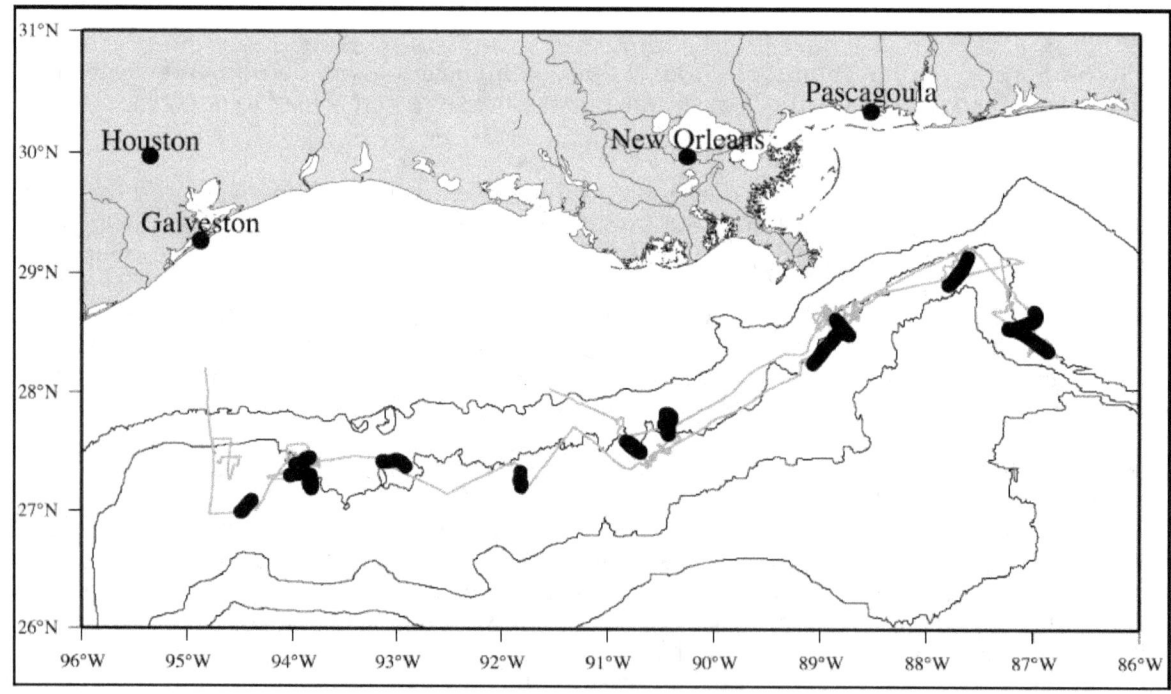

Figure 3.1.8. Locations of IKMT collections on SWSS 2003 WSHC cruise. The cruise track is shown together with contours for the 200, 1000, 2000, and 3000-m isobaths.

30

Table 3.1.10

Summary of IKMT and MOCNESS Tows Taken on SWSS 2003 WSHC Cruise

Tow No.	Date (mm/dd/yyyy)	Time In (UTC)	Total Time (Min)	Start Location Lat (°N)	Start Location Lon (°W)	End Location Lat (°N)	End Location Lon (°W)	Volume (m³)	Maximum Depth (m)
1	06/01/2003	03:40	158	26.9877	94.4927	27.0915	94.3847	242203	728
2	06/02/2003	03:24	106	27.2960	93.8323	27.2090	93.8190	162357	ND
3	06/03/2003	07:06	86	27.1900	93.8250	27.2638	93.8502	119240	685
4	06/03/2003	03:51	120	27.4445	93.8508	27.3582	93.9118	173180	892
5	06/04/2003	08:11	92	27.3253	93.9412	27.2968	94.0352	137157	698
6	06/04/2003	00:32	137	27.4482	93.8795	27.3947	93.9732	210286	654
7	06/04/2003	03:47	125	27.4005	93.9387	27.4565	93.8452	191531	708
8	06/05/2003	02:45	118	27.3783	92.9163	27.4372	92.0028	177319	728
9	06/06/2003	05:50	154	27.4355	93.0177	27.2060	93.1245	207955	ND
10	06/06/2003	03:03	168	27.3350	91.8153	27.4222	91.8112	240213	750
11	06/08/2003	03:03	154	27.5992	90.8285	27.5080	90.6868	265598	809
12	06/09/2003	06:23	118	27.5072	90.6835	27.5855	90.7860	211325	544
13	06/10/2003	01:59	168	28.2530	89.0648	28.4030	88.9360	249920	723
14	06/11/2003	06:10	138	28.4270	88.8998	28.5458	88.7950	194451	630
15	06/12/2003	02:40	170	28.9167	87.7667	29.0450	87.6667	280877	778
16	06/13/2003	07:05	123	29.0435	87.6658	29.1497	87.6057	197926	602
17	06/13/2003	04:00	125	28.6905	86.9807	28.6113	87.0368	203810	572
18	06/14/2003	06:27	181	28.5917	87.0458	28.5545	87.2262	275536	789
19	06/14/2003	01:40	179	28.3598	86.8562	28.4720	87.0233	277065	815
20	06/14/2003	04:56	142	28.4777	87.0328	28.5550	87.1780	212981	359
21	06/17/2003	03:39	150	28.6250	88.8458	28.5043	88.7650	232812	407
22	06/17/2003	07:22	151	28.4955	88.7235	28.6113	88.8298	239471	778
M	06/18/2003	03:08	127	28.6978	88.7693	28.5875	88.7625	7302	800
23	06/19/2003	01:32	159	27.8243	90.4422	28.6648	90.4155	279050	610
24	06/19/2003	04:34	154	27.6548	90.4230	27.8330	90.4263	261888	722
25	06/20/2003	07:34	126	27.8330	90.4263	27.7367	90.4650	231377	410

M=MOCNESS trawl

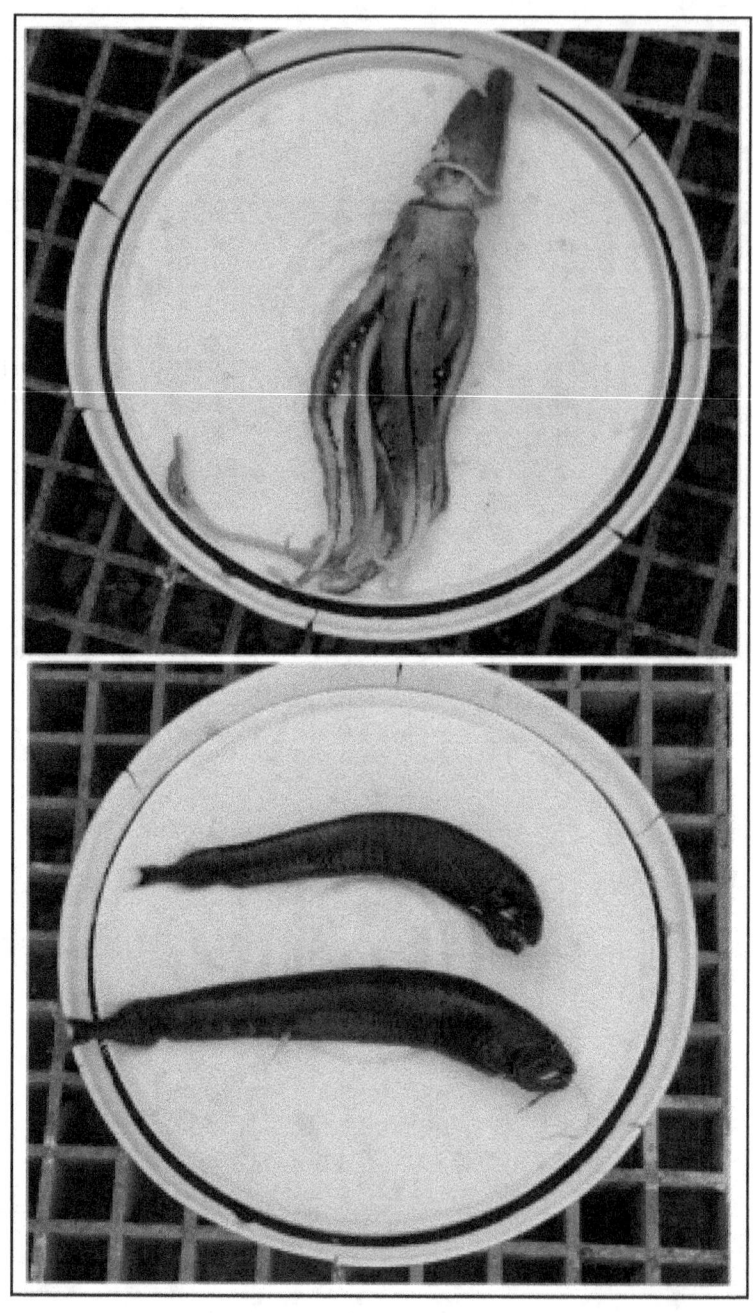

Figure 3.1.9. Histioteuthid squid (upper panel) and fang-tooth blackfish (bottom panel) from IKMT collections near 94°W. The white collection bucket lid is 12" (30 cm) in diameter.

38kHz ADCP Backscatter: A Tool for Tracking Deep Scattering Layers

The 38kHz ADCP provided the ability to track the diel vertical migration of the main deep scattering layer (DSL). Each evening before the trawl went in, the backscattering data for the previous 24 hours were plotted as a function of time to give a visualization of the timing for daytime descent and nighttime ascent of the DSL. Figure 3.1.10 shows one example. On most days, several distinct layers were seen, suggesting that different organisms have different biorhythms or use different environmental cues that trigger their diel vertical migration. Generally the migrating layers began to descend between 30 to 60 minutes before sunrise from the surface to between 400 and 450 m depths. The main DSL was present at this depth horizon for most of the daylight hours, and then some of its component organisms ascended to the surface again from 0 to 60 minutes after sunset. The main DSL averaged deeper than 450 m when the ship was in clear blue surface water; its daytime depth in Eddy Sargassum was 500-550 m, compared to just 300 m in the DeSoto Canyon cyclone.

The IKMT trawling each night was targeted for depths from 400-600 m and 600-800 m. Since these two depth zones were sampled in an area of convergence (Eddy Sargassum) as well as in an area of divergence (DeSoto Canyon cyclone), the trawl collections from these two hydrographic boundary conditions should include representatives of the deep scattering non-migrating species that will be correlated with the backscatter intensities in the deep layers.

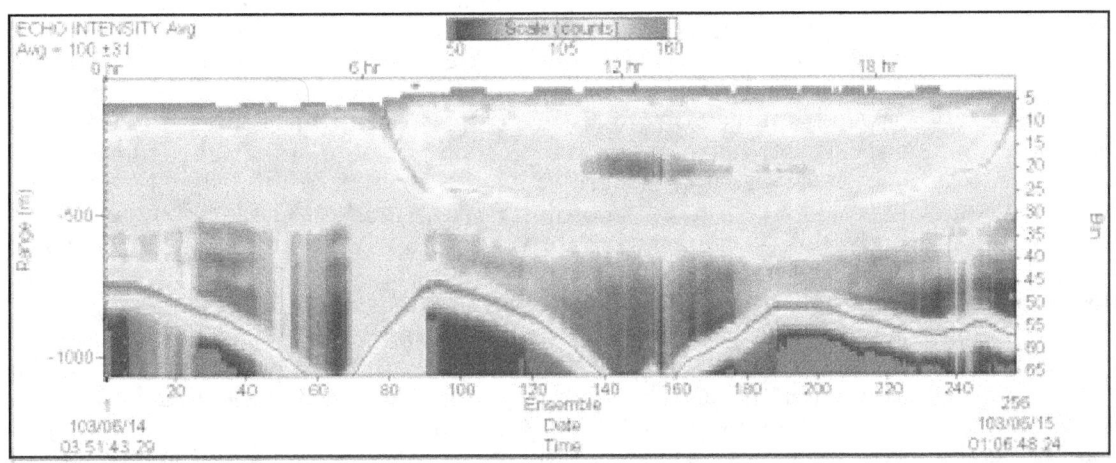

Figure 3.1.10. Plot of backscatter intensity from the 38 kHz ADCP. It shows the daytime descent (starts down 6 hr into the record) and evening ascent (back up at end of the record) of the deep scattering layer in the eastern Gulf of Mexico. This 21 hour record begins 03:51 UTC on 14 June and ends 01:06 UTC on 15 June. Bottom depth is shown by the high intensity return at depths >700 m. The bright green zone between ~5.5-7.5 hrs into the record comes from a low signal-to-noise period when the ship transited at a speed over ground of more than 6 knots.

33

3.2   D-tag Cruise 2003

The SWSS 2003 D-tag cruise was conducted from 3-24 June 2003 aboard the R/V *Maurice Ewing* (cruise EW0303). The *Ewing*, operated by Lamont-Doherty Earth Observatory (LDEO), was made available to SWSS by the National Science Foundation. Cruise EW0303 consisted of two entirely separate legs. The D-tag leg immediately followed an LDEO-project leg during which calibrated recordings were made of the *Ewing* airgun arrays under a separate authorization from NOAA Fisheries to the National Science Foundation/LDEO. The D-tag leg of cruise EW0303 began out of Gulfport, MS, and ended in Galveston, TX. During 9-22 June 2003, in the controlled exposure experiment (CEE) portion of the D-tag cruise, the R/V *Ewing* was joined by the seismic source vessel M/V *Kondor Explorer*, made available by the International Association of Geophysical Contractors (IAGC) and a coalition of industry sponsors. This vessel's cruise also consisted of two components, associated with the MMS sponsored SWSS and EARS projects. The EARS buoy component was to calibrate *Kondor* airguns under a separate authorization. The SWSS component was in support of the SWSS D-tag/CEE work under NOAA Fisheries permit 981-1707 issued to Dr. Peter Tyack of WHOI. This summary reports on the D-tag/CEE work only; persons interested in the EARS component should contact MMS for information. Additional information associated with this cruise is in Section 4.3 (D-tag analyses).

The primary goals of the SWSS 2003 D-tag/CEE study were to conduct controlled exposure experiments (CEEs) of an industry standard airgun array and to improve the technology used to conduct CEEs. Each CEE was composed of a pre-tagging period before a D-tag is attached to a sperm whale, a pre-exposure period after the tag is attached and prior to the onset of the controlled sound source, an exposure period during which a sound is transmitted in a controlled fashion to the tagged whales, and a post-exposure period during which the behavior of the animal is observed after the sound is turned off. Real-time display of information was used extensively to maneuver the source vessel into the correct geometry for the sound exposure. As part of conducting CEEs, a secondary goal of the cruise was to characterize the signals received from the *Kondor* source array on a calibrated recording device (the LDEO spar buoy and/or D-tags attached to the spar buoy; this is separate from the work with the bottom-mounted EARS buoys).

In addition to the primary goals related to CEEs of airgun transmissions, baseline data also were collected in which tagged whales were not deliberately exposed to sounds. Skin samples were retrieved on seven occassions from the D-tag suction cups after they released from the animal. These were retained for genetic analysis. On 13 occassions, in approaching and inspecting whales, photographs of flukes or photogrammetry images were taken. Visual and acoustic observers on the observation vessel made continuous observations of the behavior of sperm whales. Surfacing positions and group compositions were recorded, and the locations of fluking whales were passed to the acoustics team. The acoustics team tracked the bearing to these whales using passive tracking, and informed the visual team when whales ceased clicking and were therefore about to surface. The acoustics team also recorded and logged sounds of interest such as codas, other natural sounds, and seismic transmissions from ongoing activities. Finally, environmental measurements were made using XBTs, and videotape was taken for an MMS documentary.

SWSS Principal Investigators (PIs) who participated on this cruise were Mark Johnson (Field Party Chief), Patrick Miller, Aaron Thode (3-D passive acoustic tracking PI) and, after transfer from *Gyre* on 9 June, Dan Engelhaupt (genetic analyses PI). Terry Ketler of Interactive Educational Network was the PI for the video documentary work. Additionally, Carol Roden of MMS participated in the cruise aboard the *Kondor*. Table 3.2.1 lists the D-tag science team aboard the *Ewing* and their duties. Table 3.2.2 lists the LDEO science team aboard the *Ewing* and their duties. Table 3.2.3 lists the science team and duties aboard the *Kondor*.

34

Table 3.2.1

The SWSS 2003 D-tag Cruise: D-tag/CEE Science Team on R/V *Maurice Ewing*
(PI Institutional Affiliations are Given; Other Personnel were Affiliated Through WHOI)

Personnel	Description
Dr. Mark Johnson	Field Party Chief, tagger, data analysis (WHOI)
Dr. Patrick Miller	Tag boat observer, data analysis (U. of St. Andrews, UK)
Alessandro Bocconcelli	Tag boat driver, VHF tracking, deck operations
Kenneth Alex Shorter	Tag preparation, tag data management
Maria Elena Quero	Visual coordinator, data manager
Michela Podesta	Visual data recorder, assistant data manager
Valeria Teloni	Acoustic coordinator, data manager, GIS display
Matt Grund	Acoustic observer, GIS display
Natacha Aguilar de Soto	Acoustic observer
Sue Rocca	Acoustic observer
Amy Beier	Tagging coordinator on flying bridge, tissue handling
Dee Allen	Visual/acoustic observer, permit compliance
Todd Pusser	Lead visual observer
Irene Brigga*	Visual/acoustic observer
Kara Buckstaff	Visual/ acoustic observer
Anna Nousek	Visual/ acoustic observer
Suzanne Yin*	Visual/ acoustic observer
Dan Engelhaupt	Playback coordinator, tissue handling (U. of Durham, UK)

* Also served on *Kondor* as visual observers (separately)

Table 3.2.2

The SWSS 2003 D-tag Cruise: LDEO Science Team on R/V *Maurice Ewing*

Personnel	Description
Dr. John Diebold	Field party chief – LDEO calibration work
Chris Leidhold	Science officer
Ethan Gold	Systems Admininstrator
Emily Chapp	Acoustics Technician, helped with D-tag acoustic tracking

The biology team on-board the *Ewing* and *Kondor* were listed as co-Investigators of permit 981-1707 issued to Dr. Peter Tyack by NOAA Fisheries (formerly National Marine Fisheries Service). The permit specifically authorized the research activities conducted during the cruise, including approaching whales for tagging, observing whales during focal follows, and exposing whales to controlled levels of sound. The permit included requirements that no marine mammals or sea turtles be exposed to sound levels above 180 dB re 1µPa RMS, that every effort be made to ensure that animals are disturbed as little as possible, and that no activities be conducted that might cause significant harm to whales. To comply with the permit, Dr. Tyack and co-investigators developed a detailed protocol to mitigate possible harm related to the tagging or sound-playback activities. The protocol is given in the Appendix to this report. All parties throughout the cruise followed this protocol closely.

Chronological Summary
The track of the D-tag leg of cruise EW0303 is shown in Figure 3.2.1 (top panel). A summary of tagging and CEE activities is given in Table 3.2.4. After leaving Gulfport, MS, on the evening of 3 June, the science team spent June 4-8 working on baseline tagging and coda playbacks. During this period, a D-tag was attached to one whale in the DeSoto Canyon region. Weather was too rough to attempt a coda playback with this whale. Several of the days had bad weather. There was no success in attaching a D-tag after multiple approaches on June 8.

On June 9, the *Kondor* and *Ewing* rendezvoused and Dan Engelhaupt transferred from *Gyre* to *Ewing* to fill the critical role of playback coordinator. The *Kondor* was outfitted with a towed SEAMAP hydrophone array and a team of visual observers to assure that no marine mammal or sea turtle would be exposed to sound levels above 180 dB re 1μPa RMS, as is specified in the Tyack permit. Dr. Douglas Nowacek coordinated the *Kondor* observer team. The *Kondor* propulsion system was very noisy on the towed array, but after several iterations the *Kondor* team was able to detect sperm whales out to approximately 1.5 km. The much quieter research vessel *Ewing*, in contrast, had detection ranges estimated to be greater than 8 km.

On June 9, the EARS buoys were deployed from the *Kondor*. Calibration of the *Kondor* sources was attempted. This calibration was not completed because beaked whales were sighted within the mitigation range defined by the mitigation protocol (Appendix). The ships then proceeded to conduct the D-tag/CEE component of the cruise.

June 10-12 were marked by rough weather, making tagging operations difficult. No tags were deployed on June 10. Tags were deployed on June 11 and 12. However, these were too late in the day for there to be sufficient daylight to conduct a CEE. Having a tag on the whale allowed the *Ewing* and *Kondor* to conduct a trial "dry-run" of the CEE procedure. The overall CEE process was streamlined. These tag data also are valuable as baseline/control data in the SWSS data set.

Table 3.2.3

The SWSS 2003 D-tag Cruise: Multi-Purpose Science Team on M/V *Kondor Explorer*

Personnel	Description	Institution
Dr. Douglas Nowacek	Permit compliance, observation coordinator	WHOI
Carol Roden	Visual observations for permit compliance	MMS
Sandy Sawyer	Visual observer	IAGC
Craig Douglas	Acoustic systems	SEAMAP
Dr. Aaron Thode*	3-D tracking of sperm whales	SIO
Dr Joal Newcomb,	EARS buoy PI and Team Leader	NRL
Jim Showalter	EARS buoy	NRL
Terry Ketler**	Documentary filming PI	IEN

NRL = Naval Research Laboratory   IEN = Interactive Educational Network
 * Transferred to *Ewing* on June 16   ** Worked on *Ewing* from June 16-22

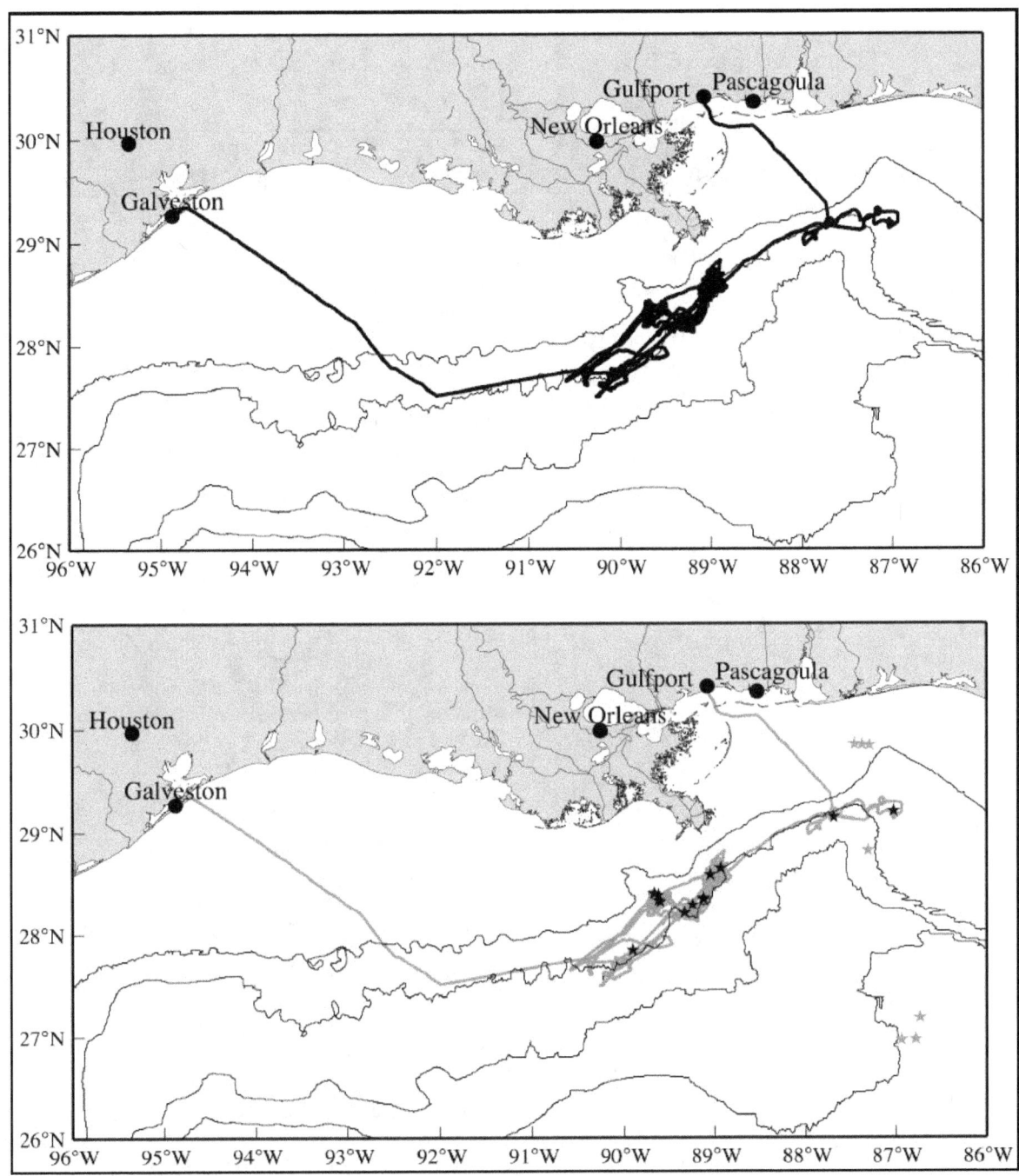

Figure 3.2.1. D-tag cruise track of R/V *Maurice Ewing* for SWSS 2003 (upper) and locations of XBT drops (lower). Locations of XBT drops made during the D-tag/CEE leg of cruise EW0303 are shown at the black stars. Those of the leg immediately preceeding the D-tag/CEE leg are shown at the gray stars. The 200, 1000, 2000, and 3000-m isobath contours are shown.

Table 3.2.4

Daily Summary of Tagging and CEE Activity During D-tag Cruise

Date	with whales?	# tags deployed	# CEEs	Comments (times are CDT)
June 3	n/a	n/a	n/a	Departure PM from Gulfport
June 4	y	0	n/a	Tag-deploy arm repaired
June 5	y	1	n/a	4:50 deployment, bad weather arrives
June 6	y	0	n/a	Weather too rough for tagging
June 7	y	0	n/a	Weather too rough for tagging
June 8	y	0	n/a	Several approaches, whales avoided *R2* tag boat
June 9	n	0	n/a	Rendezvous with *Kondor*. Calibration day, halted due to mitigation
June 10	y	0	0	Tagging was attempted, but it was too rough
June 11	y	1	0	Weather too rough AM to tag, late attachment allowed only a test-run CEE
June 12	y	1	0	Rough weather until 1630 made CEE impossible
June 13	y	1	1	CEE start delayed due to rough weather, but CEE was accomplished later in the day
June 14	y	2	1	Poor VHF tracking placement made the CEE difficult, W. Neptune arrives in delta area
June 15	n	0	0	No whales, calibration trial with spar buoy
June 16	y	2	1	CEE halted during ramp-up due to mitigation, tags detached from whales just after mitigation call
June 17	n	0	0	No whales all day in MRC
June 18	n	0	0	No whales all day in MRC, rendezvous with Gyre
June 19	y	1	0	Aborted CEE due to nearby ongoing seismics and inability to VHF track tagged whale
June 20	y	0	0	Whales avoided *R2* on over 5 approaches
June 21	y	0	0	Storms and lightning prohibited tagging
June 22	y	2	1	Storms AM. One tag detached before CEE. CEE was OK, but VHF tracking was again poor. *Kondor* departed in PM to EARS buoys
June 23	n	0	n/a	Searching for whales during return transit
June 24	n/a	-	n/a	Arrive dock in Galveston
TOTAL	15/20	11 / 80.5 hrs / 7 w/ skin	4/13	4 CEEs (June 13, 14, 16, 22); 16th not to full-array 4 days rough weather AM (June 10, 11, 12, 21); 3 days no whales (June 15, 17, 18), 1 day no tag-out on whale (June 20), 1 day poor VHF + nearby seismics (June 19)

On June 13 a whale was tagged in the morning and the first CEE was conducted later in the day when visibility conditions improved sufficiently for effective visual mitigation off the *Kondor*.

On June 14, a second CEE was conducted with two whales tagged. The tags were placed rather low on these animals, so VHF reception was very intermittent. This made it difficult to direct the *Kondor* toward the tagged whales. Nonetheless, loud seismics were heard on the recovered tags.

Also on the 14th, an industry vessel, the *Western Neptune*, began a planned survey across the 1000-m contour off the Mississippi Delta. Its transmissions began about the same time that the *Kondor* began its controlled exposure. This timing means that the pre-exposure data on this CEE is still valid for the CEE data analysis.

To find whales that were less recently exposed to ongoing seismics, the ships moved back to the Mississippi River Canyon (MRC) where many whales had been followed just days before. By 1400 CDT on June 15, no whales had been found. The LDEO spar buoy was deployed and the signature of the *Kondor* array was recorded on that buoy. Conditions were quite good for this received-level characterization, and the *Kondor* was driven to within 100 m of the buoy. LDEO acquired and analyzed over 250 shots from the buoy. A D-tag attached to the buoy also recorded these sounds. This will be a useful means to ground-truth levels received on whales during CEEs. The D-tag also showed that the "deep" hydrophone on the buoy was actually at about 150-m depth rather than the 500-m depth of the cable. A planned second broadside oriented pass at 1000-m range was canceled due to sighting of mesoplodont beaked whales within the mitigation range defined by the mitigation protocol (Appendix).

The ships continued to move west. Two large animals were found on the morning of June 16. Both whales were tagged. A CEE was begun, but 15 minutes into the ramp-up, a *Kogia* and then a beaked whale were sighted within the mitigation range defined by the mitigation protocol (Appendix), so the transmission was stopped. The tags detached early from both whales just after the mitigation stop.

The MRC was searched for whales on June 17 and 18, but with no detections. The ships then moved east to a group of whales that had been followed by the *Gyre*. This area had been avoided because of ongoing seismics from the *Western Neptune*, but the search areas further to the west had been exhausted. On June 19, one whale was tagged, but the tag slipped so low that VHF tracking was impossible. The CEE was aborted because the *Kondor* could not be directed adequately to provide a sufficient exposure to the tagged whale in the presence of the ongoing seismics.

On June 20 multiple whales were approached with no success tagging. June 21 was stormy, and lightning prohibited tagging. On the last potential day of CEEs, June 22, the team waited out a long series of storms until the weather broke. Alex Shorter tagged two whales in rapid succession. Although one tag detached from one of the whales, a CEE was successfully accomplished with the other. While transiting to Galveston on June 23, the team searched for whales to the west of the MRC, but made no detections. The final day of work by the *Kondor*, also on June 23, was at the EARS buoys and was conducted under a separate authorization.

Summary of Data Collection

During EW0303, a total of 11 sperm whales were tagged. The on-animal recording time was 80.5 hours. The new version-2 D-tags provided higher resolution and lower noise sensor and acoustic sampling. The average deployment duration from the new tags was almost 8 hours compared to about 4 hours for the older tags. The baseline data set will be useful to describe the natural behavior of sperm whales in the Gulf of Mexico. As in 2002, both bottom and mid-water feeding by sperm whales were recorded. Of particular interest this year are the first all-night data sets te team has recorded. These will help to round-out the understanding of diel behavior of sperm whales. Data on more extensive shallow dives and social behavior were collected than in previous years, which will greatly expand the coda data set. The new version of D-tag records undistorted clicks to 48 kHz. This will improve analyses of the acoustic structure of sperm whale clicks.

Out of 13 days with the *Kondor* available for CEEs, nine days had no CEEs (Table 3.2.4) due to bad weather (4 d), no whales (3 d), no successful tagging (1 d), or poor VHF tracking due to the

39

presence of ongoing industry seismics (1 d). Four CEEs were attempted with 6 whales tagged. Three were completed with 4 whales tagged. As noted in Table 3.2.4, these CEEs (on June 14, 19, and 20) were conducted on tagged animals that were difficult to track using the VHF signal. The location of these tagged whales will be deduced by linking click bottom-echoes to bathymetry, by assessing time-arrival differences of the *Kondor* array on the tagged whale versus the *Ewing* towed array, and through detailed inspection of the movement data recorded by D-tag. On the fourth (the CEE of June 16), the seismic source did not reach full power due to a mitigation stop because of sightings of *Kogia* within the mitigation range defined by the mitigation protocol (Appendix). These tags also subsequently detached early from the whales, but their data may be useful to assess immediate responses to ramp-up. Preliminary estimates of received levels during the accomplished CEEs ranged from 145-155 dB, but the exact levels will be examined during the data analysis effort.

D-tag recordings will be linked to part of the over 376 hours of high-quality sperm whale recordings from the SEAMAP array. These recordings include over 850 codas and numerous sounds with unusual characteristics, such as rapid click trains. Visual observers logged 4,430 fixes on 810 different surfacings of sperm whales, using three BigEyes and two data recorders for optimum visual tracking when tags were deployed. All this information was integrated and logged in a real-time GIS display. This display was particularly useful for the tagging and playback coordinators.

Seven tissue samples were collected on D-tag suction cups. The team collected 13 high-quality photo-ID shots, of which 3 were D-tagged whales (sw164a, sw167a & sw167b), two were S-tagged in SWSS 2002, and 8 were other whales that fluked during approaches for D-tagging. A total of 6 different satellite-tagged whales were sighted. LDEO staff measured 23 XBT profiles in support of tag deployments, although 4 were tests or had bad data (Table 3.2.5; Figure 3.2.1, lower panel).

Aaron Thode recorded roughly 24 hours on an autonomous towed depth-logging recorder synchronized with the SEAMAP array (see section 3.4). Data were collected from a pass of the *Kondor* firing its airguns past the LDEO spar buoy. Terry Ketler obtained footage from both *Kondor* and *Ewing* to use in the video being prepared for MMS.

Tagging Effort

Two different D-tag designs were used in SWSS 2003. Tag type 1 was identical to that used in SWSS 2002. It was comprised of a D-tag version 1 with 2 GBytes of FLASH memory and 12 bit audio resolution. Type 1 tags attached to the whale with 2 nitrile rubber suction cups of diameter 95mm. A passive vacuum pump was included in the tag to periodically reinforce the vacuum in the cups. The tags were programmed to sample audio at 32 kHz and sensors at 48 Hz, giving a recording time of 12 hours. The audio sensitivity was -153 dB re μPa meaning that a signal with 153 dB re μPa peak pressure would produce a .wav file recording with peak levels of ±1. This is also the clipping level of the tag, meaning that 153 dB re 1 μPa is the highest peak level after input filtering. The sensor suite on the tag consists of an accelerometer (3 axis), magnetometer (3 axis), pressure, and temperature.

Type 2 tags comprised a D-tag version 2 with 3.3 GBytes of FLASH memory and 16 bit audio resolution. These tags were attached with 4 nitrile rubber suction cups in a square arrangement, each of diameter 60mm. No pumps were included in the design. Audio was sampled at 96 kHz and the sensitivity was approximately -192 dB re μPa (a clipping threshold of 192 dB re μPa). Sensor sampling-rate was 50 Hz with the same sensor suite as D-tag Version 1, plus a new conductivity sensor. The tag uses a loss-less compression scheme, called *x3*, developed at WHOI to greatly extend the recording-time x sampling-rate product. With the settings used, a recording time of about 16 hours was expected. The version 2 D-tag had not been deployed on a wild

40

Table 3.2.5

Location, Date, Time, and Depth of the 15°C Isotherm at XBT Stations

Filename	Date (mm/dd/yyyy)	Time (UTC)	Latitude (°N)	Longitude (°W)	15°C depth (m)	Notes
ew030301.xt5*	05/27/2003	01:28	26.968	-86.777	-	1
ew030302.xt5*	05/27/2003	01:31	26.968	-86.777	-	1
ew03032.xt5*	05/27/2003	01:39	26.967	-86.933	462	4
ew03033.xt5*	05/27/2003	16:58	27.183	-86.733	447	4
ew03034.x7d*	06/02/2003	06:35	29.849	-87.450	-	2
ew0303_4.x7d*	06/02/2003	11:14	29.843	-87.368	-	3
ew0303_5.x7d*	06/02/2003	11:19	29.843	-87.367	-	2
ew0303_6.x7d*	06/02/2003	15:56	28.828	-87.299	-	2
ew0303_7.x7d*	06/02/2003	18:48	29.838	-87.286	-	2
ew0303a1.xt7	06/05/2003	16:54	29.203	-87.024	184	5
ew0303b2.xt7	06/06/2003	13:05	29.150	-87.683	170	-
ew0303b3.xt7	06/06/2003	13:39	29.150	-83.050	-	3
ew0303b4.x7d	06/07/2003	08:42	28.350	-89.117	216	-
ew0303b5.x7d	06/08/2003	12:37	28.325	-89.598	205	-
ew0303_8.x7d	06/09/2003	02:16	28.407	-89.665	206	-
ew0303_9.x7d	06/09/2003	19:59	28.392	-89.621	222	-
ew0303c1.x7d	06/10/2003	00:02	28.342	-89.622	233	-
ew0303c2.x7d	06/11/2003	20:23	28.294	-89.239	297	-
ew0303c3.x7d	06/12/2003	08:03	27.847	-89.906	270	-
ew0303c4.x7d	06/14/2003	08:00	28.210	-89.325	301	-
ew0303c5.x7d	06/15/2003	09:12	28.652	-88.934	242	-
ew0303c6.x7d	06/16/2003	16:18	28.590	-89.042	213	-
ew0303c7.x7d	06/17/2003	08:15	28.365	-89.120	273	-

* Leg of cruise EW0303 that immediately preceded the D-tag/CEE cruise; included here to provide near-in-time temperature data in other parts of the Gulf
1. Tests only: no data
2. Shallow profile; never reaches 15°C
3. Bad data, repeated
4. Deep Gulf profile
5. Failed below ~300 m

animal prior to the experiment but had been proven in pressure tank testing at WHOI. The new attachment method was a variant of a system tested successfully on a captive dolphin in Florida over winter 2002-3. See Section 4.3 for additional information on the D-tags.

Both tag types were delivered using a 46-ft carbon fiber pole cantilever-mounted to the bow of a RHIB. Two boats were carried on the *Ewing* for this purpose: the aluminium-hulled *R2*, owned by MMS, and the fiberglass *Balena*, a Novurania brand RHIB owned by WHOI. The *R2* had two 135 hp two-stroke Mercury outboard engines and a pair of transom-mounted 24V electric trolling motors. On the *Ewing*, the *R2* was hung from the starboard-side CTD winch that had an A-frame. An unfortunate consequence of this was that CTD measurements were logistically awkward, requiring moving the *R2* to the stern of the ship to clear the winch, so none were taken.

The second RHIB carried on the *Ewing*, the *Balena*, is maintained at Woods Hole Oceanographic Institution and carries two counter-rotating 4-stroke Yamaha 110 hp outboard motors. The *Balena* was stowed on the B-deck of the *Ewing* on its trailer and lowered using the port-side crane. Protruding metal-work on the ship made movement of the *Balena* delicate especially in bad weather. However, the crew of the *Ewing* handled the operation skillfully.

The *R2* was deployed on 11 days while the *Balena* was used on 4 days. The quiet engines of the *Balena* made it the boat of choice to approach whales for tagging. However the *R2* is a sturdier boat and was more straight-forward to deploy and so was used whenever the weather was poor. The *R2* engines are noisy but relatively quiet successful approaches were possible using the electric motors. Unfortunately both the controller and, later, the propellers of these motors failed during the cruise. The controller was replaced with equipment from the *Ewing* but the propeller breakages ultimately rendered the motors unusable. Both outboard motors on the *R2* showed various alarm signals more-or-less continuously throughout the cruise but performed adequately. Apart from the electric motors, there were no significant failures with either boat.

After an early breakage was repaired by *Ewing* engineering staff, the tag delivery system worked well throughout the cruise and was swapped between the *R2* and *Balena* as needed. Crew aboard the RHIBs was Alex Bocconcelli (driver), Patrick Miller (observer and permit fulfillment), Mark Johnson and/or Alex Shorter (taggers), and Natacha Aguilar (trainee observer).

In addition to tagging, the RHIB crew took video for photo-identification and sizing of whales. No fecal samples were found. A total of 11 tags were delivered in 13 good-weather days with sperm whales. Overall, the whales semed more difficult to approach than in the two previous years, having a tendency to make repeated shallow dives to avoid the RHIB. As a result, 55 approaches were required to deliver the tags. Because many groups were approached, a larger number of takes, which in this case are close approaches, were recorded under Tyack's permit. Table 3.2.6 gives a summary of tag carries. Figure 3.2.2, upper panel, shows a map of deployment locations.

Both tag designs included a release that vents the suction cups after a programmable time, usually when the memory on the tag is full. Although tags often released prior to the programmed time due to poor skin condition or social rubbing, two tag carries (sw165a and b) were sufficiently long to require active releasing. Despite the smaller number of tag carries this year as compared to SWSS 2002 (11 this year, 19 last year) the total on-animal time increased from approximately 64 hours in 2002 to 80 hours this year. As a result, the average tag carry was 7.5 hours this year, improving over previous years. Most long carries were achieved with the smaller and lower profile type 2 D-tag. Section 4.3 contains additional information on the tags.

On June 15, an experiment was performed to characterize the receive level of the airgun array on the *Kondor*. This was attempted in an area free of marine mammals and primarily involved the Lamont Doherty acoustic telemetry buoy. A type-2 tag was strapped to the deep hydrophone and set to record at 96 kHz sampling-rate. The tag was recovered from the buoy after the experiment and the tag data were saved as data-set lw166a. The tag recording will be compared to the signals recorded by LDEO from the spar buoy to check the calibration of the buoy hydrophone and to

Table 3.2.6

Summary of D-tag Deployments for SWSS 2003

Focal ID	Date (mm/dd/yyyy)	Time (UTC)	Latitude (°N)	Longitude (°W)	Hours on Animal	Tag Type	Sample Rate (kHz)
sw156a	06/05/2003	15:06	29.217	87.211	4:50	1	32
sw162a	06/11/2003	22:26	28.139	89.419	1:02	2	96
sw163a	06/12/2003	22:54	28.397	89.684	6:45	2	96
sw164a	06/13/2003	14:47	28.334	89.618	13:32	2	96
sw165a	06/14/2003	18:35	28.480	89.054	~16:30*	2	96
sw165b	06/14/2003	18:38	28.480	89.054	~16:30*	2	96
sw167a	06/16/2003	20:26	27.720	90.069	~3[1]	2	96
sw167b	06/16/2003	21:07	27.688	90.094	~2[2]	2	96
sw170a	06/19/2003	16:35	28.671	89.001	9:50	2	96
sw173a	06/22/2003	19:46	28.643	88.992	0.53	1	32
sw173b	06/22/2003	19:49	28.643	88.992	5:45	1	32
				TOTAL:	80.5		

* released after recording complete at 16:20
[1] data not yet extracted from malfunctioning tag
[2] no data collected due to battery malfunction

provide a higher frequency characterization of the airgun signal (the Lamont Doherty system has a bandwidth of about 10 kHz compared to the tag bandwidth of 46 kHz). The tag also provided valuable information on the depth and movement of the deep hydrophone on the buoy. Because there was a substantial surface current, the hydrophone did not hang to its full depth of 500 m but rather trailed behind the surface expression at a depth, determined from the tag, of 150 m.

Seismic Activities Using the M/V *Kondor Explorer*
The industry coalition contributed the seismic source vessel M/V *Kondor Explorer* that was used in the CEE. The towed airgun array on *Kondor* had 31 airguns of which three were spares (Figure 3.2.3). The volume of the airguns was 3090 cubic inches. All of the active transmissions of the *Kondor* were recorded.

During the SWSS 2003 D-tag/CEE leg of cruise EW0303, there were five seismic shooting periods: four playbacks for CEE and one calibration of the *Kondor* array. The total shooting time was 5.23 hours for the playbacks (1 hour, 2 hours, 14 minutes, and 2 hours) and 3.2 hours for the calibration. These times include the ramp up. A mitigation protocol was implemented on the source vessel *Kondor* and supported by the visual and acoustic teams on board the *Ewing*. The seismic shooting locations are shown in Figure 3.2.4.

The starting time of the ramp up for each seismic event (playback or calibration) was communicated to the acoustic team by the playback coordinator. After this, the acoustics team continuously monitored the seismic signals arriving on the SEAMAP array towed by the *Ewing*. This was implemented simultaneously with the normal sperm whale acoustic passive tracking. Thus three acousticians were present for data collection. The seismic playbacks were recorded at

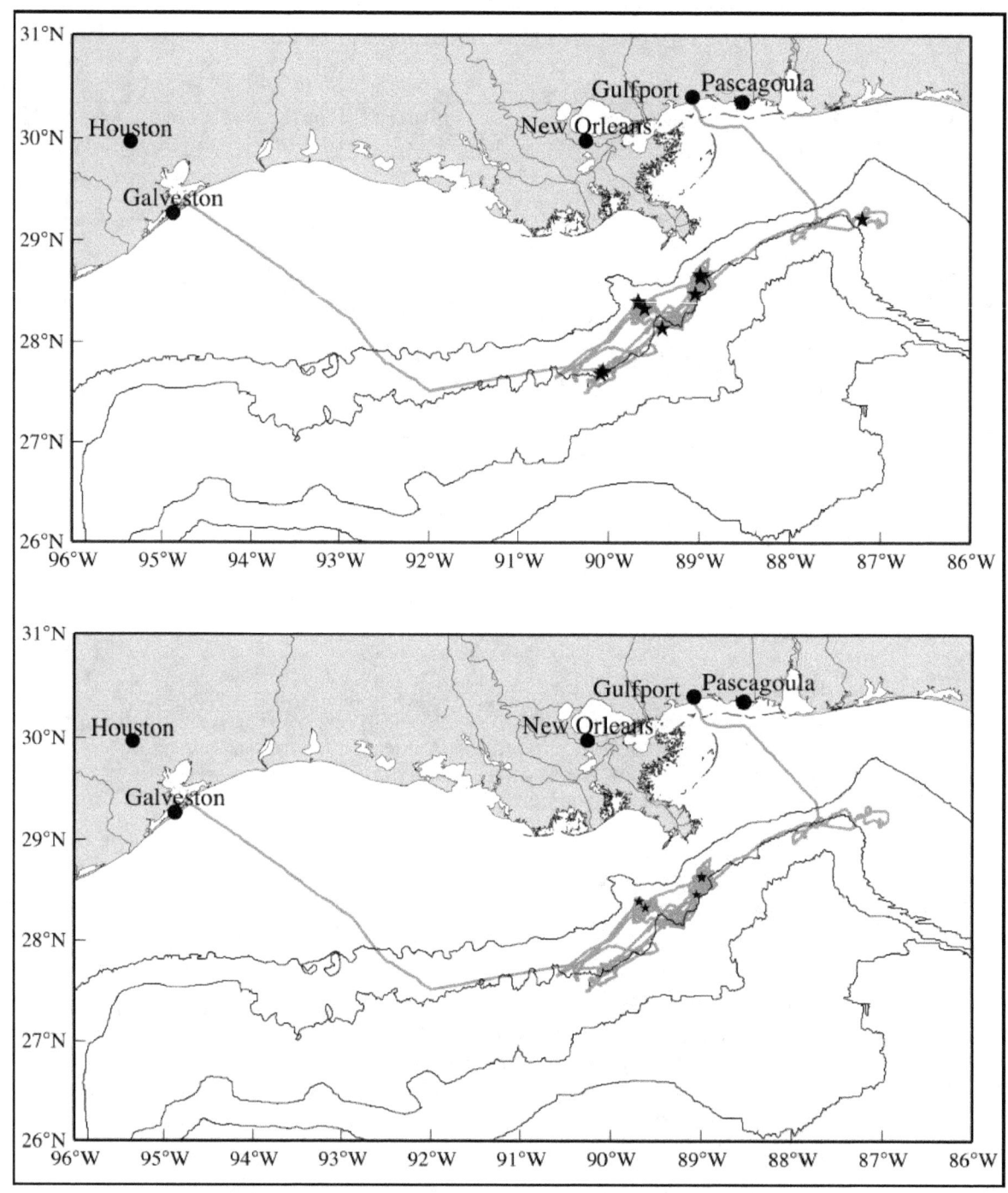

Figure 3.2.2. Locations of D-tag deployments (upper) and skin samples (lower) superimposed over the cruise track.

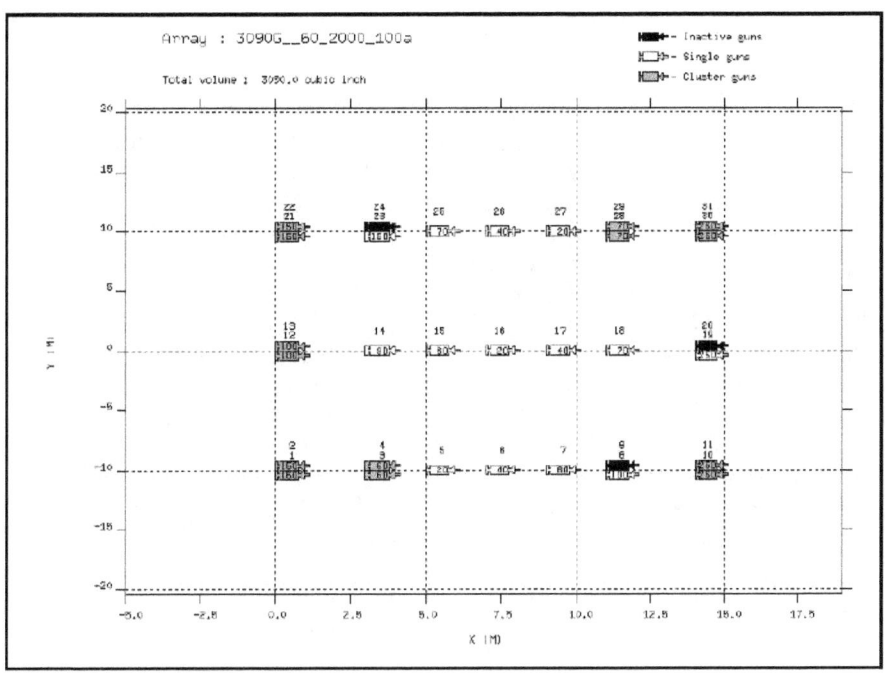

Figure 3.2.3. Dimensions of the airgun array towed by the *Kondor*.

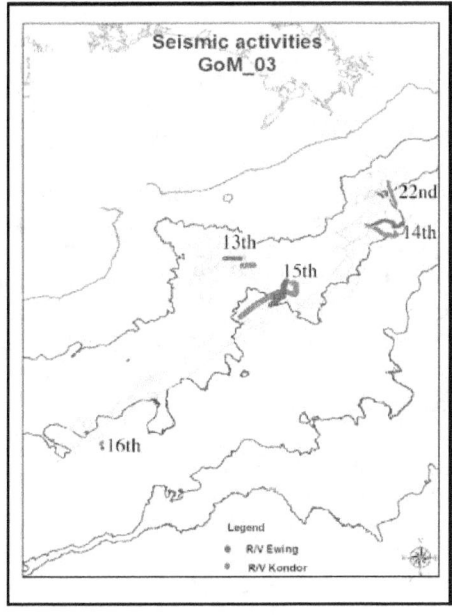

Figure 3.2.4. Source vessel *Kondor* (red) in relation to the observation vessel *Ewing* (blue) while the *Kondor* airguns were active.

45

a 96kHz sampling rate and the calibration at 48kHz. The sensitivity of the system was adjusted when necessary to avoid clipping on the recording system, without reducing the sperm whale tracking capacity.

Frequent samples of the seismic signals were analyzed in real time with the SEAMAP Cetacean Monitoring System (CMS) to get peak amplitudes (in dB) and peak frequencies. The analysis was made on the full pulse and also separately on the direct arrival and the first return of the signal. The results were stored in a database with spatial and temporal references by means of the software *Logger* (IFAW). A preliminary calibration of the system was done on the basis of data provided by SEAMAP, followed by a full calibration of the system CMS-Alesis digital recorder. The data are still under analysis, but preliminary results indicate maximum received levels around 150 dB re 1μPa. They also confirm last year's observations on the presence of medium and high frequencies on the direct arrival, with recorded peak frequencies up to 15 kHz. Depending on the distance to the seismic source, the analysis of the frequency distribution of the overall pulse showed results similar to the direct arrival or to the returns.

GIS-based Tactical Display
A new data logging system was used during the SWSS 2003 CEEs. The system required several new software components to allow central logging of all observation and navigation data, and also to allow real-time viewing of the data, as it is collected, via an ArcView Geographic Information System (GIS). This system was created in a collaboration between Woods Hole Oceanographic Institution and NATO Undersea Research Center.

Primary functions of the GIS Tactical Display were: real-time support to the tagging operations, coordination during CEE, and fieldwork planning both before and during the cruise. A new NMEA-based logging and real-time display system was used for the first time during SWSS 2003. The system worked well, after several on-board upgrades.

Two major requirements were achieved: the ability of the tagging and playback coordinators to always have a direct and up-to-date overview of the situation and an easily accessible work station for tracks planning and quick-look overviews. Two GIS Tactical Displays, receiving the same data source, were used in different locations. On the flying bridge the display was used by the visual team and the tagging and playback coordinators during the daylight operations. In the acoustic lab the display was used by the acoustic team and for the day-by-day planning.

Data visualized on the map were ship tracks, from both the observation vessel and the seismic source vessel, the visual sightings plotted as focal follow and survey layers, the acoustic detections, the number of acoustic contacts (number of sperm whales heard) plotted using the position of the ship instead of by slots of time. The acoustic categories (e.g., codas and trumpet or the anthropogenic noise) were plotted in the same way. The location of each tagging attempt (successful or not, as the first point) and the monitoring effort (visual and acoustic) were plotted as well. Pre-collected georeferenced data, such as sighting data and oil platform locations or even satellite images, were easily added to the map.

GIS tracking tool components: An *NMEALogTool* was written to simultaneously log many NMEA serial data streams. This tool also was responsible for broadcasting these data to several real-time GIS systems throughout the ship. This tool logged navigation and observation data streams continuously from 6/04 through 6/24, with less than 0.05% scheduled down time for system upgrades and maintenance, and no unexpected down time.

An acoustic tracking entry tool, *AcLogger*, was created to allow acoustic tracking data entry. The user interface collected data and converted this data to an NMEA serial stream for logging and display. A visual sightings entry tool, *Visual-MMI*, was written to facilitate visual sighting data entry. Data was entered and converted to an NMEA serial data stream, which was suitable for logging and display.

Finally, a GIS to NMEA interface, *NMEA_IF*, was implemented to create and update ArcView shape files, allowing real-time data viewing with the GIS. This tool parses many data strings and presents the data to ArcView in rich tables. Many of the data fields from the entry tools are included in these shape files, allowing detailed real-time data inspection. The ESRI ArcMap (ArcView 8.3) was the software successfully used for desktop geographic mapping and real-time data visualization.

GIS tracking tool conclusions and suggestions for future improvements: The SWSS 2003 D-tag/CEE cruise demonstrated the feasibility of RF serial modems for transmitting NMEA data. During playbacks, the position of the M/V *Kondor Explorer* was plotted in real-time on the GIS workstations aboard the R/V *Ewing*. It is possible to display the tag boat position in a similar way. More importantly, the modem also can provide a data stream in the other direction. So, the latest sightings and acoustic bearings can be viewed in real-time on the tag boat to more directly facilitate tagging. Critical elements include a new rugged lightweight map display and a compact battery powered GPS and RF modem system.

The current system can only stream data over serial cables. Most modern ships are wired with Ethernet. Some, including the *Ewing*, even have shipboard wireless networks. Adding a UDP broadcast capability to *NMEALogTool* and *NMEA_IF* facilitates moving GIS displays to different areas of the ship. One obvious benefit would be providing the ship's bridge with a map during night-time acoustic tracking. Another benefit would be moving visual workstations indoors during foul weather, or during radio tracking. One phase of the D-tag tagging effort that is not plotted in real time, and not logged in a uniform way is RF beacon tracking. A new RF tracking system is currently in development.

Passive Acoustic Monitoring
The primary objectives of the acoustic team were to support the animal tracking during tagging operations, provide behavioral observations during CEEs, and conduct passive tracking. The acoustic monitoring was organized in four-hour shifts providing 24-hour coverage when the array was deployed, with different efforts between day and night. Of over 445 total hours of navigation, the acoustic monitoring covered 376 hours, showing the ability of this system and team of observers to track whales through the night for early morning operations.

In Day Mode (06:00 a.m. to 08:00 p.m. local time), when close and continuous contact with the visual team is required, detailed tracking of sperm whales with descriptions of dive behavior and direction changes was performed. In this mode, two operators acted to fill the acoustic data entry form and manage communication with the flying bridge. In Night Mode (08:00 p.m. to 06:00 a.m. local time), the priority was to follow the animals until daylight. Only one observer was required. At night, the logging was limited to significant acoustic events such as codas, creaks, trumpets and slow clicks.

In both modes, a five-minute timeout was set to record sounds such as ship noise, seismic activities, biological disturbances, or other sounds that might be interfering with the acoustic monitoring and to estimate the number of sperm whale contacts at that time. This last information was logged to provide a quick measurement of the presence of animals in the study area, especially during the night when detailed animal tracking was not performed. Also, the number of animals clicking at a certain time can be used as one factor to measure simultaneous diving events to investigate possible synchrony in diving patterns between sperm whales.

The acoustic team comprised five people with an additional part-time observer after June 16. The shift schedule was organized to always have two people on duty during the day and one during the night. Occasionally, an observer was involved with parallel activities, such as system set up and tagging, but the number of available people was sufficient for these absences for short periods.

Two towed arrays were available on board with listening and recording equipment and computer software for bearing estimation. The SEAMAP array, a four element array with 300 m of tow cable and a pressure sensor, was used for the entire cruise during all the tracking operations. The WHOI array was kept as a backup. Deployment was performed mainly by the crew with the ship winch; this proved to be fast and convenient. The array was recovered on board in cases of night-time tag recovery or for high-speed transit to new areas. At the beginning of the cruise, an additional weight of 12 kilos was added in order to increase the depth of the array. This depth was always shown on the real-time display as the Depth Acquisition Unit. The array depth ranged between 15 and 60 m, depending on the tow-speed.

The maximum tow-speed for the SEAMAP array was specified at 8 knots. Reasonable levels of detection range were obtained for towing speeds up to 6 knots. The manufacturer's audio-analysis tool, provided with the SEAMAP array to monitor the array, was the Cetacean Monitoring Software. This software proved to be less suitable as a click detector compared to other available software, such as *Rainbow Click*. The main concern was the presence on the bearings screen of "echos", sometimes at more than 40 degrees apart from the real source and mainly with high amplitude levels. This discrepancy caused an over estimation of the number of acoustic detections in the first few days of the cruise. The problem was solved by using additional software (AudioMonitor, developed by Walter Zimmer at SACLANTCEN) to discriminate between "echos" and positive acoustic detections.

A positive innovation for the recording system consisted of the use of a multi-channel hard disk recorder, the Alesis adatHD24XR. With this recorder it was possible to save sounds as.wav files directly into hard drives of 120 GB capability. These files were afterwards downloaded and stored in daily folders into external hard drives. The standard recording mode was fixed at 48 kHz with two channels. But, as soon as the tag was on the animal, the recordings were switched to 96 kHz for collecting high quality sound cuts. The beginning of each recording session (every 3 hours at 48 kHz and 1.5 hours at 96 kHz) was synchronized with the acoustic data entry time to the second and a detailed spreadsheet was continuously updated during the fieldwork. A total of about 520 GB of recordings was collected during this cruise.

A new acoustic data entry form for the real-time passive acoustic monitoring, the AcLogger, was used on this cruise for the first time. Its design had been based on previous fieldwork experiences (SWSS 2002 D-tag/CEE and Sirena sea trials) with the aim to support sperm whale tracking during tagging operations and to collect acoustic behavioral observations. As with the data coming from the visual observations, all the entries made with AcLogger were automatically saved to the NMEA Server. Daily directories holding 10-minute files organized the acoustic logging outputs together with all the other outputs while a few filters were made to extract the most significant acoustic information.

The entry form consisted of six straightforward Tabs, each one of which worked for a specific objective. These were the Sperm Whale Tab, the Generic Tab, the Array Tab, the Recorder Tab, the Effort Tab, and the Note Tab. The use of the AcLogger was organized through two different levels, based on the operation mode. During the day, when two operators were on watch, the AcId in the Sperm Whale Tab, which is a numeric code assigned to distinguish single or group of animals streaming on the screen, also worked to automatically update the History Window. This window proved to be particularly useful by showing time, type, bearing and side of the first and of the last commit for each AcId. This helped the acoustic observer to better estimate when an animal was going to stop clicking and to advise the visual team of an upcoming surfacing or to monitor the animal movements when diving and to guide the workboat in the right direction.

During the night, while not transiting to a new working area, the acoustic effort was concentrated on staying with a group of animals until the daylight operations. The data logging was actually limited to significant acoustic events only and to animal counting.

A considerable number of codas and coda exchanges were observed during this cruise. Most of them were concentrated near the Mississippi Delta area at less then 30 nm from the coast on the 700-m depth contour. From a preliminary review of the acoustic logging outputs, roughly 870 coda events were recorded, with most events containing several individual codas. In particular, the 4 and 9 equal spaced clicks pattern seemed to be the most frequent codas. Moreover, fast series of clicks were observed together with codas production. This peculiar vocalization seemed to be related to surfacing activities. About 250 of these events occur in the recordings and further analysis is needed to understand their structure and position within sperm whale vocalizations. Additionally, 551 creak events were logged, 22 slow-click series, and one trumpet.

Visual and VHF Tracking
The Visual Team consisted of 8 people split in two squads of 4 each. The teams alternated on watch on the *Ewing* flying bridge from first daylight to dark. Each squad included one recorder, two observers at 25x150 binoculars (BigEyes) and one observer at 7x50 binoculars (regular binoculars). As is noted below, three BigEye observers usually worked simultaneously when the team was with whales. The third BigEye also was placed to cover portions of the water that were blocked by the other two BigEyes.

Communication between the recorder and observers was done through headset radios. Two laptop computers were used on the flying bridge for sighting, environmental, effort, and navigation data logging. A third laptop, running a GIS software, was available for plotting visual contacts, acoustic contacts, the R/V *Ewing* track and the M/V *Kondor* track.

The two laptops ran the old data logging system (Logger 2000) for the first two days of the D-tag cruise. Once the new system was entirely set up, VisualMMI was connected to the NMEA Data Logging System and the GIS was the main system for data recording. The new Data Logging System was designed with tools that were lacking in the previous data logger. For example, it provided calculated fields for range from both regular binoculars and BigEyes reticules, a configuration table that allowed setting the calculation from different heights and for different conversion factors, and different port settings for NMEA coms. The new system allowed the use of a third machine easily accessible to the tagging coordinator. This was used to coordinate the visual, acoustic, and tagging teams with the *Ewing* bridge for maneuvering the vessel in the best way for tracking sperm whales, independently from data loggers.

Three different operational states for the visual teams were applied throughout the cruise: (a) searching for whales, (b) tagging operations, and (c) focal follow. When searching for whales, the personnel positions consisted of the portside BigEyes operator, the starboard BigEyes operator, the data recorder with naked-eye observations, and the naked-eyes/regular binocular observer. In this state, visual observers scanned the entire sighting angle of 360 degrees with the main goal of detecting sperm whale presence. Any other species observed was recorded but no extra effort, such as leaving the planned route and maneuvering towards the sighting contact, was dedicated to identify those species or estimate group sizes. During search status, teams followed a 2hrs on/2hrs off schedule. A 30-minute rotating schedule was used to cycle each team member between the four personnel postitions on the flying bridge. This schedule helped to prevent eyestrain and maintain vigilance.

When engaged in tagging operations, the personnel positions were the portside BigEyes operator, the starboard BigEyes operator, the data recorder, the naked-eyes/regular binocular observer with permit compliance activities during approaching, and the tagging coordinator. Once the team was with whale(s) and the weather was acceptable, the tag boat was launched. During this phase the goal of all the effort was to direct the tag boat as close as possible to a potential target whale. The tag boat was fed both with visual and acoustic information via VHF radio by the tagging coordinator, who also coordinated ship's operations and maneuvering with the bridge. Data relative to the range and bearing of sperm whale(s) present in the area was recorded. This information was crucial during tagging operations to direct the tag boat to a potential target whale, and during playbacks for positioning the M/V *Kondor* appropriately. Each time an animal fluked up (starting a deep dive), the acoustic lab was alerted so the whale could be tracked underwater by passive acoustics.

Focal follow operations commenced once a whale was tagged or when only one animal was in the area. The second visual team was notified to go to the flying bridge. The second team was dedicated to data collection on other sperm whale(s) or on other focal whales in the case where two tags were deployed.

The tagged whale became the focal whale, and the search watch schedule was abandoned. At least 6 people were required to cover the different tasks during a focal follow. Three people from one team were dedicated to the focal whale while three people from the other team were dedicatedto other sperm whale(s), if any, present in the area. At least one observer was dedicated to detecting and locating VHF signals from the tagged whale. When two tags were out at the same time, both visual teams were on watch to cover all tasks required and to double the effort.

On a total of 18 usable trial days (the first day was considered a test and setting up day), about 15.5 were actual working days on the flying bridge for a total of 220.8 hours. Visual effort was not conducted only during adverse weather conditions. Successful contacts with sperm whales characterized about 14.5 working days out of 15.5. Sperm whales were visually located for a total of 810 surfacings, with 4430 fixes made. A summary is given in Table 3.2.7.

Tagging and Playback Coordinator
Critical for tagging and carrying out CEEs are the roles of the Tagging Coordinator and the Playback Coordinator. The Tagging Coordinator coordinated all the information between the tagging boat, bridge, acoustic lab, and visual team and communicated with the tag boat and the *Ewing* bridge. The Playback Coordinator used the GIS-based display to direct the *Kondor* to an appropriate location for controlled-exposure experiments.

The coordination of tagging and playback operations during the WHOI 2003 D-tag cruise was significantly improved over last year's efforts as a result of the integration of the visual MMI, acoustic data feed, and the GIS display. This system allowed both coordinators to see real-time information for sperm whales both above and below the water and to make immediate decisions regarding the placement of the *Ewing*, *Kondor*, and tagging boat accordingly. Overall, the setup worked extremely well.

The tagging coordinator was able to quickly relay pertinent acoustic and visual information to the RHIB to maximize the small window of time sperm whales were at the surface between dives. The direct ship's phone line between acoustics, the bridge, and the tagging coordinator was a huge benefit as this eliminated the use of the VHF radio to maintain contact with all departments, thus reducing the amount of chatter the RHIB receives and the background noise that "steps on" the VHF radio tracking transmitter signal. However, both the RHIB and the *Kondor* were linked by VHF radio contact and required additional information once the first tag was on a whale and a second tagging attempt or a CEE was underway. These remained sources of "chatter" for the coordinators. Although the modest solution was to warn the trackers before the coordinators started talking, this is still a valid problem that may require some attention especially when tags sit low on whales and so do not give out many signals.

Table 3.2.7

Summary of Visual Effort During SWSS 2003 D-tag Cruise
(For *Physeter macrocephalus* only.)

Date (mm/dd/yyyy)	Visual Contacts	Total Fixes	Earliest Sighting (CDT)	Latest Sighting (CDT)	Effort (hrs)
06/04/2003	82	288	09:52	20:01	13.00
06/05/2003	88	457	06:02	15:48	13.00
06/06/2003	0	0	-	-	2.00
06/07/2003	3	3	13:34	19:54	7.30
06/08/2003	45	45	06:55	17:46	13.75
06/09/2003	20	193	16:00	20:10	13.75
06/10/2003	48	324	06:25	12:59	13.75
06/11/2003	58	389	07:09	19:41	13.75
06/12/2003	58	458	07:40	20:09	13.00
06/13/2003	34	476	07:35	19:57	13.75
06/14/2003	77	309	10:08	19:52	13.75
06/15/2003	3	7	06:38	06:44	13.75
06/16/2003	26	573	06:45	19:28	13.75
06/17/2003	0	0	-	-	11.25
06/18/2003	11	61	18:48	19:55	12.75
06/19/2003	83	365	06:27	20:05	11.75
06/20/2003	36	147	06:47	17:59	10.75
06/21/2003	32	93	06:28	12:20	7.00
06/22/2003	106	242	06:43	20:07	9.00
Total	810	4430			220.80

The playback operations also went well. The ability to have the *Kondor*'s course and speed automatically plotted in real time was extremely beneficial as it eliminated the need for a visual observer to fix an approximate *Kondor* position. It was also a valuable tool that allowed the coordinator to alter the course of the *Kondor* when whales were detected in the mitigation range defined by the mitigation protocol (Appendix). The use of hand-held radios on the *Kondor*'s flying bridge seemed problematic with regards to ship-to-ship communication when the two ships were separated by some distance. A base radio with proper antenna for the flying bridge of the seismic vessel is recommended for future cruises.

Tissue Collection/Genetic Typing
Tissue sampling during the D-tag cruise was primarily focused on the opportunistic collection of sloughed skin occasionally found attached to the D-tag suction cups placed on sperm whales Table 3.2.8 gives a summary of samples collected, and Figure 3.2.2, lower panel, shows a map of the locations. A total of seven sloughed skin samples from seven D-tagged sperm whales were collected during the four-week cruise. While sloughed skin obtained from D-tags has proven fairly reliable in the past, sloughed skin in general can be quite difficult to amplify given the DNA's somewhat degraded nature. On two occasions, skin samples were obtained from two

51

Table 3.2.8

Tissue Collection/Genetic Typing Samples Collected During 2003 D-tag Fieldwork
(Sample number code gives the date (yymmdd) followed by the consecutive number for multiple
samples taken on any given day (01 to 02).)

Sample Number	Tag Number	Group Number	Approx. # Whales in Area	Latitude (°N)	Longitude (°W)
03061201	SW163A	1	12	28.397	89.684
03061301	SW164A	2	8	28.334	89.618
03061401	SW165A	3	20	28.480	89.052
03061402	SW165B	3	20	28.480	89.052
03061901	SW170A	4	12	28.671	89.001
03062201	SW173A	5	25	28.643	88.992
03062202	SW173B	5	25	28.643	88.992

members of two groups (group numbers 3 and 5; see Table 3.2.8). In the first of the two instances, tagged/sampled whales were found in a cluster formation separated by less than 100 meters. In the second instance, the two tagged/sampled whales were separated by less than 200 meters. Degrees of relatedness will be tested between whales found within all sampled clusters and groups.

The combination of D-tagging and genetic sampling continues to provide an in-depth examination of sperm whales found throughout the northern Gulf of Mexico. Molecular sexing, microsatellites, and mitochondrial DNA sequencing provide a rich set of information that can be directly integrated with the dive profiles of D-tagged whales and incorporated into the analysis of population and social structure. The combination of genetics and WHOI D-tag dive profile data may perhaps shed light on how related and unrelated whales found within groups in the northern Gulf of Mexico coordinate both deep foraging and shallow dives.

<u>Collection of Received Level Data on Spar-buoy Hydrophones</u>
On 15 June 2003, time was allocated during the SWSS leg of cruise EW0303 for calibration of the *Kondor* seismic source used for the CEEs. The calibration device was the spar buoy that was assembled a few days before the cruise by Spahr Webb of Lamont-Doherty Earth Observatory. This buoy suspends two hydrophones connected to digitizing and RF telemetry electronics designed by Spahr Webb and Alan Nance. The RF signal can be recorded, one channel at a time, on command, aboard the host vessel, in this case *Ewing*, with one of four different gain settings and selectable sampling rates up to 25 kHz. In addition to the signal, the RF telemetry includes positions from an onboard GPS set. The source array of the *Kondor* consisted of three strings of 10 SSI G guns each, including 7 2-gun clusters and 3 spares. Total volume was 3090 cu. in., fired at a nominal 2000 psi.

The *Kondor* calibration run took place in water about 1000 meters deep over a gentle slope. The two hydrophones were suspended on cables 18 meters and 500 meters long. Fortunately, one of WHOI's type 2 D-tags had been tie-wrapped onto the string just above the deep hydrophone. The depth transducer of the D-tag showed that the "deep" hydrophone was in fact consistently at a depth of 150 m. This can only be due to drift-induced drag, which is the result of a differential between motion of the buoy and the deeper waters in which the hydrophone was located. Before the run was begun, drift was determined by the *Ewing* bridge to be about 2 knots towards the NE (047°). The initial calibration pass was set to run in this direction.

The first pass was carried out without complications or problems. The source array ramp-up was recorded as well as the entire pass (Figure 3.2.5, upper panel). Due to the rate of buoy drift, the pass took longer than planned. As the closest point of approach (CPA) was neared, it became apparent that there would not be enough time to complete the shooting pattern as planned. Shortly after CPA, therefore, *Kondor* began a hooklike turn to the left, in an effort to get into a position to record some shots with the calibration buoy abeam before darkness halted the activities for mitigation purposes. This maneuver was just completed when a beaked whale was sighted. The shooting was stopped for mitigation, and *Kondor*'s airgun array and the spar buoy were recovered. Although curtailed for mitigation, a few dozen useful shots were recorded during this side shot pass of the calibration run (Figure 3.2.6, lower panel).

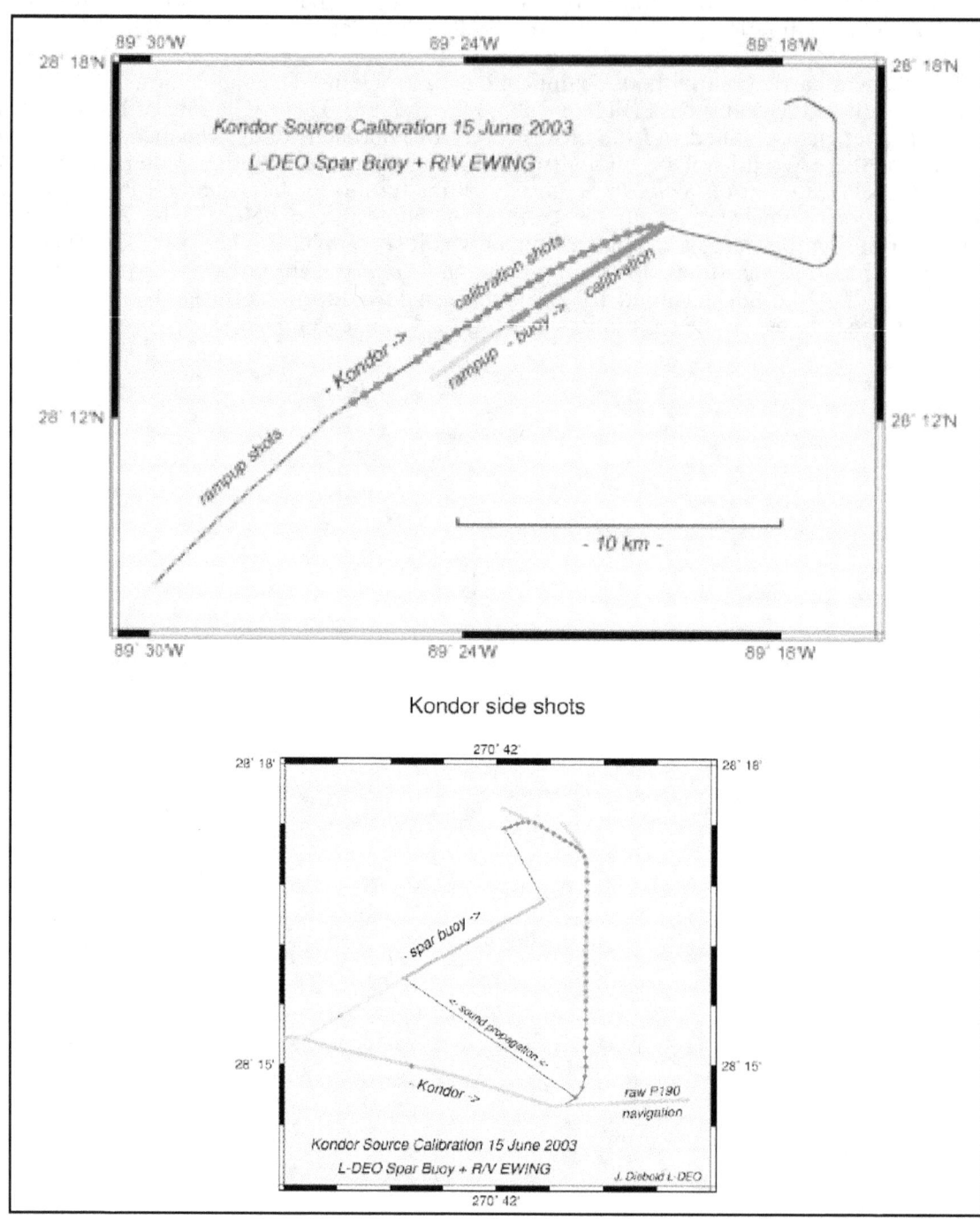

Figure 3.2.5. Track of the *Kondor* and spar buoy during the calibration run on 15 June 2003. Upper panel: continuous track of the *Kondor* during the entire run (thin line) and track of the buoy during the pass in the direction of the drift. Lower panel: the side shot portion of the calibration. Positions of individual shots recorded aboard *Ewing* are shown as dots along the *Kondor* track; green for ramp-up shots, red for full-array calibration shots. The corresponding positions of the spar buoy while recording these shots are similarly shown along the buoy's track.

3.3   S-tag Cruise 2003

The S-tag cruise was conducted aboard the R/V *Gyre* (cruise 03G07) from 26 June through 14 July 2003. The cruise left Galveston, TX, at approximately 2300 CDT on 25 June 2003 and put into Pascagoula, MS, at approximately 0830 CDT on 14 July 2003, where the science team disembarked. *Gyre* returned to Galveston, TX, at approximately noon on 18 July 2003, where several of the Texas-based science team members completed demobilization of the vessel. Field work consisted of tagging sperm whales with satellite-tracked radio tags, associated video work, photo-ID, and biopsy sampling. In addition, surveys for sperm whales were conducted using passive acoustics and visual observations, samples were collected for habitat characterization, and videotape was taken for an MMS documentary. SWSS Principal Investigators (PIs) who participated in this survey were Ann Jochens (Field Party Chief), Bruce Mate (Tag Team Leader), and Dan Engelhaupt (Biopsy). Terry Ketler of Interactive Educational Network was the PI for the video documentary work. These PIs and their supporting teams, together with Bill Lang and Sarah Tsoflias of MMS, constituted a 25-person science party (Table 3.3.1). Additional information associated with this cruise is in Sections 4.1 (S-tag analyses), 4.2 (genetic analyses), 4.6 (habitat characterization: eddy-forced variations), and 4.7 (habitat characterization: currents).

During the cruise, 15 sperm whales were tagged and 15 biopsy/skin samples were obtained. The cruise team searched for sperm whales both acoustically and visually when conditions allowed. In water depths greater than approximately 700 m, where sperm whales might be encountered, acoustic "observers" monitored for vocalizing (diving) sperm whales for over 260 hours using two towed Ecologic hydrophone arrays. Visual observers searched the sea surface with BigEye binoculars for over 130 hours (generally between 06:30 and 20:30 CDT each day) to locate sperm whales that were at the surface. Two rigid-hulled inflatable boats (RHIBs) were used: RHIB-1 for tagging (OSU tag boat *Puffin*) and RHIB-2 (*R2* RHIB) for support and photo-identification. Additionally, 5 CTD stations were made, 48 Deep Blue XBTs provided profiles of temperature in the upper 760 m, and 75 samples were filtered and analyzed for chlorophyll content. Ocean current velocities in the upper 300 m and upper 900 m were monitored continuously with hull-mounted 153 kHz and 38 kHz ADCPs. Near-surface water from the ship's hull depth of 3.5 m was pumped continuously through SeaBird temperature and conductivity sensors and a Turner Designs Model 10 fluorometer to log surface temperature, salinity, and chlorophyll fluorescence once per minute.

The cruise track is shown in Figure 3.3.1. It consisted of three parts. During 26 and 27 June, after *Gyre* left Galveston, the ship headed south to 27°20'N, 93°55'W, which was one region frequented by whales tagged in 2002 where sperm whales also had been observed on the SWSS 2003 WSHC cruise. A meeting was held on 26 June to discuss small boat operations, fueling protocols, and safety. Shortly before arriving at the first station, the two hydrophone arrays were deployed, and a CTD cast was made. Due to engine problems that could not be repaired at sea, the ship returned to port, arriving about 1230 local time on 27 June. Repairs were made and *Gyre* headed back out to sea at approximately 1630 local, heading for a way point at 27°30'N, 92°50'W. This was a region with historical and satellite tag observations and where whales also were observed during the SWSS 2003 WSHC cruise in early June.

On 28 June, the hydrophone arrays were deployed about an hour prior to arrival at the way point. The visual team commenced observations about 1000 CDT. At about 1940 CDT, two whales were detected at approximately 27°6'N, 92°40'W, first acoustically, then visually. However, it was too late to launch small boats. Acoustics stayed with the whales until about 2330 CDT when acoustic contact ceased. On 29 June, due to bad weather east of 90°W, the search for whales proceeded in the region bounded by the 26° and 27°N latitude and 92 and 93°W longitude lines. At about 1600 CDT, the hydrophone arrays were pulled in and a CTD cast was made at 26°57.7'N, 92°48.1'W, before a planned run to the east to get behind the bad weather trough.

Table 3.3.1

Science Personnel for SWSS 2003 S-tag Cruise Aboard the R/V *Gyre*

Description	Personnel	Institution
Field Party Chief	Ann E. Jochens (Oceanography team leader)	TAMU
Tagging crew	Bruce Mate (Tag team leader)	OSU
	Mary Lou Mate (Video)	OSU
	Ladd Irvine (Boat driver)	OSU
	Dan Engelhaupt (Biopsy/genetic typing)	U. Durham, UK
Visual Observers	Joel Ortega (Team leader)	OSU
	Elizabeth Zúñiga	OSU
	Rhoni Lahn	OSU
	Bill Lang	MMS
	Laura Opsommer	OSU
	Andrew Wigton	ExxonMobil
Acoustic team	Tom Norris (Team leader)	OSU
	Sarah Tsoflias	MMS
	Trent Apple	OSU
	Anurag Kumar	OSU
	Elizabeth Zele	OSU
Photo-ID crew	Dan Lewer (Boat driver/photographer)	OSU
	Bruce Miller (Photography)	OSU
	Terry Ketler (Video)	IEN
Oceanography	Elizabeth Mitchell	TAMU
	Alicia Salazar	TAMU
TAMU Techs	Eddie Webb (Electronics Technician)	TAMU
	Willie Flemings (Electronics Technician)	TAMU
	Bill Green (Deck Engineer)	TAMU
	Marty Bohn (Deck Engineer)	TAMU

Unfortunately, weather conditions worsened into Tropical Storm Bill, which was centered to the south and a bit east of the ship (see Figure 3.3.1). It was forecasted to move NNW at 11 knots, which would have put the ship right in the path of the storm. With high seas predicted within all of the study area, *Gyre* headed back into Galveston for safe harbor, with arrival at about 1530 CDT on 30 June 2003. Time in port was used to check out the small boat operations, add enhancements to the *R2* launch system, and make enhancements to computer systems and communications.

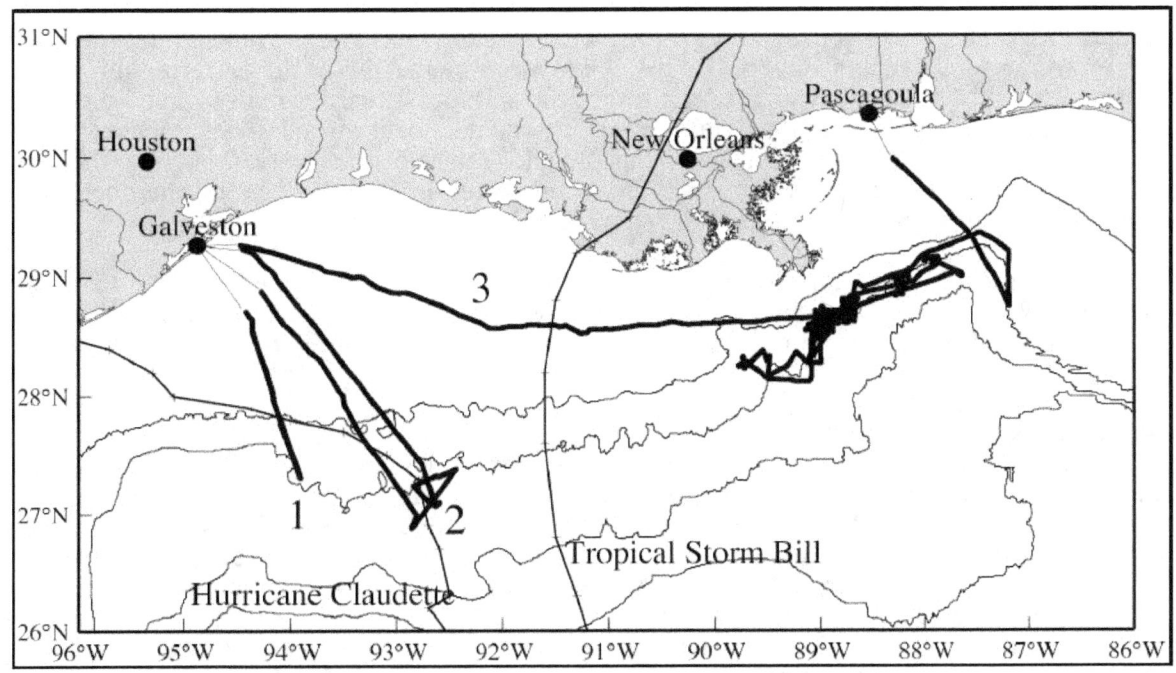

Figure 3.3.1. Cruise track for SWSS 2003 S-tag cruise, R/V *Gyre* 03G07, conducted 26 June – 14 July 2003. The thick part of the track shows the locations of the temperature, salinity, and fluorescence taken from approximately 3.5 m below the sea surface and logged approximately once per minute. The three phases of the cruise are indicated by the numbers 1 (covering the period June 26-27), 2 (June 28-30), and 3 (July 1-14). The tracks for Tropical Storm Bill (29 June-1 July 2003) and Hurricane Claudette (8-16 July 2003) are shown. The bathymetric contours shown are for the 200, 1000, 2000, and 3000-m isobaths.

The third part of the cruise began on 1 July 2003. *Gyre* left the dock at about 1800 CDT and headed for the way point at 28°40'N, 89°00'W to begin the search for sperm whales in the region of the Mississippi Canyon and off-shelf of the Mississippi River Delta. By 0730 CDT on 3 July, the way point, which was part of an area off-shelf of the Mississippi River near where sperm whales had been detected on the SWSS 2003 WSHC and D-tag/CEE cruises, was reached. This also was an area where, shortly before and during the cruise, several whales tagged in 2002 had been located through satellite transmissions. The ensuing 11 days were spent working with animals over the slope in the northeastern Gulf. The RHIBs were launched on every day except 13 July, because no whales were seen or heard that day. Thunderstorms and choppy seas were prevalent. On some days, this weather caused the small boats to be launched later or to be brought in earlier than planned. Minor repairs were made to the engines of both RHIBs, but caused tagging downtime of just a few hours, as some repairs were done after the day's work was completed. Much of the time, sperm whales were found in widely dispersed groups that were spread out over several kilometers. On multiple occasions, clusters of 2-3 and up to 8 whales were seen within these larger groups. At least one whale tagged off the delta later was observed near the canyon. The region that consistently had numerous whales was centered near 28.6°N 89°W.

Tropical Storm Claudette crossed into the Gulf of Mexico from the Caribbean Sea on 11 July 2003, and made landfall southwest of Galveston near Port O'Connor, TX, on 15 July 2003

57

(Figure 3.3.1). This storm generated high seas in the western Gulf and prevented the S-tag cruise from returning to Galveston, TX, on 16 July. Seas were increasing in the eastern Gulf, making launch of small boats problematical. As a result, the ship put in earlier than planned on 14 July and at Pascagoula, MS, rather than Galveston. The science team disembarked, rented vehicles, and departed variously for New Orleans, Houston, and Galveston and on from there to their final destinations. *Gyre* returned to Galveston, TX, about noon on 18 July. Several members of the Texas-based science team demobilized the ship from the S-tag cruise.

All S-tag, Photo-ID, and Biopsy/Genetic Typing activities were conducted in accordance with federal permits from the NOAA Fisheries to Bruce Mate of Oregon State University (permit 365-1440-01) and to Dan Engelhaupt of the University of Durham (permit 909-1465-01).

Oceanographic Habitat

The habitat characterization work was coordinated by Ann Jochens. The sea surface height (SSH) analyses, provided by Robert Leben of the Colorado Center for Astrodynamics Research, University of Colorado, supplemented the historical and S-tag sperm whales sighting data that were used to determine where to go to search for whales. Selected SSH fields for the period of the S-tag cruise are shown in Figure 3.3.2. During the time when the cruise was in the western Gulf (26-29 June 2003), there was a weak anticyclonically (clockwise) circulating feature along 27°N and west of 93°W. In the eastern Gulf, the SSH fields showed a large deepwater anticyclonic Loop Current Eddy (LCE) adjacent to the upper slope off the Mississippi River (Figure 3.3.2; feature in red-orange). This LCE had been present during the SWSS 2003 WCHC cruise conducted just prior to the S-tag cruise. Satellite altimeter data indicated this LCE had a SSH anomaly of greater than 40 cm and that to its north there was an area of cyclonic circulation (feature in dark blue) where SSH dipped as low as –20 cm. Strong currents of order 3 knots were generated at the northern periphery of the LCE. During the S-tag cruise, this LCE moved southward as the cruise progressed, reducing the amount of water that was being pulled off the shelf into deeper waters. As a result, the S-tag cruise encountered less low salinity, higher chlorophyll, "green" water than had the WSHC cruise.

The locations, dates, times, and 15°C isotherm depths of the CTD and XBT stations are given in Table 3.3.2. Figure 3.3.3 shows a map of the locations. Of the five CTDs taken, two were in the western Gulf and three were in the eastern Gulf. The temperature-salinity profiles for the CTDs are shown in Figure 3.3.4. All show evidence of entrainment and mixing of water masses in the upper waters, as indicated by the vertical variability of the T-S profiles in waters warmer than ~20°C. Reflecting the stronger eddy features in the east, the vertical variability is greater in the eastern profiles than the western profiles. All show the Gulf-wide characteristic tight T-S profile below about 17°C. The three stations taken in the eastern Gulf were all taken within the cyclonic circulation feature; none were taken in the LCE. However, CTDs 3 and 4 show the influence of the LCE, which during the WSHC cruise had been farther up on the slope, in the salinities > 36.6 near the 26 kg·m^{-3} contour, as is typical of the Subtropical Underwater mass brought into the Gulf by LCEs. Additionally, CTD 5 shows the influence of shelf water that was drawn off-shelf by the LCE. This is seen by two effects: the very low (< 30) salinity in the upper 20 m of the water column and the eroded (~36.4) salinity maximum at about 26 kg·m^{-3}. CTD data were reviewed by the acoustics team to make sure ship speed was appropriate to keep the hydrophones below any shallow sound channels, such as was caused by the strong stratification at CTD 5 due to the low salinity water layer. XBT stations were taken approximately every 10 nm.

Temperature, salinity, and fluorescence from a depth of ~3.5 m were logged once per minute throughout the cruise. The sample locations are shown in Figure 3.3.1, which gives the cruise track. The fluorometer was malfunctioning on 10-11 July, so no fluorescence data were collected for about 24 hours. There also were some periods when prolonged operation in green water lead to biofouling artifacts on the cuvette, but post-cruise analysis shows that for most of the time

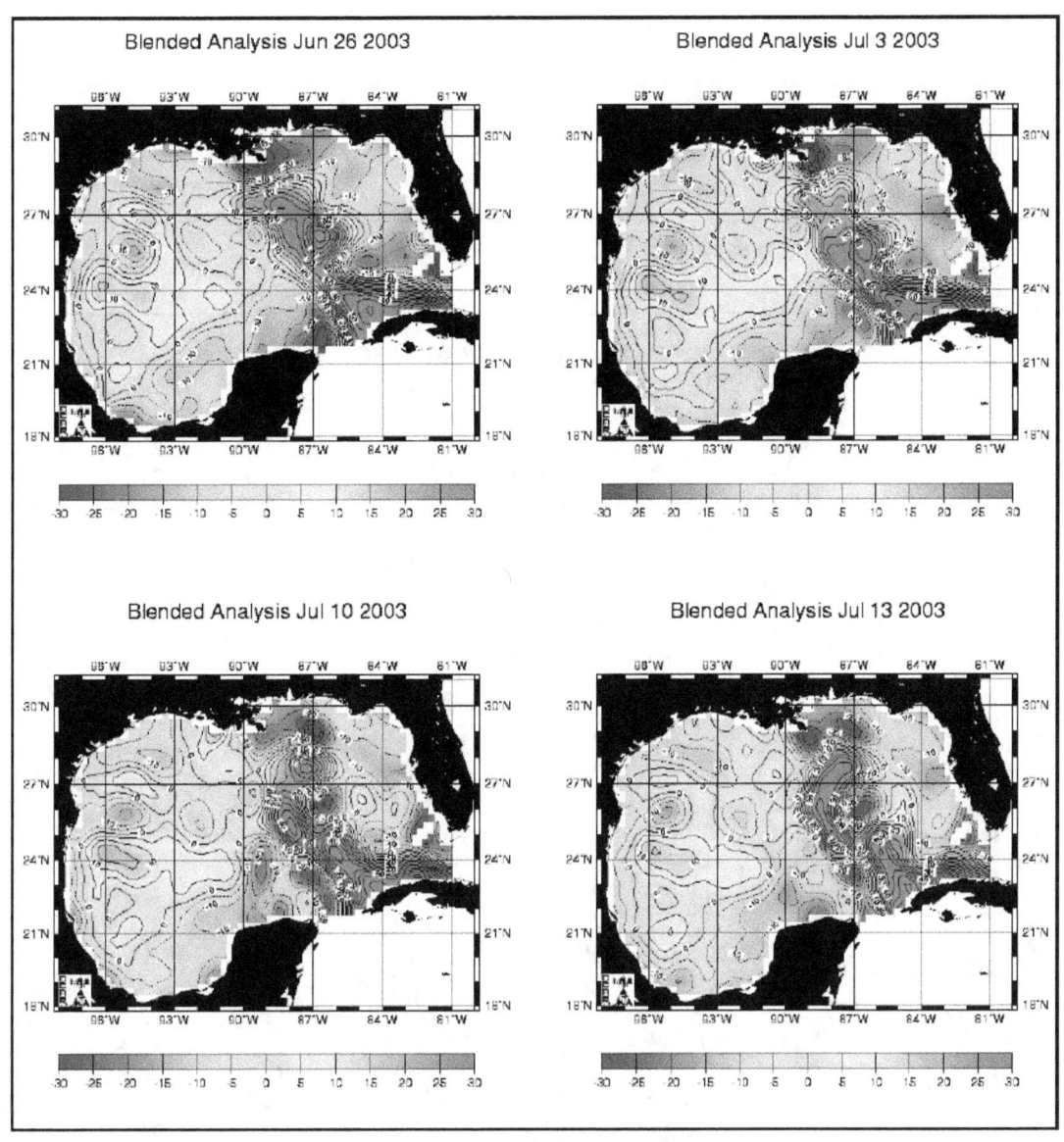

Figure 3.3.2. Sea surface height fields for the period 26 June through 13 July 2003 during the SWSS 2003 S-tag cruise.

spent in the eastern Gulf, the flow-through fluorescence record will be useful for describing habitat. The locations, dates, and times of the chlorophyll samples are given in Table 3.3.3, with the map of locations given in Figure 3.3.5. The samples will be used to calibrate the continuous fluorescence data. ADCP data generally were collected continuously along the track in water depths of ~15 m or greater for the 150 kHz ADCP and ~35 m or greater for the 38 kHz ADCP.

Table 3.3.2

Summary of Hydrographic Stations on SWSS 2003 S-tag Cruise
(XBTs 6, 10, and 23 were bad, so they were Re-Shot as XBTs 7, 11, and 24.)

Description	Date	Time (UTC)	Latitude (°N)	Longitude (°W)	Water Depth (m)	15°C Depth (m)	XBT Probe Type
CTD 1	06/27/2003	00:32	27.3097	93.9057	851	240	
XBT 1	06/28/2003	18:20	27.5030	92.8292	939	167	Deep Blue
XBT 2	06/28/2003	20:08	27.3538	92.7328	975	207	Deep Blue
XBT 3	06/28/2003	21:34	27.1943	92.6758	1106	222	Deep Blue
XBT 4	06/29/2003	08:13	27.2445	92.8363	1101	213	Deep Blue
XBT 5	06/29/2003	12:47	27.3415	92.5442	935	222	Deep Blue
XBT 7	06/29/2003	18:09	27.0193	92.7365	1307	241	Deep Blue
XBT 8	06/29/2003	19:59	26.8800	92.8508	1371	247	Deep Blue
CTD 2	06/29/2002	22:21	26.9617	92.8010	1545	224	
XBT 9	07/03/2003	12:09	28.6653	89.0155	727	242	Deep Blue
CTD 3*	07/03/2003	12:40	28.6682	88.9982	750	232	
XBT 11	07/05/2003	15:36	28.7015	88.7163	1208	228	Deep Blue
CTD 4	07/06/2003	03:57	28.7338	88.7527	1025	223	
XBT 12	07/06/2003	05:43	28.7742	88.5672	1101	231	Deep Blue
XBT 13	07/06/2003	06:46	28.8318	88.3893	937	219	Deep Blue
XBT 14	07/06/2003	08:34	28.8862	88.2070	1334	226	Deep Blue
XBT 15	07/06/2003	09:02	28.9367	88.0192	1565	220	Deep Blue
XBT 16	07/06/2003	10:18	28.9903	87.8385	1549	185	Deep Blue
CTD 5	07/06/2003	11:54	29.0438	87.6760	1607	161	
XBT 17	07/06/2003	17:30	29.1583	87.8673	970	200	Deep Blue
XBT 18	07/07/2003	03:08	29.0407	88.0023	960	207	Deep Blue
XBT 19	07/07/2003	04:52	28.9485	88.1628	1090	216	Deep Blue
XBT 20	07/07/2003	19:22	28.6248	88.8513	1102	252	Deep Blue
XBT 21	07/08/2003	06:33	28.5543	89.1272	530	254	Deep Blue
XBT 22	07/08/2003	09:09	28.6662	89.0037	600	243	Deep Blue
XBT 24	07/08/2003	10:22	28.7405	88.9937	560	200	Deep Blue
XBT 25	07/08/2003	13:25	28.6253	88.8533	1098	265	Deep Blue
XBT 26	07/09/2003	05:03	28.6498	89.0005	744	248	Deep Blue
XBT 27	07/09/2003	07:36	28.4453	88.9967	988	236	Deep Blue
XBT 28	07/09/2003	09:12	28.2837	88.9895	1152	227	Deep Blue
XBT 29	07/09/2003	10:23	28.2793	89.1130	1038	221	Deep Blue
XBT 30	07/09/2003	12:29	28.4825	89.0517	960	251	Deep Blue
XBT 31	07/10/2003	04:11	28.2870	89.1087	1016	214	Deep Blue
XBT 32	07/10/2003	05:35	28.3650	89.2192	699	197	Deep Blue
XBT 33	07/10/2003	09:00	28.1600	89.4948	1027	213	Deep Blue
XBT 34	07/11/2003	04:51	28.1313	89.3070	1051	208	Deep Blue
XBT 35	07/11/2003	06:34	28.1193	89.1177	1171	220	Deep Blue
XBT 36	07/11/2003	08:26	28.2825	89.0825	1037	223	Deep Blue
XBT 37	07/11/2003	10:11	28.4493	89.0813	722	215	Deep Blue
XBT 38	07/11/2003	11:55	28.6135	89.0543	547	233	Deep Blue
XBT 39	07/12/2003	03:48	28.9450	88.6280	446	224	Deep Blue
XBT 40	07/12/2003	05:54	28.9627	88.4365	814	237	Deep Blue

60

Table 3.3.2

Summary of Hydrographic Stations on SWSS 2003 S-tag Cruise (continued)

Description	Date	Time (UTC)	Latitude (°N)	Longitude (°W)	Water Depth (m)	15°C Depth (m)	XBT Probe Type
XBT 41	07/12/2003	07:39	29.0213	88.2528	869	200	Deep Blue
XBT 42	07/13/2003	00:55	29.2098	87.9377	426	205	Deep Blue
XBT 43	07/13/2003	02:35	29.2620	87.7567	439	189	Deep Blue
XBT 44	07/13/2003	04:20	29.3247	87.5790	366	174	Deep Blue
XBT 45	07/13/2003	06:18	29.3340	87.3825	601	206	Deep Blue
XBT 46	07/13/2003	08:00	29.2392	87.2245	777	206	Deep Blue
XBT 47	07/13/2003	09:49	29.0760	87.1875	972	205	Deep Blue
XBT 48	07/13/2003	11:53	28.9047	87.1832	923	208	Deep Blue
XBT 49	07/13/2003	16:33	28.9620	87.2963	1165	241	Deep Blue
XBT 50	07/13/2003	18:20	29.0895	87.3845	1338	237	Deep Blue
XBT 51	07/13/2003	19:57	29.2178	87.4625	1093	216	Deep Blue

*CTD 3 was taken 0.92 nm from XBT 9 to allow comparison of Deep Blue XBTs with CTD.

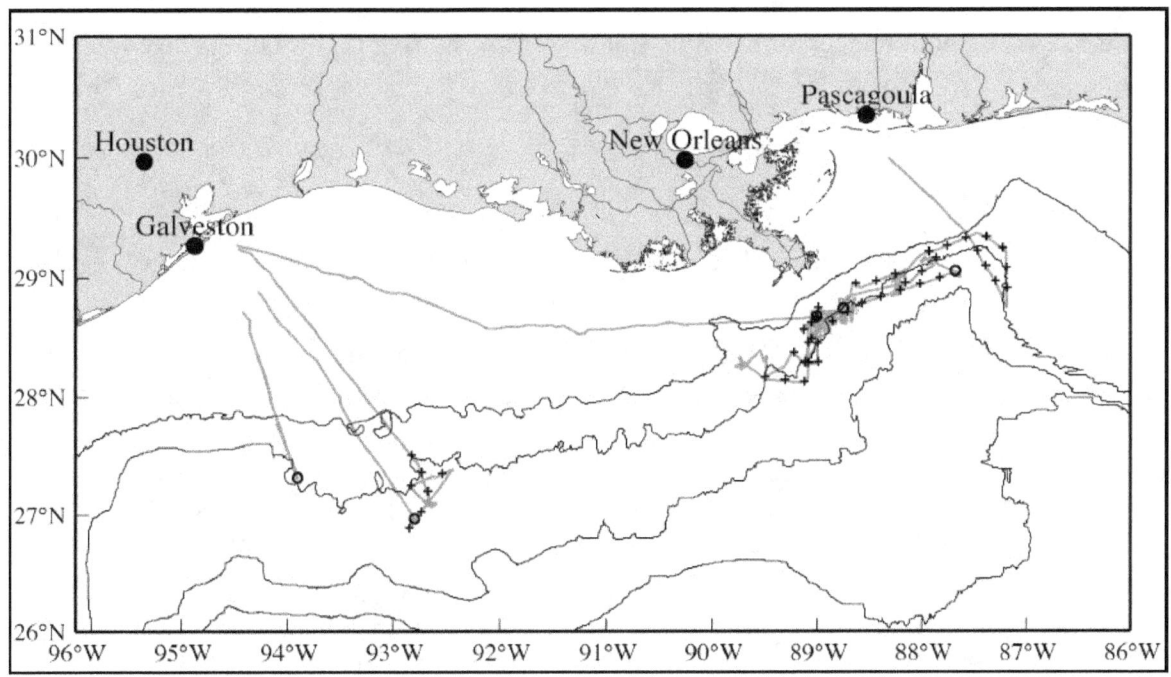

Figure 3.3.3. Locations of XBT (crosses) and CTD (circles) stations, superimposed on the cruise track (gray line), taken during SWSS 2003 S-tag cruise.

61

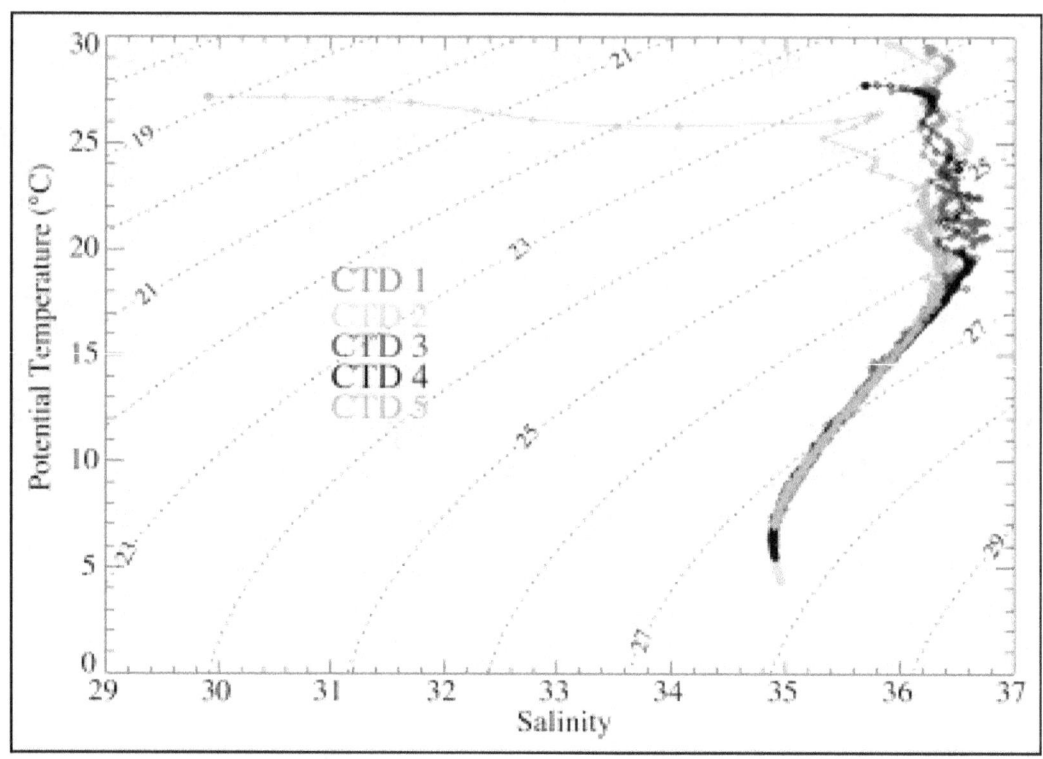

Figure 3.3.4. Potential temperature-salinity diagrams for the five CTD stations taken during the SWSS 2003 S-tag cruise. Contours of potential density anomaly (σ_θ) in kg·m^{-3} also are shown.

Table 3.3.3

Chlorophyll Stations for the SWSS 2003 S-tag Cruise

Date	Time (UTC)	Nearest Station	Latitude (°N)	Longitude (°W)
06/26/2003	22:55		27.3776	93.9371
06/27/2003	00:14	CTD 1	27.3116	93.9080
06/28/2003	18:35	XBT 1	27.4926	92.8189
06/28/2003	21:43	XBT 3	27.1835	92.6714
06/29/2003	08:13	XBT 4	27.2446	92.8365
06/29/2003	12:47	XBT 5	27.3416	92.5441
06/29/2003	18:02	XBT 7	27.0292	92.7281
06/29/2003	19:57	XBT 8	26.8762	92.8478
07/2/2003	12:08		28.8649	92.0990
07/2/2003	19:04		28.6001	91.7475
07/2/2003	23:00		28.5619	91.1324
07/3/2003	02:56		28.6052	90.4868
07/3/2003	07:02		28.6228	89.8549
07/3/2003	12:20	CTD 3	28.6661	89.0043

62

Table 3.3.3

Chlorophyll Stations for the SWSS 2003 S-tag Cruise (continued)

Date	Time (UTC)	Nearest Station	Latitude (°N)	Longitude (°W)
07/3/2003	17:09		28.5990	89.1096
07/4/2003	20:08		28.6268	88.9820
07/4/2003	21:57		28.6347	88.9379
07/5/2003	00:10		28.5917	88.9221
07/5/2003	05:06		28.6434	88.7703
07/5/2003	08:58		28.8040	88.6336
07/5/2003	13:17		28.6676	88.6774
07/5/2003	14:23	XBT 11	28.7022	88.6669
07/5/2003	17:01		28.7480	88.7663
07/5/2003	18:56		28.6997	88.7704
07/5/2003	20:51		28.6357	88.7419
07/6/2003	00:58		28.7234	88.7541
07/6/2003	03:38	CTD 4	28.7319	88.7568
07/6/2003	06:49	XBT 13	28.8340	88.3817
07/6/2003	07:54	XBT 14	28.8871	88.2039
07/6/2003	09:03	XBT 15	28.9373	88.0172
07/6/2003	10:18	XBT 16	28.9907	87.8354
07/6/2003	11:32	CTD 5	29.0448	87.6772
07/6/2003	19:33		29.1649	87.8971
07/6/2003	23:06		29.1369	88.0017
07/7/2003	03:06	XBT 18	29.0422	88.0012
07/7/2003	04:47	XBT 19	28.9499	88.1551
07/7/2003	17:14		28.6326	88.9187
07/7/2003	19:19	XBT 20	28.6247	88.8494
07/8/2003	01:33		28.7079	88.8290
07/8/2003	06:33	XBT 21	28.5539	89.1280
07/8/2003	09:10	XBT 22	28.6673	89.0028
07/8/2003	10:19	XBT 24	28.7497	88.9913
07/8/2003	13:36	XBT 25	28.6173	88.8522
07/8/2003	17:21		28.5757	88.9203
07/8/2003	23:28		28.6510	88.9397
07/9/2003	05:06	XBT 26	28.6506	89.0032
07/9/2003	07:43	XBT 27	28.4319	88.9963
07/9/2003	09:12	XBT 28	28.2822	88.9894
07/9/2003	10:23	XBT 29	28.2794	89.1137
07/9/2003	12:29	XBT 30	28.4831	89.0515
07/9/2003	18:12		28.5319	88.9620
07/9/2003	22:28		28.6865	89.0456
07/10/2003	05:35	XBT 32	28.3653	89.2196
07/10/2003	09:00	XBT 33	28.1599	89.4951
07/10/2003	17:03		28.2570	89.7364
07/11/2003	04:39		28.1311	89.3306
07/11/2003	06:35	XBT 35	28.1195	89.1158
07/11/2003	08:26	XBT 36	28.2848	89.0827
07/11/2003	11:55	XBT 38	28.6137	89.0542

Table 3.3.3

Chlorophyll Stations for the SWSS 2003 S-tag Cruise (continued)

Date	Time (UTC)	Nearest Station	Latitude (°N)	Longitude (°W)
07/11/2003	19:13		28.7379	88.7207
07/11/2003	23:06		28.7901	88.6878
07/12/2003	03:05		28.9094	88.6618
07/12/2003	03:49	XBT 39	28.9422	88.6241
07/12/2003	06:08	XBT 40	28.9725	88.4095
07/12/2003	08:03	XBT 41	29.0351	88.2077
07/12/2003	17:11		28.8508	88.2534
07/12/2003	21:11		29.0191	88.2147
07/13/2003	01:02	XBT 42	29.2140	87.9210
07/13/2003	02:26	XBT 43	29.2576	87.7724
07/13/2003	04:23	XBT 44	29.3269	87.5723
07/13/2003	06:18	XBT 45	29.3341	87.3808
07/13/2003	08:00	XBT 46	29.2387	87.2236
07/13/2003	09:49	XBT 47	29.0743	87.1875
07/13/2003	11:53	XBT 48	28.9030	87.1830
07/13/2003	18:03		29.0700	87.3719

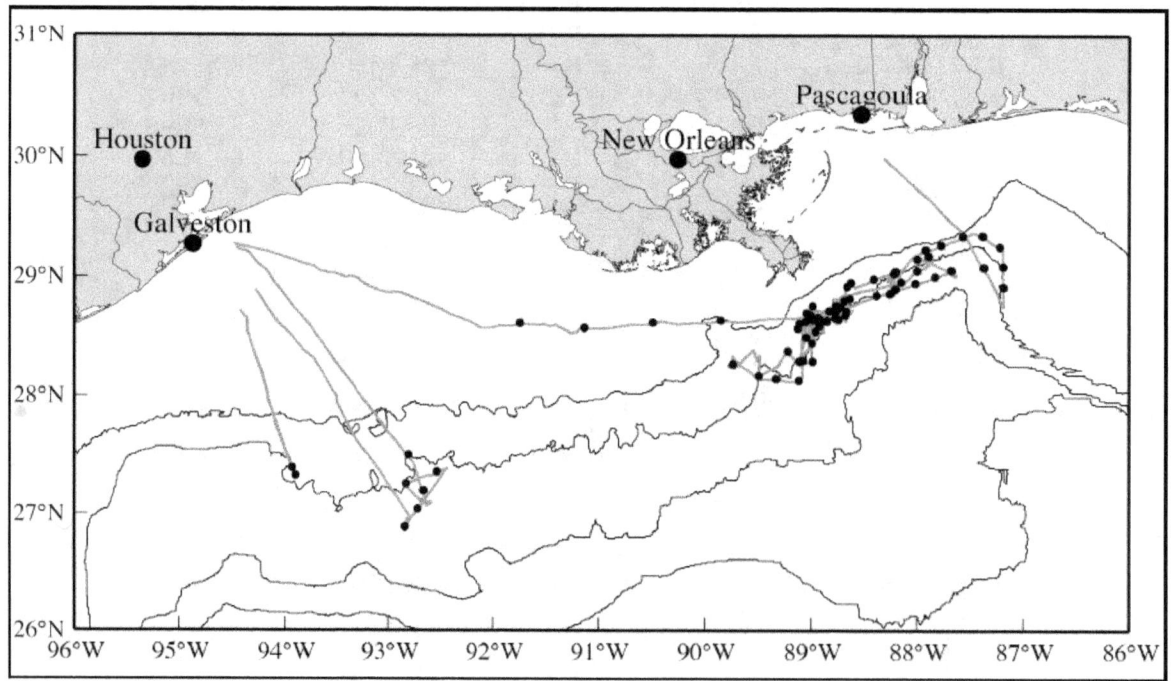

Figure 3.3.5. Cruise track (gray line) and locations of chlorophyll stations (circles) taken during the SWSS 2003 S-tag cruise.

64

<u>Visual Monitoring</u>
The visual observation team consisted of six people and was coordinated by Joel G. Ortega-Ortiz. During survey/search mode, at least three observers were on watch during daylight hours from the *Gyre's* flying bridge. Two observers used BigEye 25x150 binoculars, while a third observer kept watch with naked eye or 7x50 binoculars and entered data into the computer. The observers on the BigEye binoculars searched a 100 swath, from 90 (abeam) to 10 past the bow on the opposite side. Observers rotated positions every 30 minutes. The six observers worked 1.5-hr shifts followed by a 1.5-hr rest period. This schedule was used to minimize observer fatigue and yet ensure continuity of whale tracking. The range to each sighting was estimated using reticles etched into the right eyepiece of the binoculars, and horizontal bearings were measured using a radial measurement scale at the base of the BigEye yoke. Search effort, sighting conditions, and cetacean sightings were recorded using the computer program *Logger*. *Logger* is a data collection and display program written by Douglas Gillespie and made available by the International Fund for Animal Welfare.

Once a group of sperm whales was detected, the visual team worked in coordination with the acoustic team to maximize the effectiveness of S-tagging and photo-ID operations. This involved plotting the locations of groups of whales in real time using the *Logger* mapping program, and monitoring patterns of acoustic detections, movement, and behavior. Locations (or inferred locations) of animals were communicated by VHF radio to the tagging and photo-ID RHIB boats to direct them into areas where whales were likely to surface. RHIBs were guided using software, developed by Joel Ortega at OSU, that provided bearing and approximate distance to the whales relative to the RHIB boat. The visual team suggested course and speed changes to the bridge to keep the *Gyre* in a position to maintain visual and acoustic coverage of whale groups, which typically could be spread over several miles.

The visual team searched for sperm whales on all 14 days when the ship was in regions that might have sperm whales. A total of 130.86 hours were spent by the observers either on survey effort or tracking whales (Table 3.3.4 and Figure 3.3.6). This effort includes only the time when the computer was operating on the flying bridge and does not account for the survey watch with naked eye from the either the bridge or the flying bridge during rain.

A total of 579 sightings of sperm whales were recorded (Figure 3.3.7). However, when the vessel was in tracking mode, many of those sightings were of the same individual, i.e., re-sights. Additionally, 40 sightings of other cetacean species were recorded during the cruise (Table 3.3.5 and Figure 3.3.8).

<u>Acoustic Monitoring, Detection, and Tracking</u>
The acoustic team consisted of five people and was coordinated by Thomas Norris. A shift system was established to provide 24-hr coverage while ensuring that "observer fatigue" did not impact performance. Thomas Norris and Ricardo Antunes, who was acoustic coordinator for the SWSS 2003 WSHC cruise, met prior to the cruise in Galveston, TX, on 24 June to review acoustic equipment and protocols. Sarah Tsoflias, who participated as an acoustic observer on the WSHC cruise, provided some continuity and overlap in protocols between the two 2003 SWSS cruises on *Gyre*.

Hardware/Software: The passive acoustics monitoring system consisted of two matched hydrophone array systems assembled by Ecologic UK Ltd. Each array had sections consisting of 2 hydrophone elements (Benthos AQ-4) and respective pre-amplifiers (Magrec) that provided 30dB of gain and a 100Hz high-pass filter. The elements were positioned 3-m apart, and each was housed in a polyurethane tube, approximately 10-m long, that was filled with non-toxic oil. The hydrophone array was attached to 400 m of strengthened tow cable with a hair fairing sheath

Table 3.3.4

Visual Survey Effort by Day on the SWSS 2003 S-tag Cruise

Day	Hours
26 June 2003	2.82
28 June 2003	10.04
29 June 2003	8.98
3 July 2003	10.30
4 July 2003	1.97
5 July 2003	12.92
6 July 2003	11.53
7 July 2003	9.39
8 July 2003	11.90
9 July 2003	10.96
10 July 2003	12.49
11 July 2003	11.94
12 July 2003	6.00
13 July 2003	9.62
Total	130.86

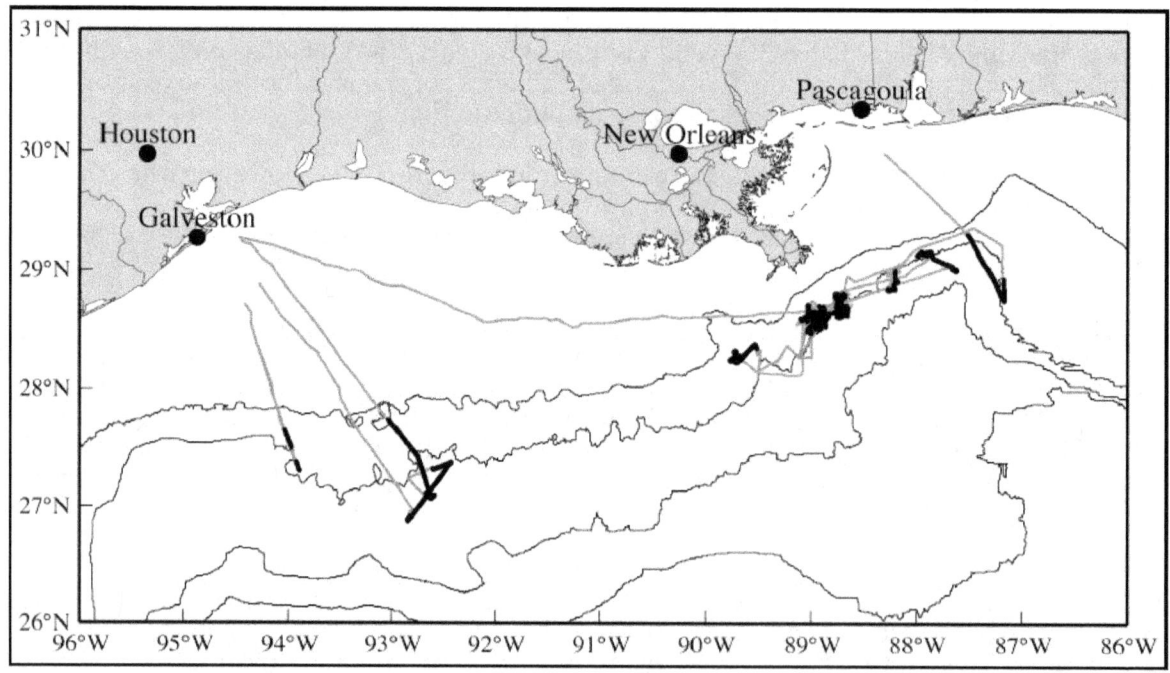

Figure 3.3.6. SWSS 2003 S-tag cruise track with the track during the visual survey effort (thick black line) superimposed. Contour lines are for the 200, 1000, 2000, and 3000-m isobaths.

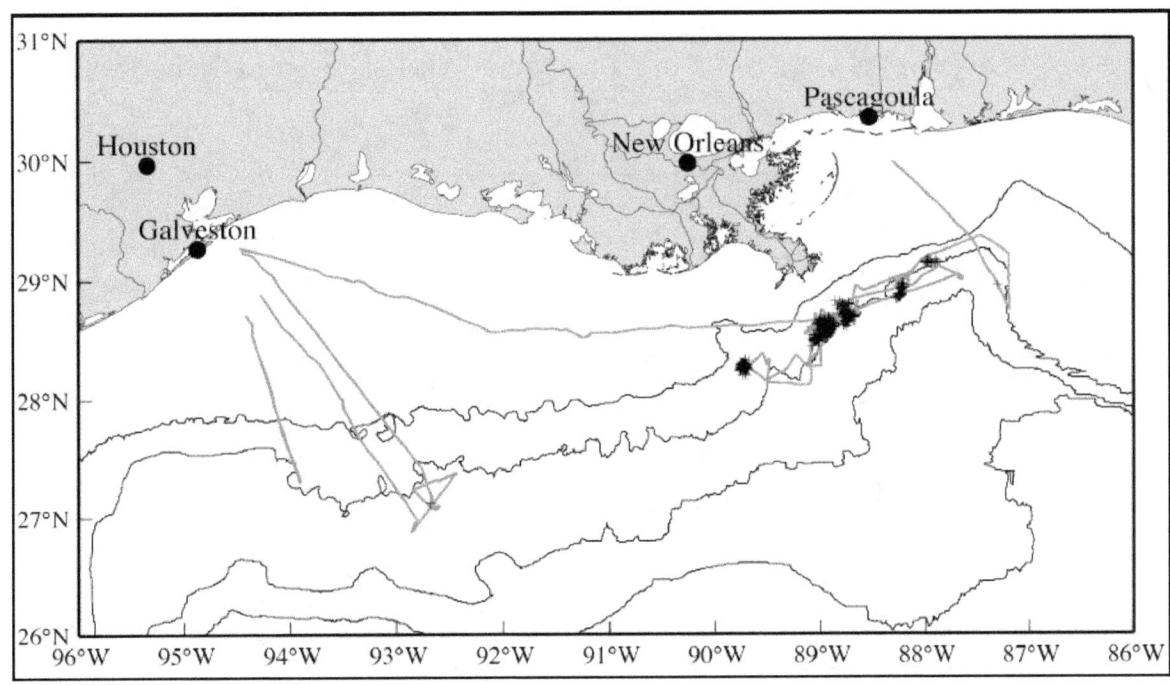

Figure 3.3.7. Cruise track line (gray line) and locations of sightings of sperm whales (crosses) recorded during the SWSS 2003 S-tag cruise. Contour lines show the 200, 1000, 2000, and 3000-m isobaths.

Table 3.3.5

Sightings of Cetaceans Other Than Sperm Whales

Species	# Sightings
Pilot whale	6
Pantropical spotted dolphin	5
Kogia sp.	4
Risso's dolphin	1
Rough-toothed dolphin	1
Unidentified dolphin	21
Unidentified whale	2
Unidentified beaked whale	1
Total	40

Table 3.3.6

Locations of Sightings of Cetaceans, Other Than Sperm Whales, Recorded During the SWSS
2003 S-tag Cruise

Speices Names	Longitude (°N)	Latitude (°W)
kogia sp	-87.670	29.027
kogia sp	-89.723	28.295
kogia sp	-88.741	28.675
Pantropical Spotted Dolphin	-92.626	27.153
Pantropical Spotted Dolphin	-92.824	26.961
Pantropical Spotted Dolphin	-88.657	28.673
Pantropical Spotted Dolphin	-87.633	29.017
Pantropical Spotted Dolphin	-88.881	28.564
Pilot Whale	-93.031	27.727
Pilot Whale	-89.707	28.289
Pilot Whale	-89.687	28.284
Pilot Whale	-88.922	28.648
Pilot Whale	-88.915	28.648
Pilot Whale	-88.721	28.750
Risso's Dolphin	-89.020	28.634
Rough-toothed Dolphin	-88.107	29.089
Unidentified Beaked Whale	-88.683	28.798
Unidentified Dolphin	-93.013	27.707
Unidentified Dolphin	-92.966	27.658
Unidentified Dolphin	-92.889	27.570
Unidentified Dolphin	-92.762	26.990
Unidentified Dolphin	-87.882	29.163
Unidentified Dolphin	-87.882	29.167
Unidentified Dolphin	-87.864	29.136
Unidentified Dolphin	-88.910	28.587
Unidentified Dolphin	-88.936	28.609
Unidentified Dolphin	-88.940	28.645
Unidentified Dolphin	-89.021	28.504
Unidentified Dolphin	-89.693	28.288
Unidentified Dolphin	-89.675	28.261
Unidentified Dolphin	-89.529	28.363
Unidentified Dolphin	-89.509	28.312
Unidentified Dolphin	-88.956	28.656
Unidentified Dolphin	-88.932	28.650
Unidentified Dolphin	-88.737	28.691
Unidentified Dolphin	-88.726	28.722
Unidentified Dolphin	-87.426	29.156
Unidentified Dolphin	-87.446	29.190
Unidentified Whales	-87.880	29.141
Unidentified Whales	-87.456	29.207

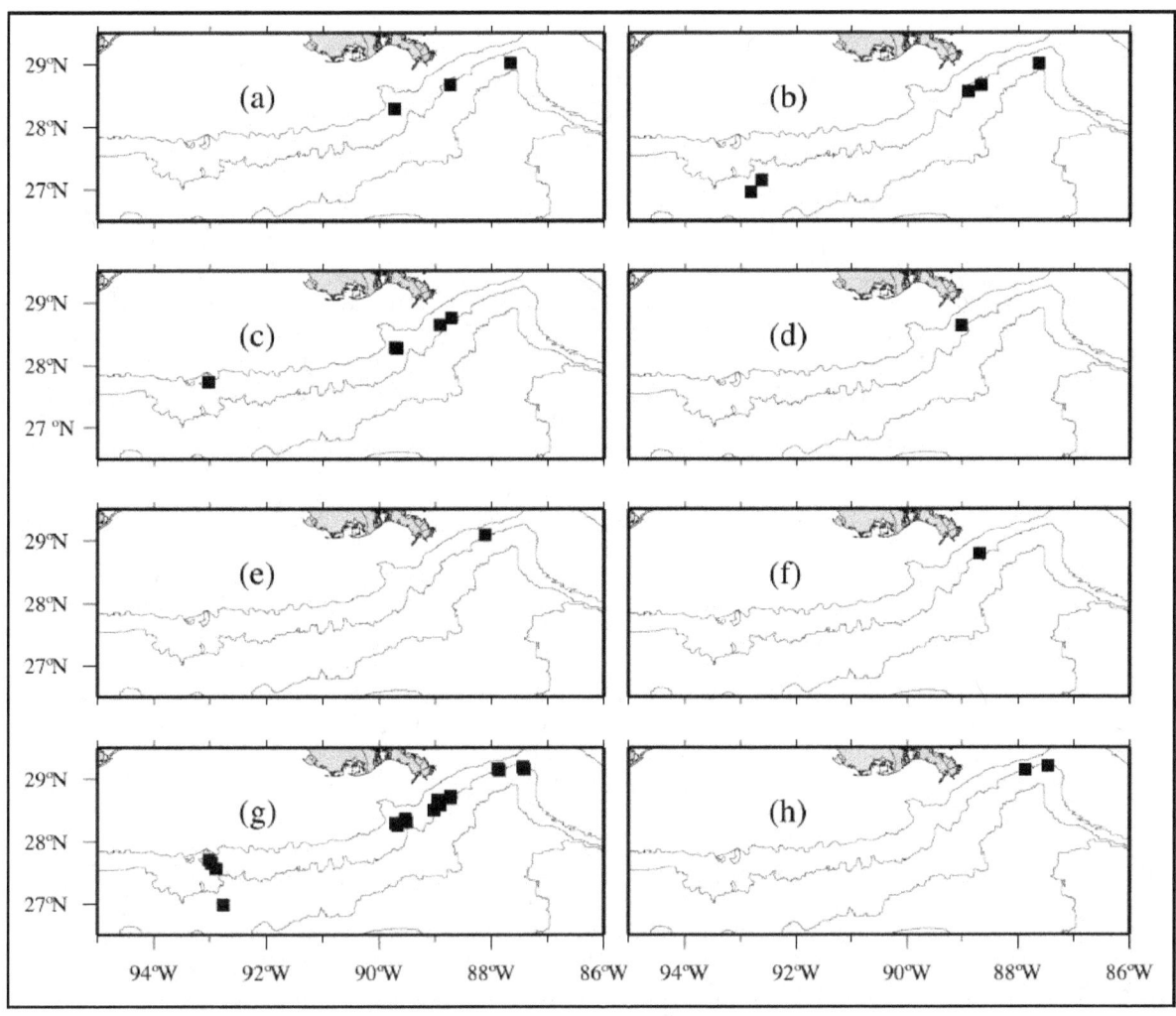

Figure 3.3.8. Sightings of cetaceans, other than sperm whales, recorded during the SWSS 2003 S-tag cruise. Shown are (a) *Kogia* sp.; (b) pantropical spotted dolphin; (c) pilot whale; (d) Risso's dolphin; (e) rough-toothed dolphin, (f) unidentified beaked whale; (g) unidentified dolphin; (h) unidentified whales. Contour lines indicate the 200, 1000, 2000, and 3000-m isobaths.

to reduce cable strumming noise. Each array was equipped with depth sensors (Keller PA-9SE-50 50bar 4-20mA sensor). Depth readings were displayed on panel meters (Asahi Keiki A5000 display units) in the acoustics lab. Software for the depth sensors was developed by Ricardo Antunes on the SWSS 2003 WSHC cruise. Data were logged in the acoustic *Logger* database.

The dual hydrophone array configuration was used to form a two-dimensional (i.e., in x and y) array to eliminate the right-left ambiguity that usually results with a single linear array. The second array also could be used as backup if the primary one failed. The hydrophone arrays were deployed at their maximum cable length of approximately 375 m. Hydrophone tow depths depended on tow speed and cable length. With the cable fully deployed, the hydrophone elements towed at an approximate depth of 35 m at ship speed of 5 knots. Tow depth increased to over 100 m when the ship slowed to 2-2.5 knots. During transit, *Gyre* typically maintained a speed of 6-7 knots resulting in a tow depth of 20 m. At this speed, self-generated noise from the ship and tow-cable often was severe enough to reduce effective detection of sperm whales at distances greater than ~1 km. Hence, operations were adjusted to provide intensive listening periods at slower speeds, as described under "Animal Tracking" below.

Each hydrophone array fed into the acoustic acquisition system in the acoustics lab via a deck cable of the same specifications as the tow cable. The primary acoustic monitoring laboratory was located in a dry lab aft of the computer room on the 01 deck of the R/V *Gyre*. The acoustic acquisition system consisted of an adjustable amplifier/high-pass filter box (Ecologic), an external USB soundcard (Creative Labs Extigy SB0130), and two desktop computers independently running signal processing and data-logging software. Output from the hydrophones could be monitored in real-time using headsets or with high quality speakers in the acoustic lab. A cross-over and equalizer provided signal conditioning capabilities for real-time signal monitoring only; this did not affect the signal characteristics of recorded signals.

Signal acquisition, processing and data-logging software consisted of *Rainbow Click, Logger,* (written by Douglas Gillespie and available from the International Fund for Animal Welfare), and *Ishmael* (written by Dave Mellinger of NOAA/PMEL Newport, Oregon). *Rainbow Click* and *Ishmael* provided real-time signal acquisition, processing, signal display and bearing-to-source calculation capabilities. *Logger* was used for acoustic, location, and environmental data acquisition and display as well as providing sperm whale tracking capabilities. All three programs ran continuously during monitoring. *Rainbow Click* and *Ishmael* were used primarily to monitor hydrophone signals, calculate bearings-to-source (sperm whales), and display bearing-based tracks of animals. *Rainbow Click* calculates bearings to the sound source (whale) from the time-of-arrival delay for individual clicks detected at the two hydrophone elements of a single linear array. It then displays this on a time-bearing plot using dots with different colors to represent potentially different animals. *Ishmael* provides real-time spectrographic display capabilities as well as the capability to calculate bearings of a common signal from two hydrophone elements. *Logger* is designed to automatically record acoustic data (48 kHz sample rate, based on a user defined sampling schedule), acquired GPS data, and displayed tracks of the research vessel and bearings to animals. Scored data (e.g., relative loudness of whales and noise, estimated number of whales detected) were entered manually into *Logger*. Continuous recordings also could be made manually (48 kHz sample rate, 2-channels) using *Logger*. Acoustic data from *Logger* were written automatically to the hard disk on the computer running the software. These were later backed up manually on CD's.

Hydrophone Search/Survey: A team of five acoustic personnel (acoustic monitors) provided 24-hr acoustic monitoring while underway. Acoustic monitoring was conducted during standard survey mode and searching mode, or when assisting in locating and tracking groups of sperm whales for tagging purposes. During whale survey and search modes, an acoustic monitor listened carefully to a pair of hydrophones from one of the linear arrays using stereo headphones for one minute every 15 minutes. At night, while the vessel was often in transit at a 6-7 knot speed, an alternative procedure was used, as described under Animal Tracking below. Numbers of estimated animals, relative loudness of cetacean vocalizations, and relative loudness of seismic survey and other noise were entered as scores into the *Logger* program for each listening station. In addition, during the day every two minutes a 20-second acoustic sample or during the night a 5 minute sample from every 30 minutes (48 kHz sample rate) was recorded automatically as .wav files in *Logger*. Continuous recordings were made in *Logger* of notable noises, cetacean vocalization, and other sounds of interest.

Animal Tracking: Once detected, sperm whales were tracked using *Rainbow Click* and *Logger* software. The main purpose of this effort was to provide the visual tracking team and the tagging team with information on bearings and, when possible, distances to vocalizing sperm whales. To

70

achieve this, the acoustic team made use of the dual hydrophone arrays and software on two computers. One array and its associated computer station were used to determine horizontal bearings to the source but with a left/right ambiguity, and the second array and computer station were used to resolve the left/right ambiguity. After some experience, when all acoustic contacts were not on the same side of the ship, it often was possible to differentiate which group of sperm whales was on which side of the ship. In addition, the cessation of clicking for individuals or groups of sperm whales that were being tracked was noted, and this information passed on to the visual team. Cessation of clicking usually is an indication that an animal or group of animals would soon surface. In this way the acoustics team could, on most occasions, tell the bearing and direction of sperm whales relative to the array without having to turn the ship (as is the case when using a single array). This method significantly reduced the time required to locate animals, thus enabling the RHIBs to maneuver into position, in some cases even before animals were sighted.

Night-time effort was conducted both to survey for sperm whales and to track large groups (> 4-5 animals) continuously so that the visual and tagging team were able to work with them in the morning. Night-time surveys frequently consisted of transiting along a predetermined path, determined by the chief scientists Jochens and Mate, at cruising speeds of 6-7 knots and slowing at fixed intervals (usually 20 min) to listen for a fixed period (usually 10 minutes). Thus, for every hour, there were two ten-minute periods that were closely monitored under relatively quiet self-noise conditions. Detections of sperm whales and other cetaceans were recorded in *Logger*. This information was used to determine areas for locating and tracking whales.

Small Boat Acoustic Monitoring: Each of the RHIB boats was outfitted with a hand-held directional hydrophone unit attached to a pole. Directional hydrophones were used to locate sperm whales by lowering the unit into the water and rotating the pole to allow the hydrophones to scan back and forth. Headsets allowed the operator to aurally determine the direction in which clicks appeared loudest.

Acoustically equipped RHIBs proved to be an effective method for locating and following groups of sperm whales during extended encounters. Monitoring could be performed away from the noise of the *Gyre*, and the small boats could respond and move quickly to localize animals complementing the continuous tracking of the R/V *Gyre* acoustic and visual team. RHIBs were maneuvered to create equilateral triangles that helped to localize the area at which the animals would surface in order to position the OSU RHIB boat in the best location to deploy tags.

Acoustic Tracking Preliminary Results: Approximately 262 hours of acoustic monitoring and surveying was completed over 18.5 days or 76% of the time at sea. Several days of effort were lost due to adverse weather and mechanical problems with the R/V *Gyre*. These values include time during transits to and from Galveston and the study areas during which acoustic survey effort was not undertaken in order to expedite transit times. If the total transit time was excluded, the percentage of time in which there was acoustic survey effort approaches 100%, i.e., 14 out of 14 days available to conduct effort were monitored acoustically. There were a total of 530 one-minute listening periods of 1 minute listening per every 15 minute during slow transits. Over 350 acoustic contacts of sperm whales were made during these listening periods of which 66% had at least one acoustic contact. During night-time surveys, a total of 190 ten minute listening periods, with 10 minutes of intense listening per every 30 minutes, were completed over 8 nights, while searching for and tracking whales. A histogram of qualitative scores from acoustic listening periods is given in Figure 3.3.9. A map of acoustic contacts is given in Figure 3.3.10.

In addition to monitoring for cetacean vocalizations, the presence of anthropogenic noise also was noted. The *Gyre*'s own engine and propeller sounds masked many sources of anthropogenic noise. However, the periodic noise from seismic air-gun surveys were quite common and were commonly detected during ~30% of the listening periods.

Over 200 *Rainbow Click* files were written automatically by that software on the hard drive. These files were created by *Rainbow Click* during signal acquisition and can be used to replay bearing versus sperm whale click trains in *Rainbow Click*. "Autorec" files also were written and saved automatically by *Logger* during pre-determined sampling periods or manually selected periods. These acoustic files are formatted as ".wav" files at 24 kHz bandwidth and 2 channels. However, upon review of the "Autorec" files it was determined that many did not contain useful signals, e.g., they contained only low amplitude noise. It appears that the default settings in *Logger* were changed or defaulted to an incorrect input device (a device other than the Creative Labs SB Extigy soundcard) before or at some point near the beginning of the cruise. Preliminary review indicates approximately 187 autorec files with useful audio data were saved.

In addition to these sound files, approximately 240 minutes of 2-channel acoustic recordings were made to DAT tape, including sperm whale clicks, possible codas, pilot whales, and other odontocete (mostly delphinid) vocalizations.

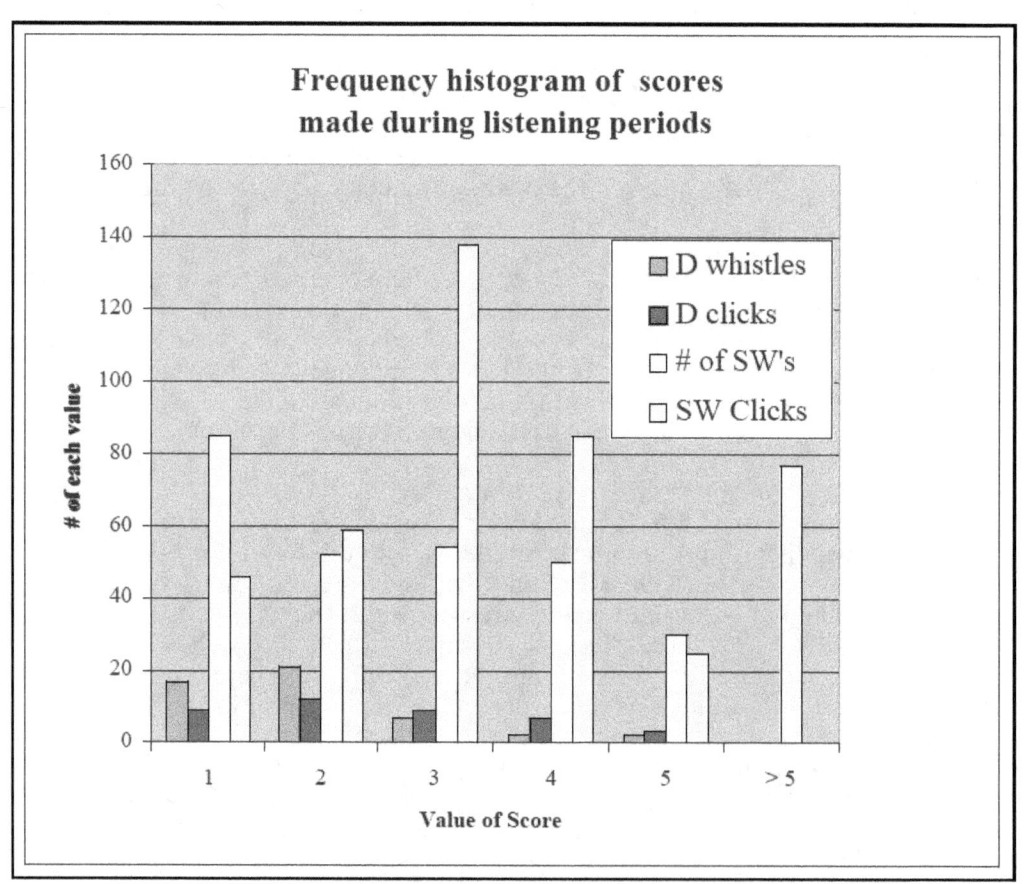

Figure 3.3.9. Histogram of qualitative scores from acoustic listening periods.

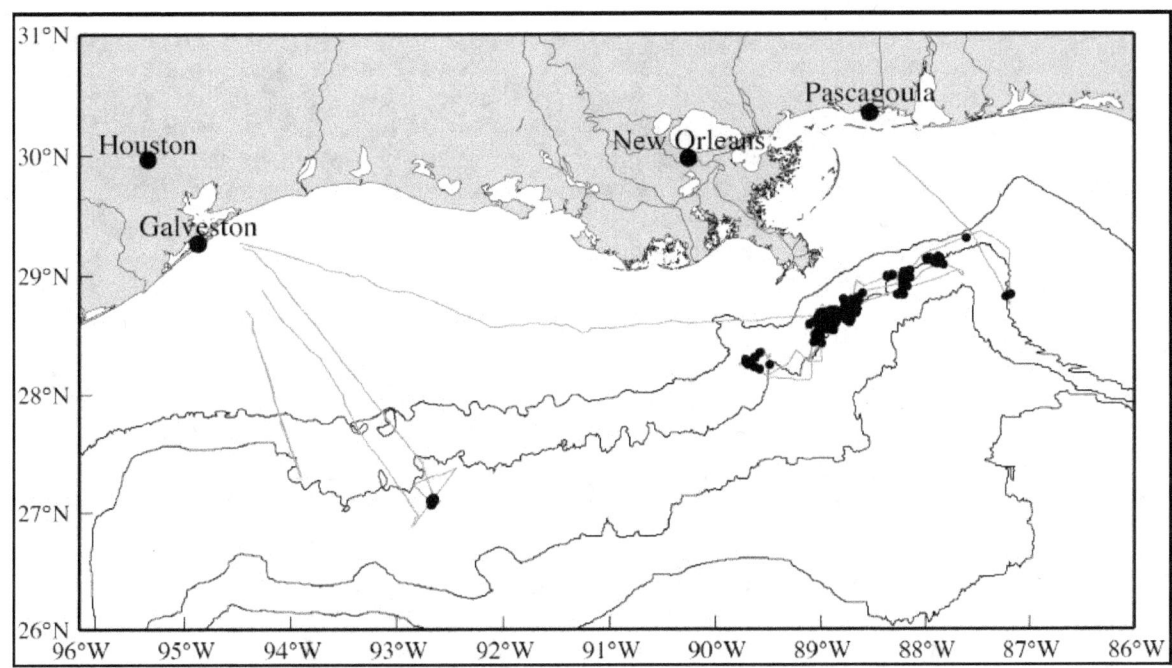

Figure 3.3.10. Acoustic contacts during the SWSS 2003 S-tag cruise.

Satellite-Tracked Tagging

Tagging of sperm whales was supervised by Bruce Mate. The tagging crew departed the R/V *Gyre* on RHIB-1 when a group of whales was spotted visually or determined to be close by the acoustic survey team. Up to five people were on the tagging boat: Ladd Irvine drove, Bruce Mate tagged, Mary Lou Mate took video of the S-tag attachment, Dan Engelhaupt took biopsies, and occasionally either Terry Ketler took video for an MMS documentary, Bruce Miller took photo-IDs, or Bill Lang observed the research for MMS. The visual and acoustics teams guided the tagging boat to the area where whales were expected to be surfacing. The acoustics team gave the tag team clues as to when the whales might surface. Because the first approach of the boat is often the best, it was important to time the approach well. Care was taken to approach slowly. Sometimes it was necessary to wait for a subsequent surfacing sequence if RHIB-1 arrived too late in the surfacing sequence or the initial approach was not successful. Tagging was accomplished at short range (<3m) using an air-powered tag applicator. Video documentation of the tagging itself was important to help evaluate placement and penetration. On the first day it also revealed problems in the application procedure due to humidity; these were subsequently remedied. A skin biopsy was attempted when feasible after tagging, most often during the same surfacing and immediately after tagging. Biopsies were obtained from 11 tagged whales. Underwater video of sperm whales was obtained during two tagging approaches.

Tags were initiated before the cruise to put them into synchrony with the satellite passes and a fixed duty cycle. Based on the tag results from summer 2001 and summer 2002, an average of 1+ good locations/day was obtained with a 4-hour transmission schedule. Under the 2001 schedule, the battery supply was used up in 137 days, while some batteries lasted for more than 12 months in 2002. To increase the likelihood of a year-round picture of movements, tags deployed in 2003 have a 4-hour per day transmission schedule but transmit only one out of every 3 days until the batteries are exhausted; this is the estimated operation for up to 12 months.

Table 3.3.7 shows the date, time, and locations where tags were deployed. Fifteen of eighteen tags were attached to sperm whales (Figure 3.3.11). As of 23 July 2003, fourteen tags had transmitted through Argos. Of the 15 whales tagged, three tags were judged "not well attached" and were not expected to last beyond a few weeks. Two of these tags were poorly attached because of humidity affecting their attachment to the pushrod system used for tag delivery. Additionally, 3 tags were lost glancing off of whales. This high rate of missing was due primarily to operating in rougher-than-ideal sea states.

Table 3.3.7

Locations of Deployments of Sperm Whale Tags During SWSS 2003 S-tag Cruise

PTT No.	Date (mm/dd/yyyy)	Time (UTC)	Latitude (°N)	Longitude (°W)	Notes
5655	07/03/2003	18:34	28.6467	-88.9979	1
1385	07/03/2003	18:42	28.6510	-89.0005	
828	07/03/2003	19:06	28.6572	-89.0091	
5654	07/03/2003	19:21	28.6668	-89.0070	2
843	07/05/2003	10:49	28.7250	-88.7211	2
833	07/05/2003	12:41	28.7315	-88.7633	
5719	07/05/2003	19:08	28.6980	-88.7648	
5720	07/06/2003	18:54	29.1402	-87.9652	2
5647	07/07/2003	10:15	28.6460	-88.9063	1
5710	07/07/2003	15:15	28.6524	-88.9080	
839	07/08/2003	14:03	28.5212	-88.9464	
848	07/09/2003	11:08	28.5083	-89.0340	1
10820	07/09/2003	11:18	28.5061	-89.0261	
829	07/09/2003	18:38	28.4822	-89.0432	
5678	07/11/2003	20:17	28.7873	-88.7583	
827	07/11/2003	20:43	28.7965	-88.7630	
826	07/11/2003	23:10	28.8050	-88.7221	
23038	07/11/2003	23:35	28.7940	-88.7242	

Notes:
1 - tag lost
2 - attachment not good

Photo-ID, Photogrammetry, and Tag Effects
Photo-ID and photogrammetry work was conducted during good weather by Bruce Miller from the *R2*, which was driven by Dan Lewer. The main objective of the photo-ID/photogrammetry effort during the S-tag cruise was to obtain identification information for the tagged whales. For this purpose, the photo-ID boat worked in close coordination with the tagging boat. After a whale was tagged, the tagging boat (RHIB-1) often moved on to look for other whales, leaving the second boat (*R2*) responsible for getting pictures of the tag and for identification of the tagged whale. Concerns developed early in the cruise about whales being sensitive to the *R2*'s outboard motor noise. As a result, the *R2* took a passive role in tagging approaches, spending

74

most of its time 50-100m behind the tagging boat. Later in the cruise, the *R2* spent much of its time helping to identify whale locations underwater by using a hand-held directional hydrophone. The bearings obtained by the *R2* were used in conjunction with the bearings from the *Gyre*'s array to triangulate a more precise location than either could accomplish without assistance.

Photos were obtained of all whales tagged in 2003, although all are not suitable for re-identification. Photos also were taken of at least five whales that had been tagged during the 2002 field season. These included one whale that had lost its tag and 4 whales with tags still attached. All of the tagged whales from 2002 looked like they were in very good condition and their tags (or tag sites) looked good as well. One tag had nearly worked its way out completely and had two gooseneck barnacles attached to it. Even this tag site looked very good.

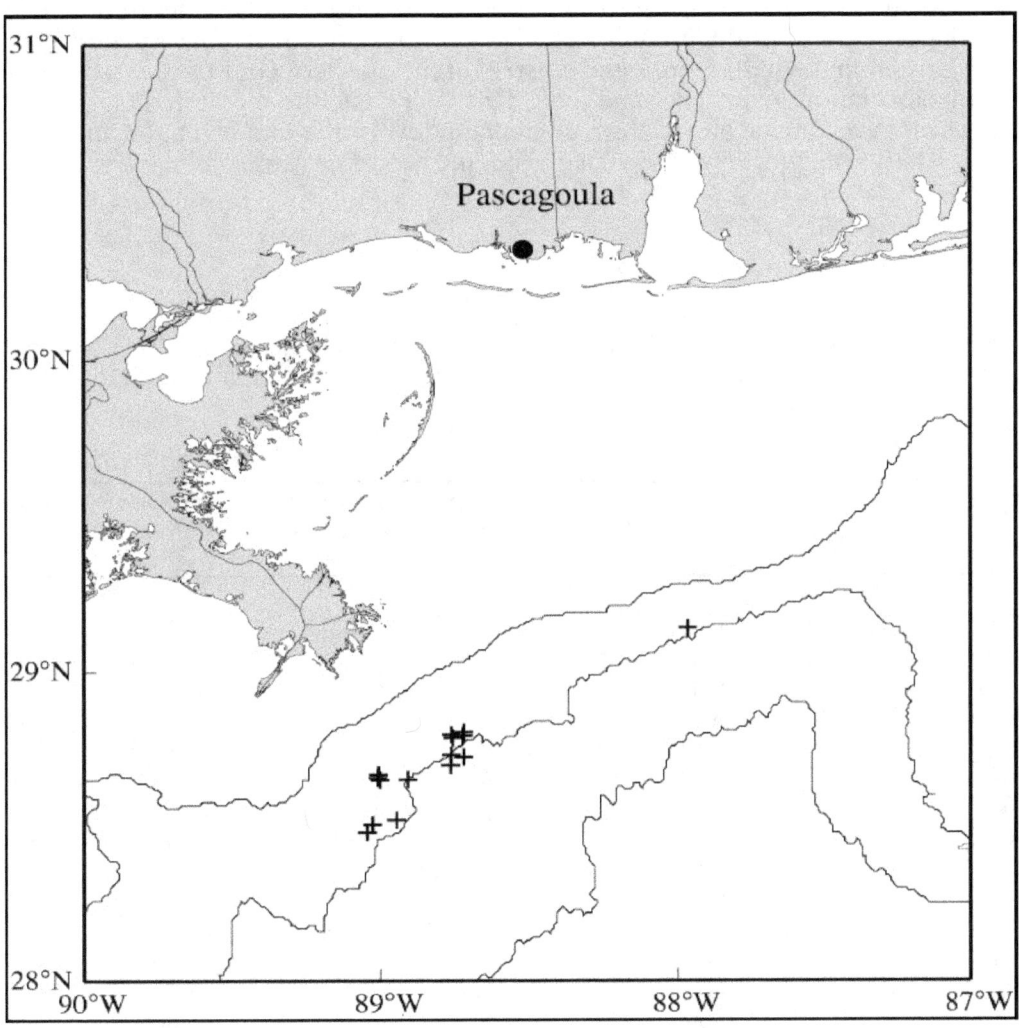

Figure 3.3.11. Locations of the 15 successful tag attachments on the SWSS 2003 S-tag cruise.

Tissue Collection/Genetic Typing

Biopsy sampling techniques were combined with satellite-monitored tagging during the second leg of the *Gyre* "S-tag cruise" in the northern Gulf of Mexico. Dan Engelhaupt conducted this work. A total of fifteen skin samples were collected during the cruise (see Table 3.3.8). Eleven biopsies and one sloughed skin sample were taken of whales tagged with satellite-monitored tags (Figure 3.3.12). Three biopsy samples were collected from whales tagged with satellite-monitored tags put out in 2002. One of the three 2002 tagged whales that was sampled this year is believed to be a key member of the female cluster that was tagged and sampled last year and fills in a very important gap in the data. All tissue samples obtained are expected to provide ample material for genetic applications. No significantly large males (whales that appear to be sexually and physically mature based on estimated sizes) were encountered and therefore none were sampled.

Overall, the combination of satellite-monitored tagging and biopsy sampling was very successful. A biopsy sample was obtained from multiple members of four groups; several of these sampled individuals have satellite tags to match. Degrees of relatedness will be tested between whales found within groups and clusters to study questions on how related and unrelated whales found within groups and clusters in the northern Gulf of Mexico maintain long or short term associations over space and time. This year's satellite-monitored tagging and biopsy sampling success was only achieved through the high levels of communication and coordination between the RHIB's tagging crew, the visual team, the acoustics team, and the *Gyre's* crew.

Table 3.3.8

Tissue Collection/Genetic Typing Samples Collected During the SWSS 2003 S-tag Cruise
(Sample number gives date (yymmdd), followed by the consecutive number for multiple samples
taken on any given day [01 to 04])

Sample #	S-tag #	Tissue Type	Group #	Approx. # Whales in Area	Latitude (°N)	Longitude (°W)
03070301	5654 or 5655	Biopsy	1	6-12	28.6467	88.9979
03070302	828	Biopsy	1	6-12	28.6572	89.0091
03070501	843	Biopsy	2	7	28.6370	88.7452
03070502	5719	Biopsy	2	7	28.6980	88.7648
03070601	5720	Biopsy	3	6	29.1402	87.9652
03070701	5655*	Biopsy	4	12	28.6604	88.9206
03070801	Unknown*	Biopsy	4	12	28.6098	88.9377
03070901	Unknown*	Biopsy	5	8-10	28.5083	89.0340
03070902	10820	Biopsy	5	8-10	28.5487	88.9961
03070903	829	Biopsy	6	8	28.4822	89.0432
03071001	1385	Biopsy	7	10	28.2684	89.7147
03071101	833	Biopsy	8	7-8	28.6016	88.8991
03071102	5678	Sloughed Skin	9	10	28.7873	88.2583
03071103	827	Biopsy	9	10	28.8050	88.7221
03071104	826	Biopsy	9	10	28.8050	88.7221

*2002 Tagged Whales

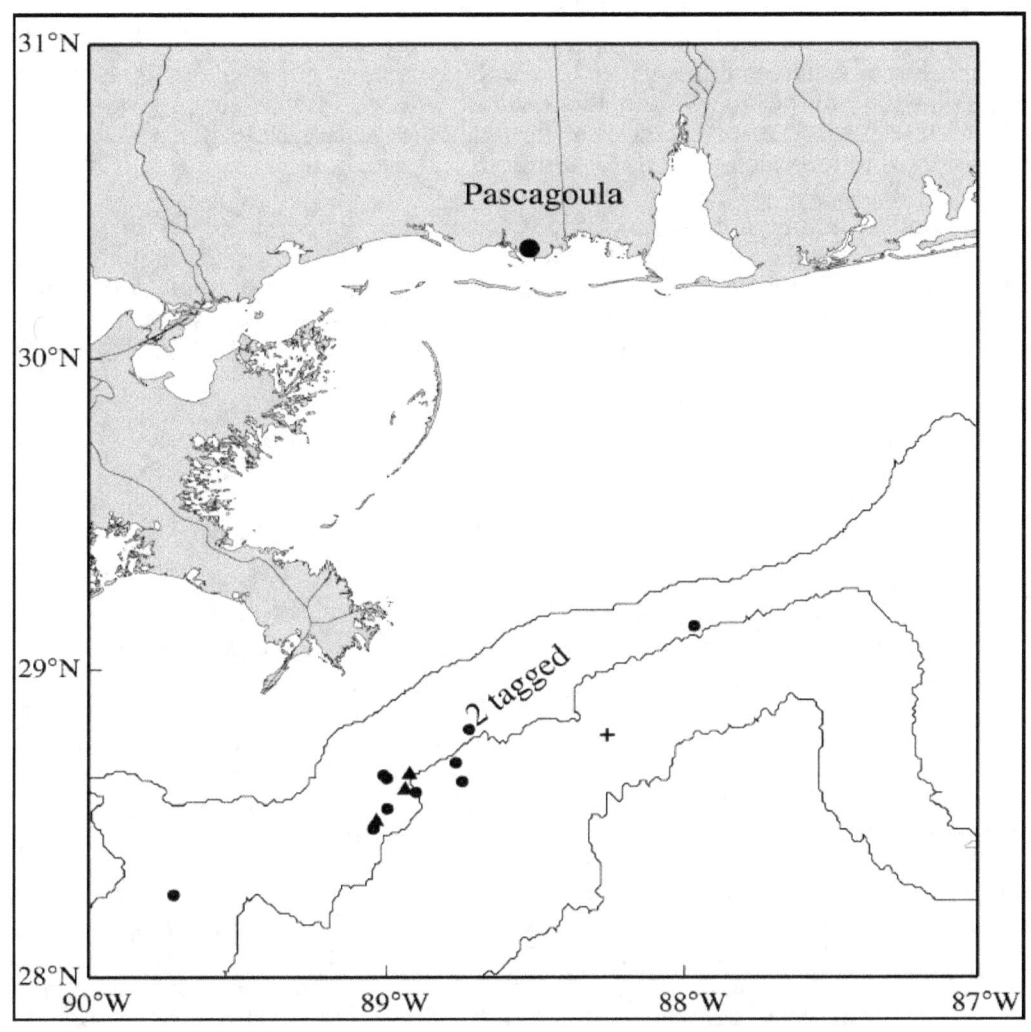

Figure 3.3.12. Locations of biopsy samples for whales tagged in 2003 (circles) and 2002 (triangles) and of the sloughed skin sample (cross). All 15 samples were collected during the SWSS 2003 S-tag cruise.

77

3.4   3-D Passive Acoustic Tracking During D-tag Cruise 2003

Field work for the SWSS 3-D passive acoustic sperm whale tracking project was performed between June 5 and 24 on the D-tag/CEE cruise. The PI, Aaron Thode, worked off two platforms: the seismic source vessel M/V *Kondor Explorer* between June 5 and June 16, and the R/V *Maurice Ewing* between June 16 to June 24. The reason for the transfer was that it was discovered that the engine noise from the *Kondor* was so intense that it was impossible to conduct effective passive acoustic monitoring from the vessel. Note that times given in this section are in local time, which was CDT. Additional information on this study is in Section 4.5.

Two deployments of an autonomous acoustic recorder were made, one each on June 18 and 21. Both recorded for about 12 hours. The recorder was attached to a rope streaming about 100 m from the end of the *Ewing* SEAMAP array. Both recordings were clipped fairly badly due to what appears to be strum on the tow rope. One of the recordings (June 18) seems to have three hours of useable data, with at least one set of sperm whale multipaths extracted from the data.

Part 1: Work from the *Kondor Explorer*
In the original cruise plan, all work for this project was planned to be performed off the *Kondor* using two data collection strategies. The first was to time-synch recordings made from the towed arrays on both the *Ewing* and *Kondor*, effectively creating a single large-aperture array with both ships. The second strategy was to deploy two widely-separated hydrophones from the *Kondor*.

Between June 4, when the PI boarded the *Kondor*, and June 8, he worked with Craig Douglas of SEAMAP Inc. to prepare the SEAMAP hydrophone array for use in the 3-D passive acoustic tracking expeiments. On June 8 the *Kondor* departed to rendezvous with the *Ewing* and to deploy and possibly calibrate the EARS buoys developed by the Naval Research Laboratory.

The Noise Problem: During June 8, the *Kondor* acoustics team realized that the noise levels of the *Kondor* were limiting the detection range of the SEAMAP array to less than a kilometer. On June 9, the *Kondor* was requested to stand off more than 2 nautical miles away from the *Ewing* because its ship noise was interfering with the *Ewing* acoustic detection. On June 10, the noise levels of the vessel were tested by accelerating the vessel speed to 6 knots through the water, then freezing both propellers in place. The background noise levels dropped by 30-40 dB. This proved that cavitation noise was the culprit. Systematic testing of various propeller pitches and shaft speeds on June 10 and 11 revealed that when only the port engine was used, and if the pitch of the propeller was set to 1 to 1.5 degrees at a fixed rpm of 200, the background noise levels could be lowered by about 15 dB while still permitting the *Kondor* to travel at reasonable speeds. From opportunistic approaches on different animals the acoustics team estimated detection ranges of 1-2 km under ideal circumstances from the *Kondor*. This was adequate to allow acoustic mitigation monitoring for controlled-exposure experiments, but made impossible the independent acoustic tracking, which was a fundamental requirement for the 3-D tracking work described here.

Because of the self-noise issue, the first strategy of coordinating vessel movement to time-synch recordings became impractical. For example, *Kondor* would have to get within 1 nautical mile of *Ewing* in order to detect the same whale on the arrays of both vessels. This was a difficult arrangement that also raised the issue of *Kondor* ship noise interfering with the sperm whale tracking from the *Ewing*. So, the first strategy was not pursued.

First Attempts at Deploying Autonomous Recorders: With the possibility of using a second SEAMAP array eliminated and ship noise issues preventing coordination between the two vessels, the one avenue remaining was to try and deploy an autonomous flash-memory recorder off the *Kondor* in such a way that the horizontal separation between the recorder and the SEAMAP array was as large as possible. Figure 3.4.1 shows an example of such a recorder.

In lieu of using fishing line, 100 m of 5/8" diameter, three-strand polypro rope was attached to the end of the working SEAMAP array, and then the recorder was attached two meters from the other end of the rope, weighting the end with a 20 lb shackle (Figure 3.4.2). As the SEAMAP array itself was 50 m long, the effective aperture of the array could have been as large as 150 m. This would have permitted tracking of animals out to about the 500-m range. An engineering test on June 12 showed that this arrangement could work and that the autonomous recorder reached depths greater than or equal to the SEAMAP array.

The disadvantage of this deployment was that the recorder could not be recovered and replaced unless the entire towed array itself was recovered. Since the array was needed for mitigation purposes, the array could be pulled in only early in the morning each day, with the result that a new configuration could only be tried once a day.

Between June 13 and June 16, as the possibility of transferring to another vessel was considered, further deployments of the autonomous recorder were made. On the deployment on June 13, the probe was attached directly to a 5/8" polypro line. The recorder began acquiring data at 20:50 CDT and was recovered at 6:04 CDT on June 14. Data were strongly clipped.

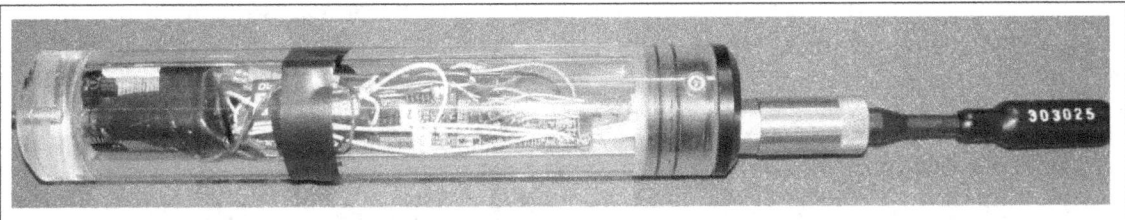

Figure 3.4.1. Example of autonomous flash-memory recorder deployed from *Kondor* and *Ewing*.

Figure 3.4.2. Flash memory recorder and depth logger attached at the end of a 100-m polypro rope. The other end was tied to the end of the SEAMAP array. Note that the hydrophone is taped to the rope as well. This unfortuantely led to clipping of the signal.

On the experiments of June 15, the probe was re-deployed, but this time with a 5-m long Kevlar 1/4" rope attached to the end of the polypro line with a swivel and with a 4 lb shackle attached to the other end of the Kevlar rope. The recorder was attached to the Kevlar rope, with the hydrophone permitted to move freely. The probe was turned on at 20:00 CDT and then recovered and reset at 7:30 CDT on June 16. Data were found to be unclipped, although a tapping noise was present.

The June 16 deployment added a radiator hose to cover the entire probe before attaching it to the Kevlar line. A few brief tests found that the flow noise was cut down further, but resonances existed in the spectra. These are hypothesized to occur due to "pipe organ" effects from the hose.

These results suggested that the recorder approach could work, provided that the data were collected on a quieter vessel. The *R/V Gyre* was in the study area conducting a concurrent survey. The initial preference of the PI was to transfer to the *Gyre*, as the passive acoustic team aboard that vessel were already using two towed arrays, and had expressed interest in working on the range-depth tracking problem. However, between June 13 and 16 the *Gyre* was located in DeSoto Canyon, which was over 100 n.m. to the east of the *Ewing* position. By the time *Gyre* came back west, the *Ewing* was heading west as well, and it became clear that by the time any transfer to *Gyre* would be possible, only 1 or 2 days of data collection might be possible. Thus, on June 16, during a lull in both tagging and the weather, the PI was transferred to the *Ewing*, along with his equipment, including the 100 m polypro rope.

Part 2: Work off the *Ewing*
The main concern about working off the *Ewing* was that tagging animals is almost always a 24-hour job, thus limiting the opportunities for pulling the *Ewing*'s SEAMAP array out of the water and attaching the rope/recorder combination to the array's end. While opportunities for deployments indeed turned out to be limited, D-tag/CEE Field Party Chief Mark Johnson went out of his way to try to accommodate the deployment needs for this project.

Other alternate deployment configurations were discussed, including whether the spare WHOI-made array on board the *Ewing* could be deployed in parallel with the SEAMAP array, or whether the autonomous recorder could be deployed independently from the SEAMAP array with a long rope. Unfortunately, the WHOI array would not have been able to be deployed deep enough to be effective without substantial weight being added to the array cable. This would have required a winch to deploy and retrieve the array. An extra winch was not available, so the WHOI array could not be used. There was not enough rope available to attempt a parallel deployment, because about 500 m of rope would have been needed to get adequate separation between the recorder and the SEAMAP array.

Thus, after discussion with Mark Johnson on how best to deploy a 3-D tracking configuration with minimum interference to D-tag activities, the PI settled on attaching an acoustic recorder to the 100 m 5/8" polypro rope to the end of the SEAMAP array, as had been done on the *Kondor*. This arrangement provided an excellent deployment geometry for range-depth tracking.

The autonomous recorder data was time-synched with the array data two ways. If whales were present in the area when the array was deployed, the recorder was activated before attaching it to the rope, and was time-synched by speaking into the recorder and a handheld VHF radio simultaneously. The hard-disk recorder for the SEAMAP array recorded the output of the VHF radio. Thus a single voice would be recorded on both acoustic datasets to permit a crude time-synchronization. If whales were not present, then the recorder was programmed to "wake" and begin acquiring data at some point in the future, usually 20:00 that same day. A dive watch was attached next to the probe, with an alarm set to go off at a time shortly after the recorder became active. By correlating the dive watch signal on both the recorder and the array, their data could be time-synced as well.

Unfortunately, this choice of deployment geometry meant that the times at which the recorder could be recovered were limited. Between June 16 and June 24, the array was only retrieved twice, permitting only two chances to collect 12 hour data sets.

The first deployment was June 18. At 14:00 CDT the array was pulled out of the water to enable a fast transit from one region to another. The recorder was attached and programmed to wake at 20:58. It was decided to try attaching the probe directly to the polypro rope once again, with a swivel inserted about 7 m in front of the recorder. Unfortunately, this led to clipping of the signal. The hydrophone also was taped to the rope. This had not been done in previous tests, but it worsened the clipping problem. The dive watch was programmed to produce an alarm at 21:00 CDT. That evening whales were located and tracking data were collected from 20:00 to 03:00 on June19. On the morning of the 19th, the D-tag team tagged an animal, but was not able to locate it until 19:00 in the evening. This prevented the CEE from taking place. To remain with animals overnight the array was not pulled in. The following morning the array was finally recovered and the probe retrieved. During June 20 about half of the data were downloaded and it became clear that portions of the data were heavily clipped by the hydrophone hitting the thick rope.

The second deployment was June 21. The SEAMAP array was retrieved in early afternoon, and a fresh recorder was attached and programmed to start recording at 20:00 CDT. At 21:00, the array was pulled in to transit to a different location. It was redeployed at midnight. The recorder was not retrieved until June 22 at 22:00 CDT. It was found that the recorder had failed when it had been knocked on the deck at 21:55 on June 21. Thus while a few hours of data were recorded before 21:55, no sperm whales were present at the time.

Data Available and Lessons Learned
The data obtained from this project consist of multi-channel recordings from the SEAMAP array during the evenings and early morning of June 16/17, 18/19, and 21/22, as well as autonomous recorder data collected between 20:00 on June 18 and ending at 3:00 on June 19. A quick preview of the June 18 set indicates that despite the heavy clipping on the recorder, there are at least three animals that might be mapped in range and depth using the recorder data. Figure 3.4.3 shows an example of sperm whale data collected on the recorder, and the output of an automated analysis of the difference in arrival times between the direct path and surface reflections for the animal visible in the spectrogram. This information is required to obtain the range and depth of the animal.

In addition, there are indications that the SEAMAP array alone might be able to perform 3-D tracking at close ranges. Since the array length is 50 m, if animals were approached within 250 m some range-depth tracking might be possible. An analysis of the June 18 array data shows that the surface and direct paths can be distinguished quite easily (Figure 3.4.4), which suggests that enough information may be available to track nearby animals. It will take more analysis to determine if this is possible.

Several factors led to the sparse data set collected during the experiments conducted here. First, it was not known how acoustically noisy (above 200 Hz) the *Kondor* was until it was measured at sea. This fact alone sacrificed 10 days of sea time. As the *Kondor* had always been used as a seismic source vessel and had never used streamers (passive arrays), there had never been an independent check of the vessel acoustics above a few hundred hertz.

Second, given the relatively short time to prepare for the cruise, it was not possible to fully test the autonomous recorders before going to sea. As a result methods for handling and attaching the recorders had to be developed and tested at sea. Trial methods for attaching the recorders led to substantial clipping noise. Additionally, the instruments suffered a few power failures (e.g. July 21) before it was realized that the components inside the recorder pressure case had to be cushioned more effectively. As the number of deployment opportunities turned out to be limited, this at-sea learning curve was costly. It is now known that a small-diameter rope (1/4" Kevlar) is the best choice, and that the recorder hydrophone should not be taped to the rope (e.g. the June 15 data). Finally, a supply of more rope, such as 500 m of 1/4" polypro or Kevlar, would permit parallel deployments of the recorder and the SEAMAP array.

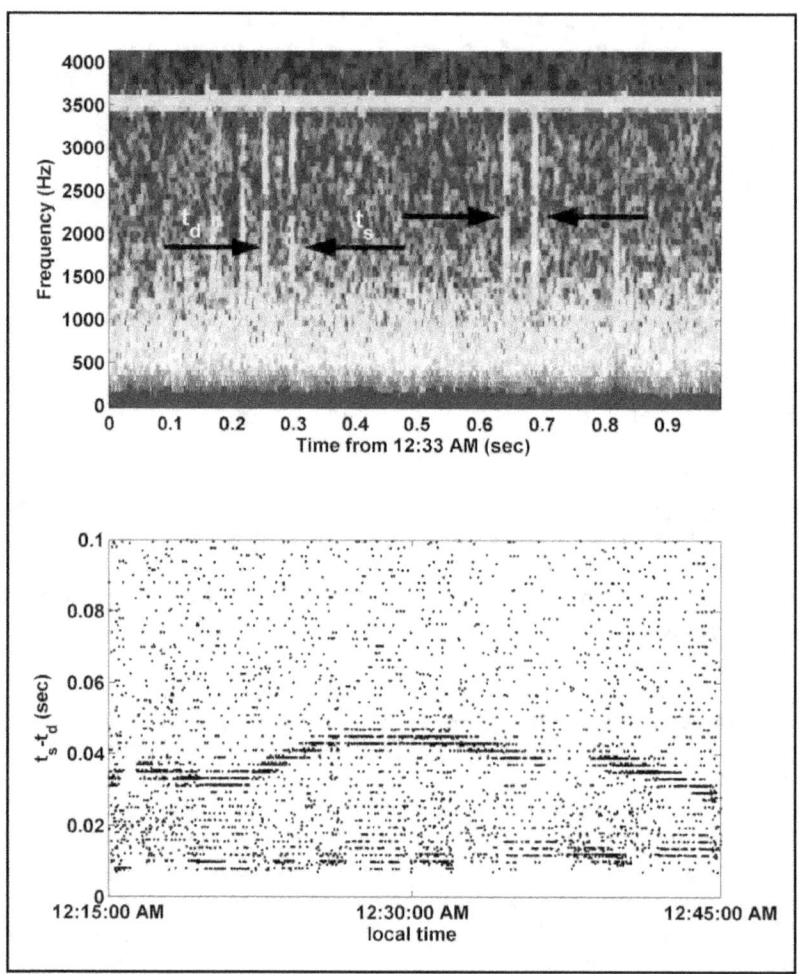

Figure 3.4.3. Examples of data collected from autonomous recorder on June 18. The upper panel shows the spectrogram of sperm whale clicks recorded when clipping levels were low. The lower panel shows the time difference between direct and surface paths for a sperm whale, extracted automatically from the data.

82

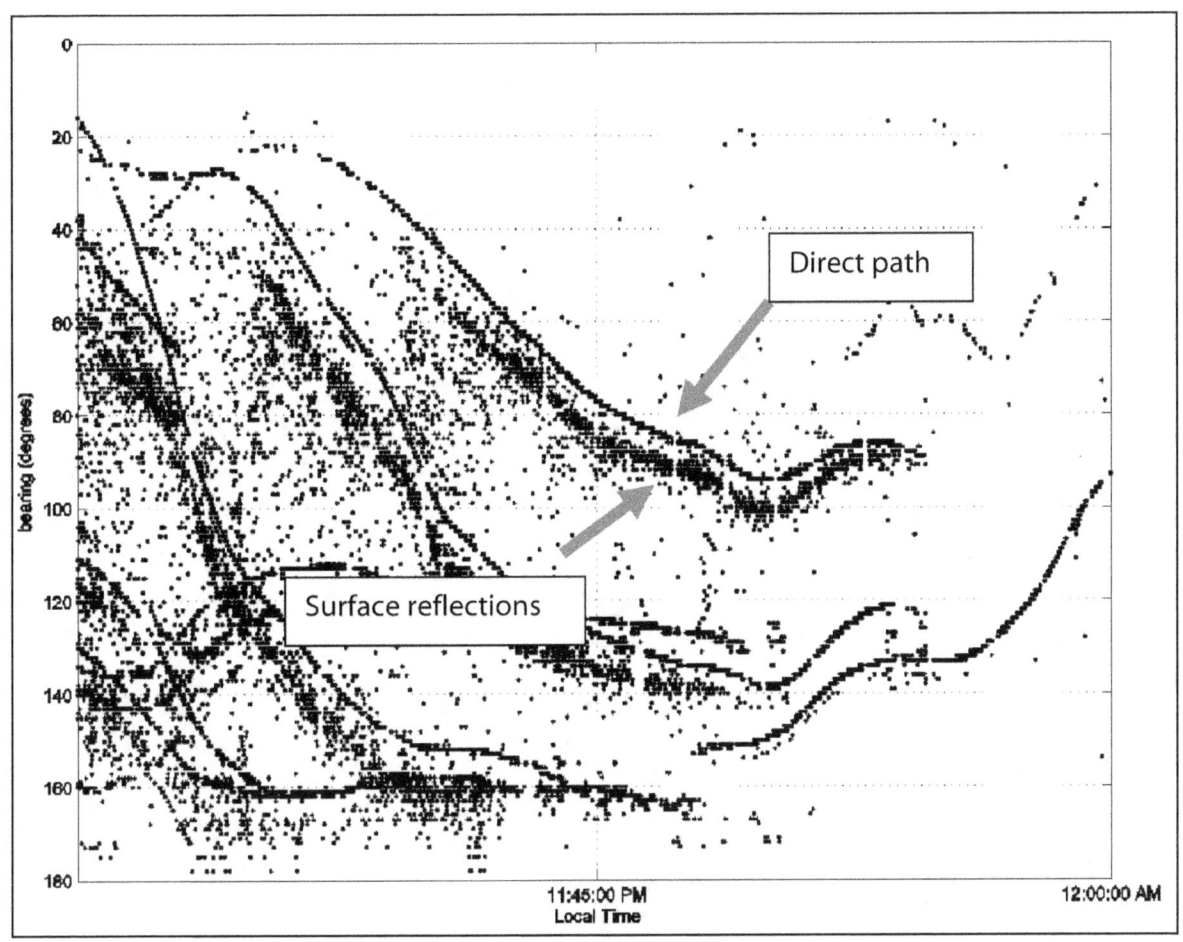

Figure 3.4.4. Plot of arrival angles detected on SEAMAP array, using elements 2 and 3 (11-m spacing), between 11:30 AM and midnight CDT on 18 June 2003. The fact that the angles between the direct arrivals and surface reflections can be distinguished suggests that the array may have collected enough information to estimate range and depth of certain animals at certain times, along with bearings. However, the array tilt would need to be estimated.

83

4 TECHNICAL SUMMARY

On 19-21 November 2003, the SWSS Workshop and Planning Meeting was held at the Shell Westhollow Technology Center in Houston, TX. Attendees were from the scientific community (SWSS, EARS, AIM, airgun calibration, and other project scientists), the federal government (including MMS, NSF, ONR, NOAA, and the Marine Mammal Commission), the geophysical contractor and oil & gas industries, and the SWSS Science Review Board. Science presentations, made over 1.5 days, provided the background information for use in planning discussions for SWSS year 3 work and in an exchange of ideas for possible studies beyond SWSS.

Year 3 planning resulted in the recommended work components of

1. S-tag cruise with additional data collection for habitat characterization, biopsy/genetic analyses, and 3-D passive acoustic tracking,
2. Mesoscale population study cruise from a motorized sailboat with biopsy/genetic analyses and limited habitat characterization data collection,
3. Enhanced D-tag/Controlled Exposure Experiment data analysis, but no cruise,
4. Data analyses, interpretations, and syntheses by all groups, and
5. Preparation of the synthesis report and data submittal and peer-reviewed publications.

Below are summaries of the SWSS presentations from the workshop; all results are preliminary.

4.1   Status Report on Satellite-Monitored Radio Tag

Dr. Bruce Mate[1] and Dr. Joel Ortega-Ortiz[1]

[1]Oregon State University, Hatfield Marine Science Center, Newport, OR 97365

SWSS research with the S-tag portion of the SWSS project is meant to describe broad-scale and longer-term seasonal movement issues, including the identification of seasonal habitats. In conjunction with the genetics program, the S-tag portion will also identify any demonstrable differences in the movements and seasonal habitats of different sex classes.

Some of the 2002 tags, at the time of this report writing, are still reporting data. For the purposes of this report, data were summarized through 15 October 2003. At that time 3,880 whale tag days of tracking data had documented 71, 298 kilometers of movements and 878,865 dives.

Because sperm whales have long surfacing times between their feeding dives, we received sufficient messages to the Argos satellite system to obtain outstanding location class accuracies. Almost half (44%) of locations were from 0 to 1,000 meters of actual location, and another 27% were zero class locations. Zero class locations do not have defined accuracies, but in our laboratory testing, we have found that over 95% of these fall within a range of 11.5 kilometers. Thus they are used with screening criteria to delete locations which would result in unusually high swimming speeds, in order to provide additional information about the seasonal whereabouts of individuals within the Gulf.

In general, animals have moved from DeSoto Canyon in the northeast quadrant of the Gulf along the slope edge to the Texas/Mexico border, with the bulk of the locations appearing within the 700- to 1,000-meter depth regime. However, several animals have ventured out into water over 3,000 meters deep, visiting the Bay of Campeche and the northwest coast of Cuba. Those animals venturing over deep water tend to be males. National Marine Fisheries Service surveys have seen females with calves out in these deepwater regions as well, suggesting the possibility that there may be both an offshore deepwater stock and a nearshore slope edge population.

Because calves have also been seen in the nearshore regions, this does not necessarily suggest an age-specific segregation pattern (i.e., juveniles vs. adults).

In conjunction with Dan Englehaupt, we are performing analyses of social affiliations over extended periods of time. In cooperation with Doug Biggs and Ann Jochens, we will conduct correlations with oceanographic parameters. To date, data confirm that sperm whales are in the upper Gulf slope region year-round and show that individuals vary in their distance from shore, depth, speed, and site tenacity. Furthermore, males tend to range more widely, move faster, and do not necessarily repeat the same seasonal use pattern from year to year.

4.2   Molecular Ecology of Sperm Whales (*Physeter macrocephalus*) in the Northern Gulf of Mexico

Dr. Dan Engelhaupt[1]

[1]University of Durham, Department of Biological Sciences, Durham, England

Background
The genetic related aspects for sperm whales occurring in the northern Gulf of Mexico during SWSS 2003 continued to provide an assessment of how populations and groups are structured, in addition to providing gender and identification information for whales outfitted with OSU's satellite-monitored radio tags (S-tags) and WHOI's digital sound recording tags (D-tags). Our component adds essential data required to fully asses the impacts that the oil and gas industry and seismic exploration may or may not have on endangered sperm whales occupying potentially critical habitat areas in the northern Gulf. Sperm whales are highly social whales that occur in small clusters to large aggregations, in some cases maintaining long-term bonds between female group members. Their dependence on acoustic communication between members and use of echolocation when feeding at depth make them vulnerable to anthropogenic noise. Could an outside noise influence disturb the dynamics of the group, or on a much larger scale, the population over time? The quantity and quality of knowledge gained from the combination of genetic (via degrees of relatedness among associates), satellite-monitored radio tagging and behavioral studies provides the essential components to accurately describe social structure on a detailed scale. Separating stocks based on geographic boundaries (e.g. northern Gulf of Mexico and the North Atlantic Ocean stocks) seems illogical given a sperm whale's enormous potential for movement. Stocks must be defined using a variety of parameters including genetics. Once stocks are defined, human-caused disturbances or mortalities that occur to a stock can be managed appropriately. Such information is vital for creating meaningful management strategies for these animals in general, and relative to petroleum exploration and production in particular.

SWAMP and SWSS Cruise Sample Analyses
Tissue samples were collected during both SWAMP and SWSS cruises throughout 2000, 2001, 2002, and 2003. Samples (including those from S-tagged, D-tagged, opportunistic and stranded whales) were genotyped using mtDNA and microsatellite techniques. Gender was determined for nearly all of these samples using molecular sexing techniques.

Population Structure: A comparative analysis of matrilineal mtDNA and biparentally inherited nuclear genetic markers (microsatellites) continues to show strong population structure for female lineages between the northern Gulf of Mexico, Mediterranean Sea, and North Atlantic Ocean stocks. This was expected given previous findings on social and reproductive behavior in this species. On a global scale, mtDNA variation is low with only 25 haplotypes discovered to date. In addition to the three most common haplotypes, the Gulf of Mexico population has two unique haplotypes carried by the majority of sampled whales. Nuclear DNA variation across oceans appears non-significant suggesting males disperse from their natal groups and spread their genes to the more philopatric females in different geographic locations.

Group Composition: The majority of sampled members from groups were predominately females, although a few groups appeared to contain only males, suggesting that bachelor groups may reside in the Gulf. Relatedness levels for individual groups suggest that the group is often unrelated, although groups did contain first-order relatives (e.g. mother-offspring pairs). Our continued analyses of the maternally inherited mtDNA control region shows that sperm whale groups are comprised of both single and multiple matrilines, which combined with the relatedness levels, may provide additional support to the hypothesis of Whitehead et al. (1991) that groups are comprised of 'constant companions and casual acquaintances'. Unfortunately, due to time constraints and other priorities, not all members within the majority of groups were sampled. However, similar results were found when we examined only those groups where 50% or more of the estimated group size was sampled.

Genetic Recommendations for SWSS 2004
Genetic techniques supply a powerful set of detailed data that can be directly integrated with both the movements of satellite-monitored tagged whales and the dive profile data of D-tagged whales. The gender of a tagged whale may prove crucial towards understanding movement patterns and dive profile data (i.e., do males and females react differently to anthropogenic noise influences?). Future work will continue to build on previous year's population and social structure results by incorporating biopsy sampling with both satellite-tagging and opportunistic sampling of whales, particularly focusing on whales of sexually mature size. This population has already been subjected to many years of human activity and there is likely to be major oil-related activity offshore here for many years to come. Social organization is an important component for sperm whale survival yet seems vulnerable to disruption by disturbance. Understanding sperm whale social organization in this putative population before it is exposed to any more disturbance, and exploring whether it is affected by offshore activity is thus a priority. Future sampling efforts should combine photo-ID and photogrammetry with every biopsy sample in order to provide estimates of both sexual and physical maturity for males and females located in the Gulf. This information is crucial towards understanding the relationships among associating whales and the extent that groups are structured over short and long terms. To increase the resolution for population structure and trans-oceanic gene flow analyses, sampling efforts should incorporate sperm whales located in additional geographic areas such as the southern Gulf of Mexico, Caribbean Sea, western North Atlantic, and Mediterranean Sea. Genetically similar or different populations may provide us with a means of a "control" group for seismic playbacks comparisons. Finally, emphasis should be placed on locating and sampling large sexually mature males found within the northern Gulf. Young calves less than a year old have been seen within mixed sex groups in the northern Gulf of Mexico, but sightings of large males appear non-existent. This will most likely require additional cruises in alternative seasons and will assist us in determining where breeding males might originate and how far they roam. A continuation of the genetic components previously described will maintain both the quality and quantity of information required for management purposes.

4.3   Studies Report on SWSS Records with the Digital Sound Recording Tag

Dr. Mark Johnson[1], Dr. Peter Tyack[1], and Dr. Partrick Miller[1]

[1]Woods Hole Oceanographic Institution, Woods Hole, MA 02543

The WHOI component of the SWSS 2003 program centered on a science cruise on board the R/V *Ewing* in June and the ensuing data analysis. The goal of the cruise was to deploy digital sound recording tags (D-tags) on sperm whales in the northern Gulf of Mexico and then expose the tagged whales to controlled levels of air-gun sound from an attending seismic survey vessel. The data set from the cruise includes a range of visual, navigation and shipboard acoustic observations in addition to the tag data. The objective in analyzing this combined data set is first to develop a baseline model for the behavior of unexposed sperm whales and then to examine the data taken from exposed animals for significant departures from baseline behavior. Here we provide an overview of the cruise and some preliminary results together with plans for data analysis in 2004.

Ewing Cruise

The cruise took place between 3 and 24 of June and made use of two vessels. The R/V *Maurice Ewing*, operated by Lamont-Doherty Earth Observatory (LDEO), acted as the observation platform while a seismic source vessel, the M/V *Kondor Explorer*, made available by the International Association of Geophysical Contractors (IAGC) and a coalition of industry sponsors, provided the controlled sound source. Two small tagging vessels, the *R2* and the *Balaena*, were operated off the *Ewing*. The procedure in the 2003 cruise largely followed that of the successful 2002 cruise on the R/V *Gyre*. However two new technologies were used in 2003 to overcome limitations found in 2002.

A new tag design, called the DTAG-2, was deployed in 2003. This tag has an extended dynamic range as compared to DTAG-1, overcoming a clipping limitation with the latter that reduces the accuracy of received level estimates for loud sounds. The physical size and mounting arrangement of DTAG-2 are also enhanced to achieve longer attachment times. In practice, both D-tag designs were used in SWSS 2003. Three DTAG-1 tags were deployed with an average attachment duration of 3.8 hours, comparable to the average of 4 hours in 2002. In contrast, the 8 DTAG-2 deployments had an average attachment duration of 8.7 hours, a dramatic improvement. The 3-phase controlled exposure experiment (CEE) design we have developed requires at least 4 hours with 6 hours being preferred. Clearly the increased longevity of DTAG-2 will enable more successful CEE trials. A concern has been raised that the new tag design is more prone to slide on the body of sperm whales than the older version making VHF tracking difficult. In fact this is not the case: 4 of 11 tags in 2003 slid down the body of the whale during deployment resulting in poor placements. Of these 1 of 3 and 3 of 8, respectively, were DTAG-1s and DTAG-2s. Poor placements typically resulted from attempting to tag in high swell and the presence of relatively thin whales, rather than due to a deficiency in the tag design.

A new data logging and real-time GIS display system was used during the 2003 cruise to handle observation and navigation data collected on the *Ewing* as well as navigation data sent from the *Kondor* via a radio modem. The system was created in a collaboration between WHOI and NATO Undersea Research Center to address a key need identified in previous cruises: the ability to display real-time navigation and observation data before and during a CEE in order to direct the source vessel accurately towards the tagged whale. The system functioned extremely well and was crucial for planning CEEs in the widespread groups of whales encountered in the 2003 cruise.

Fieldwork in 2003 was conducted under National Marine Fisheries Service (NMFS) permit 981-1707 issued to Dr. Peter Tyack. The permit included the requirement that no marine mammals or sea turtles be exposed to sound levels above 180 dB re 1μPa RMS. To comply with the permit, Dr. Tyack and co-investigators developed a mitigation protocol defining the procedure should species other than sperm whales be observed during CEEs. Beaked whales were sighted on two occasions during seismic operations and the mitigation procedure was invoked. Although this interrupted a calibration experiment, it did not curtail any CEEs: on the one occasion in which a CEE was abandoned following the mitigation procedure, the tag also released from the whale prematurely and would not have collected data through a full CEE. A key practical consequence of the 180dB mitigation radius was that the desired high level (160+dB) CEEs were not possible when the tagged whale was within a widespread group as was often the case in 2003. As no whale in the group could be exposed beyond 180dB and the available propagation models for the air-gun array were conservative, relatively low level CEEs resulted. The full-bandwidth three-dimensional propagation of signals from airgun arrays needs to be better understood and modeled for CEEs to more closely approach the permitted ceiling of exposures.

Out of 14 days in which the *Kondor* was available to perform CEEs, we conducted 3 complete experiments with a total of 4 whales, a similar success rate as in 2002 (the 2002 result was 2 CEEs to 4 whales in 11 days). Of the remaining 11 days, 8 were spent with bad weather or no whales and on one good-weather day we were unable to tag any of the whales approached. CEEs were aborted on two occasions, one due to mitigation as described above and the other due to poor VHF tracking of the tagged whale which was already in the presence of an uncontrolled seismic survey. One day in which whales were not sighted was used to perform a calibration experiment on the *Kondor* seismic array. A key limiting factor in 2003 was the formation of a large wide-spread group of sperm whales in the northern gulf perhaps in response to a pronounced eddy. This area coincided with an on-going seismic survey from vessel *Neptune*. Based upon our experimental design, to obtain independent samples of CEE response, we need to move at least 10 miles after each CEE. However, animals were scarce outside of the main accumulation and considerable time was spent trying to find whales distant from the *Neptune*. The added requirement to deploy an EARS buoy, calibrate its location, and use the *Kondor* to obtain calibrated measurements of airgun sounds also cost precious days that could otherwise have been devoted to CEEs. Nonetheless, the cruise was a success in producing high quality CEE and baseline samples at the same rate as in the 2002 cruise.

Analysis
To date, we have carried out 10 cruises focused on sperm whales in three different sites: the Gulf of Mexico, Mediterranean, and the north-western Atlantic. The combined database of 275 hours of tag recordings spanning 230 deep dives is a formidable resource for predicting the natural behavior of sperm whales. A team of scientists, post-doctoral investigators and engineers at WHOI will be working with this data in 2004. The analysis process is time-consuming on account of the density of data collected. Steps include (i) listening to sound recordings and examining them with spectral analysis tools, (ii) calculating the 3-dimensional whale track from the tag sensor measurements and ship-board observations, and (iii) assembling sounds and movements in a common geographic frame. With the results of these low-level analyses, we work to assemble a model of natural sperm whale behavior encompassing, at present, diving energetics, foraging methodology, sound source characteristics, and social organization. This natural model provides a basis with which to compare the behavior of animals during CEEs and suggests appropriate metrics for comparison. At present, we are working with the following metrics:

- Horizontal avoidance (change in heading)
- Energy investment (change in fluking rate)
- Foraging success (change in creak rate)
- Behavioral state (cessation of diving, change in foraging style, may include horizontal or vertical avoidance)
- Group dynamics (change in separation)

The 8 tag data sets collected during the 5 CEEs show received levels for the seismic source of between 145 to 160 dB re 1μPa peak-to-peak, which is equivalent to 130 to 146 dB re 1μPa RMS. Examination of the data is in a very preliminary stage. However, we offer some early results here to exemplify how the above metrics can be used to assess response. A key finding has been that the spectrum of air-gun sounds heard by tagged whales varies enormously and can include significant high frequency energy (well above 1 kHz) coinciding with the likely range of maximum hearing sensitivity of sperm whales. Such high-frequency sounds had not previously been considered likely from air-guns and a production model for these is still lacking. One of our CEE trials (sw03_173b) has energy from the direct arriving air-gun sound at frequencies up to 12 kHz. This whale remained close to the surface in a resting mode throughout the CEE and began deep diving 10 minutes after the end of the CEE. However, the behavior prior to the CEE was a mixture of resting and socializing complicating a conclusion of horizontal avoidance. Predictions of normal durations in these behavioral states from the baseline data set will help to establish the likelihood of a response.

A second CEE (sw03_165a/b) offers a possible example of horizontal avoidance. In this case, two tagged whales traveled consistently north-east before and after the CEE but changed heading to due north during the second (and louder) half of the seismic vessel approach. Both whales returned to their original track-line following the experiment. The whales performed deep foraging dives throughout the episode. Although horizontal avoidance appears to be indicated, we see little indication so far that this was costly in terms of foraging success. Baseline results concerning the normal variation in creaking and turning rates will help to establish the probability of a response, and will help in determining whether any such response may have had an adverse impact. In both CEE examples here, the key requirement is a reliable model for normal behavior. Our analysis work in 2004 will go a long way towards establishing this and, along with the CEE trials, will represent a unique and significant research product from the SWSS project.

4.4   Sperm Whale Abundance, Habitat Use, and Aspects of Social Organization in the Northern Gulf of Mexico

Dr. Nathalie Jaquet[1], Dr. Jonathan Gordon[2], and Dr. Bernd Würsig[1]

[1]Texas A&M University, 5007 Ave U, Galveston, TX 77551 USA
[2]Sea Mammal Research Unit, Gatty Marine Laboratory, University of Saint Andrews, Saint Andrews, Fife, Scotland. UK

Introduction
This report describes behavioral/photographic/acoustic findings conducted under the SWSS umbrella of research. We provide a mark-recapture estimate of population size, habitat preferences, inter and intra-year site fidelity, small-scale movements, and aspects of social organization. The findings are to be considered preliminary pending further analyses and integration with other aspects of the study.

Study Area
Our study area for the 3-week cruise of June 2003 consisted of parts of the continental slope (~500 m to 1500 m in depth) between 95°W and 86°W (Figure 4.4.1). In the text below, this area is referred to as the "northern Gulf of Mexico", although it does not encompass the entire northern Gulf.

Preliminary Results and Discussion
Distribution and habitat preference: Our intention during this survey was to spread our search effort in a consistent way to cover the entire survey area of the upper slope of the northern Gulf of Mexico between 95°W to 86°W (Figure 4.4.1). Survey tracks were designed using the Distance Program (Thomas et al. 1998). The upper slope, from the 500-m contour out to approximately 10 miles beyond the 1000-m contour, was divided into four boxes. The Distance Program was used to derive survey tracks to provide an equal level of coverage within the three eastern boxes, where sperm whale density was expected to be highest, and half that level of coverage in the western block (Figure 4.4.2 top panel). During daylight hours, sperm whale groups were followed closely for photo-identification, recording of vocalizations, and behavioral observations. Therefore, the achieved track (Figure 4.4.2 bottom panel) reflects the high concentration of whales that we encountered in the central blocks. The vessel's activity (for example, predetermined vs. random tracks, etc.) was noted regularly in specially prepared forms

90

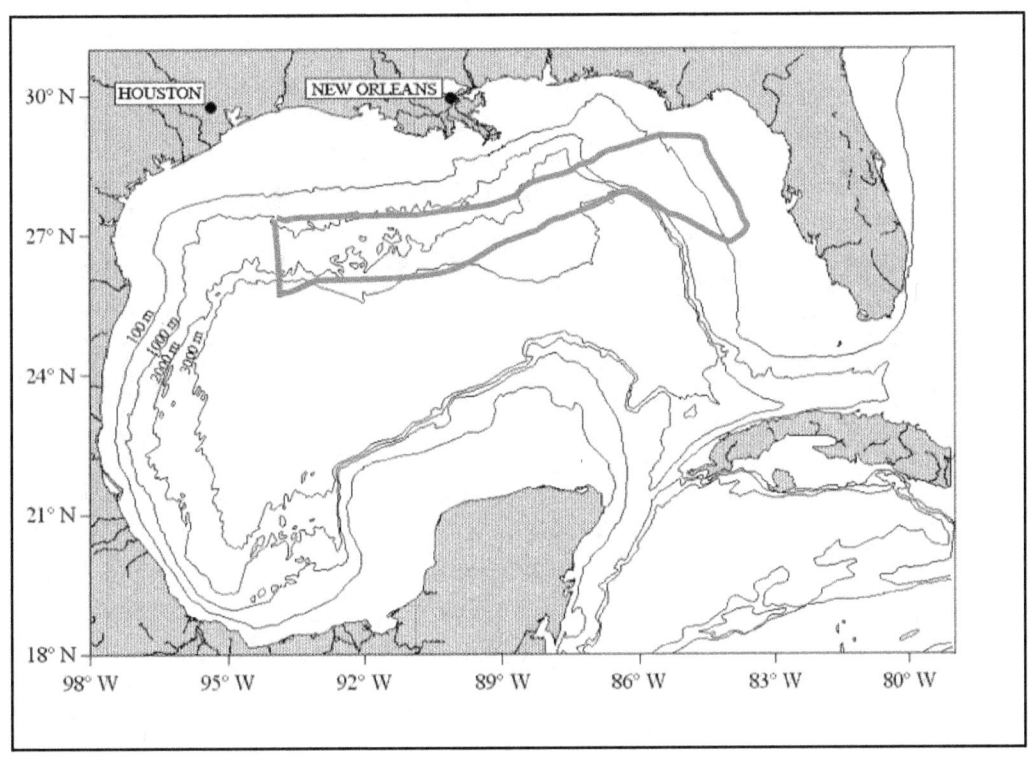

Figure 4.4.1. The Gulf of Mexico with study area outlined.

in the *Logger* Program, as were factors that might affect detectability, such as weather and underwater noise conditions. This information can be used to extract and interpret those data that might legitimately be used to assess relative abundance and habitat preferences for sperm whales. We extracted appropriate data from the 2002 and 2003 habitat characterization/photo-identification cruises and combined these with topography data in the National Geophysical Data Center's Coastal Relief Model in a Global Information System (GIS) database. Generalized Additive Modeling procedures in the R statistical software package were used to investigate the effect of bathymetry on sperm whale distributions. These showed maximum detection rates at slopes of around 6 degrees and depths of 1000-600m. Our intention is to apply the same approach to all data collected on S-tag and photo-identification cruises conducted during SWSS and, in collaboration with other members of SWSS, to include other habitat parameters in the analysis.

Abundance: Line transect techniques have been used to estimate the abundance of the many species of cetaceans which inhabit the Gulf of Mexico (Davis et al. 2000; Würsig et al. 2000). However, line transect techniques are not that well adapted for estimating sperm whale abundance. The major problem is that g_0 (the probability of encountering an animal if it is on the track line) is usually assumed to be one. As sperm whales dive for an average of 40 to 50 minutes, g_0 tends to be smaller than one. A second potential problem consists in estimating group size. Foraging sperm whales are usually spread out over several nautical miles (nm) and, due to the length of their dives, only a small proportion of the group will be at the surface at any one time. In the past, clusters, consisting of two or more individual sperm whales less than 100 m

91

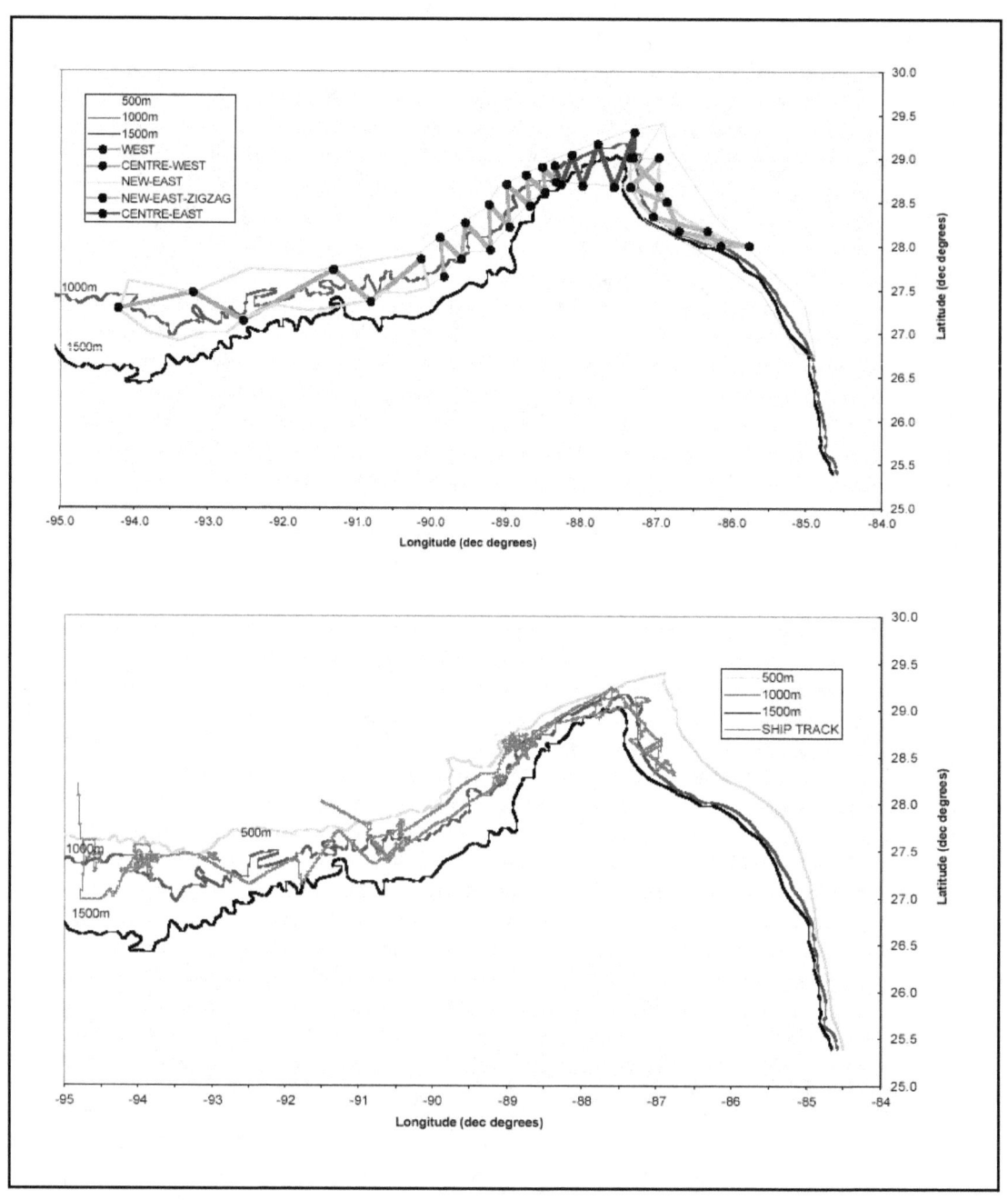

Figure 4.4.2. Survey track lines designed using the Distance Program (top) and realized track lines (below) during SWSS WSHC 2003 cruise.

apart and coordinating their movements (Whitehead and Arnbom 1987), have been used instead of groups. As sightings of clusters are not independent, abundance estimates may be biased.

Mark-recapture techniques have some advantages for estimating sperm whale abundance, as individuals older than calves can be recognized by natural marks on the trailing edge of their flukes (Arnbom 1987). With experienced photographic techniques, the majority of a population of sperm whales can be individually identified. Furthermore, mark-recapture techniques can estimate the number of individuals utilizing an area and not, as do line transects, the number of animals present in the area at any one time. Therefore, mark-recapture techniques tend to be appropriate for many long-term assessment and management purposes. However, a disadvantage of mark-recapture techniques for estimating a population size is that they can require extensive time at sea to collect sufficient data. They also require at least two sampling occasions, which often means more than one field season.

During the three weeks of field work in 2003, whenever whales were detected during daylight and the weather allowed, one or two rigid-hulled inflatable boats (RHIB) were launched to obtain photo-identifications of as many sperm whales as possible within a group. Whales were approached slowly from behind, to within about 50 to 60 meters. Photographs of the flukes were taken at the beginning of deep dives with a digital camera (Canon EOS D1) and 300 mm lens.

Before analysis, all photographs were graded for quality following the standard method described by (Arnbom 1987). This takes into consideration the angle, tilt, and focus of the fluke in the photograph. Grading is independent of amount of marking on a fluke, and thus independent of how well an individual could be recognized from a good photographic image. Image quality grading is an important step as it allows one to determine whether or not a particular image is an adequate sample to show particular types of marks. The data set used to estimate sperm whale population abundance is shown in Figure 4.4.3. As most of the identification photographs came from a short period of time, three weeks each in 2002 and 2003, the full open model described by Whitehead (1990) could not be applied. Instead, a simple open model was fit to the data (SOCPROG, Whitehead 1999). The results indicate that approximately 262 individuals utilized our study area (95% Confidence Interval = 157 to 509).

This result is consistent with previous estimates of population size for this area. The results for 2002, using a closed model due to the paucity of data, indicated that 298 individuals utilized the study area (95% Confidence Interval = 137 to 890). Therefore, by increasing the sample size and by switching to a more appropriate model, we considerably reduced the confidence intervals on the population estimate without finding a radical change in the estimate itself. During the GulfCet studies, an estimation of sperm whale abundance was also made for the northern Gulf of Mexico using line transect techniques (Davis et al. 2000). However, as their study area was larger than ours, comparisons are difficult.

The results from mark-recapture techniques, using lagged identification rates, showed that, on average, 195 (SE=122) individuals are present at any one time in the study area. These results indicate that, as has been shown for other populations of sperm whales that have been studied in detail, the home range of sperm whales span several hundred nautical miles (800 on average, Whitehead 2003), and they move extensively within their home range. These results also are consistent with the results from the S-tag tracking data that show some extensive movements within the Gulf of Mexico (e.g., see section 4.1).

However, the present results are still based on a small sample size and only two 3-week field seasons. Therefore, to gain confidence in our estimate and to reduce the standard error, data over longer time periods are needed.

Site Fidelity: Site fidelity in cetaceans is taken to refer to a tendency for individuals to spend a disproportionate amount of time in a restricted part of their home range and to return to this area in subsequent years. In this usage, the term does not preclude movements into and out of an area.

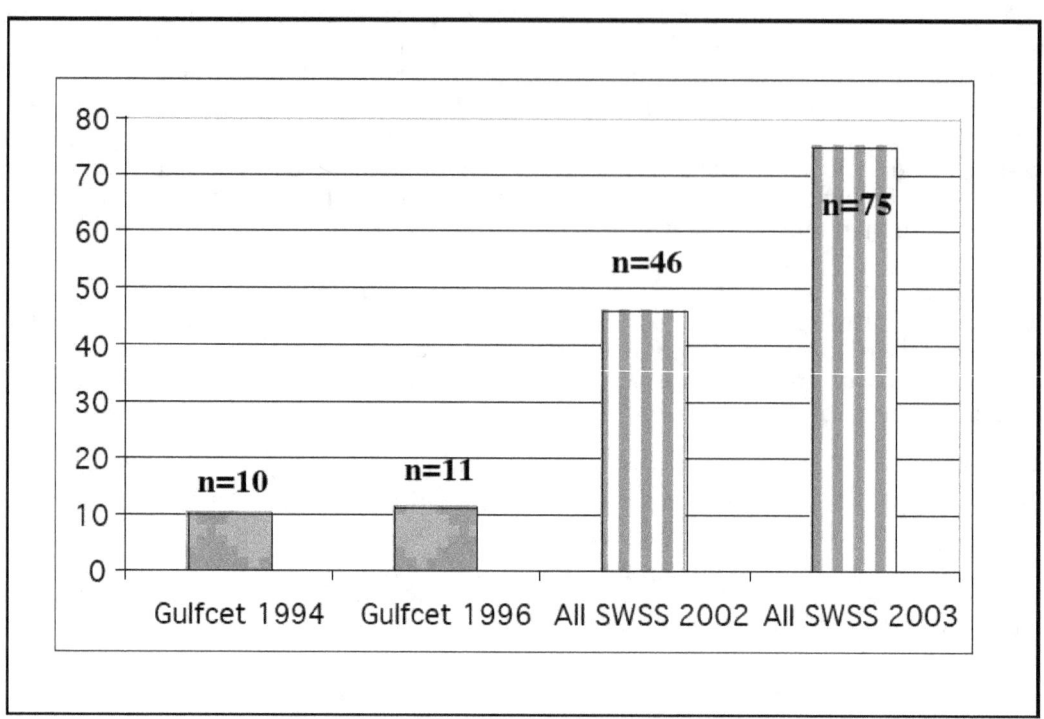

Figure 4.4.3. Number of sperm whales photo-identified each year; data set used for abundance estimates.

Before 2003, approximately 100 sperm whales were identified in the Gulf of Mexico with high quality photographs. In 2003, 75 individuals were identified. Thus, the number of identifications from 2003 represents a large percentage of all sperm whales identified in the Gulf of Mexico. Because we had a rather even coverage of the study area in 2003, we would expect that, in the absence of site fidelity, resightings of individuals in 2003 were more or less randomly distributed within the study area. As we see below, this was not the case.

Out of the 75 individuals identified during 2003, 21 had been identified during previous years, at time spans of 1 to 9 years. However, re-identifications were not random within the study area. A total of 71% of the resighted individuals were encountered between 90°W and 88°W, or the area just south of the Mississippi River Delta (MRD); and 100% were resighted between 91°W and 87°W. No resightings took place west of 91° or east of 87°, despite the extensive effort in these areas.

Figure 4.4.4 shows the mean resighting distance for identified individuals over a time span up to 9 years. In most cases, the resighting distances were less than 50 nm, which is approximately the total distance covered by an individual each day according to a variety of other studies (Whitehead 2003). The maximum resighting distance was 110 nm.

These results suggest a high site fidelity for some animals in the MRD area, and thus possibly a preferred area. The enhanced primary productivity due to the Mississippi River discharge may increase food availability for sperm whales in this area and explain this preference.

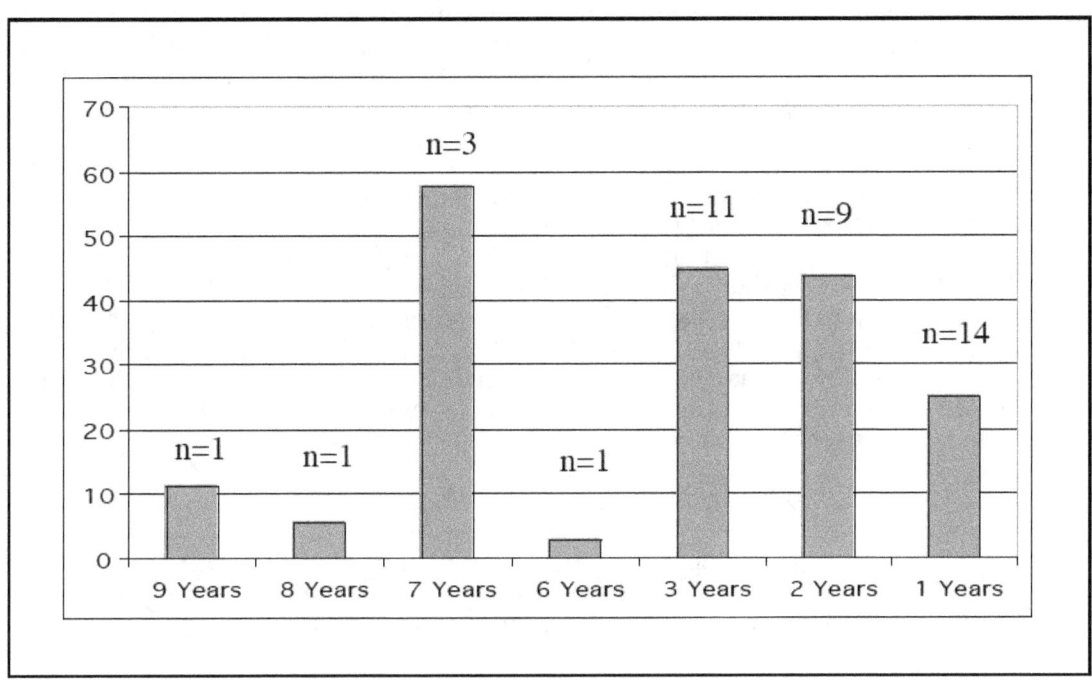

Figure 4.4.4. Mean resighting distances (in nm) for identified individuals over a time span up to 9 years. The number of individuals resighted for each time interval is shown above each bar.

Small Scale Movements: In most areas of the world, sperm whale diet is dominated by meso- and bathypelagic cephalopods (Kawakami 1980). However, as methods of effectively sampling these deep-living squid have not yet been developed (Clarke 1985), it has been impossible to directly relate sperm whale distribution or abundance to the distribution of their prey. Furthermore, as no modern whaling was conducted in the Gulf of Mexico, there are few data on sperm whale diet for this region. The little information that exists comes from stranded whales and, for the most part, still awaits analyses (Nelio Barros, pers. comm.). Thus, we do not yet know what sperm whales in the Gulf of Mexico are mainly feeding on or the distribution/abundance patterns of these prey. Consequently, it is unknown whether some areas of the northern Gulf of Mexico have higher food resources than others.

Patterns of small scale movements have been shown to provide a good indication of feeding success, inferred from the percentage of fluke-ups for which defecations are observed (Whitehead 1996; Jaquet and Whitehead 1999; Whitehead 2003). Movement patterns may thus be used to assess the food availability in a region (Jaquet et al. 2003; Whitehead 2003). In areas where food is scarce, sperm whale groups tend to travel in a straight line, whereas in areas where food resources are plentiful, groups tend to zig-zag over a much smaller area (Jaquet and Whitehead 1999; Jaquet et al. 2003; Whitehead 2003).

During the 2003 field season, eight groups of sperm whales were followed with the aid of a directional hydrophone used from a RHIB and with the help of visual and acoustic teams on the R/V *Gyre*. The position of the RHIB was recorded automatically by linking a GPS to a palmtop computer. Three of the eight groups were encountered in the western part of the study area, three in the MRD, and two in the eastern part of the Gulf. The small-scale movements for the two groups that were followed for the longest time in each area are shown in Figure 4.4.5. These results tend to suggest that, in June 2003, food resources were higher in the MRD than in the eastern Gulf. However, these results should be taken with caution as the sample size is still very low and statistical analyses could not fairly be performed.

Figure 4.4.6 shows the root mean square displacement of these eight groups of whales that were followed for 8 to 12 hours. This result suggests that in the Gulf of Mexico, sperm whales travel at an average speed of 4 km/hour. This is consistent with other studies on average speeds of female and immature groups (Gordon 1987; Whitehead 1989) and suggests that this may be an optimal speed for sperm whales (Whitehead 2003). However, this graph also shows that the displacement reaches a plateau at about 14 km, suggesting that the area over which groups zig-zag is smaller than off the Galápagos or Chile (Whitehead 2003). This result suggests that sperm whales in the Gulf of Mexico may be foraging on small but dense patches of squid. Again, more data are needed and we expect to increase sample size by collecting similar data on fine scale movements in later cruises.

Characteristics of the Sperm Whale Population of the Northern Gulf of Mexico:
1. Social organization
Sperm whales have highly developed societies (Caldwell et al. 1966) and their strong social organization allows them to communally take care of calves and defend against predators. Females and immature sperm whales form long-term (>decades) associations of on average 10-

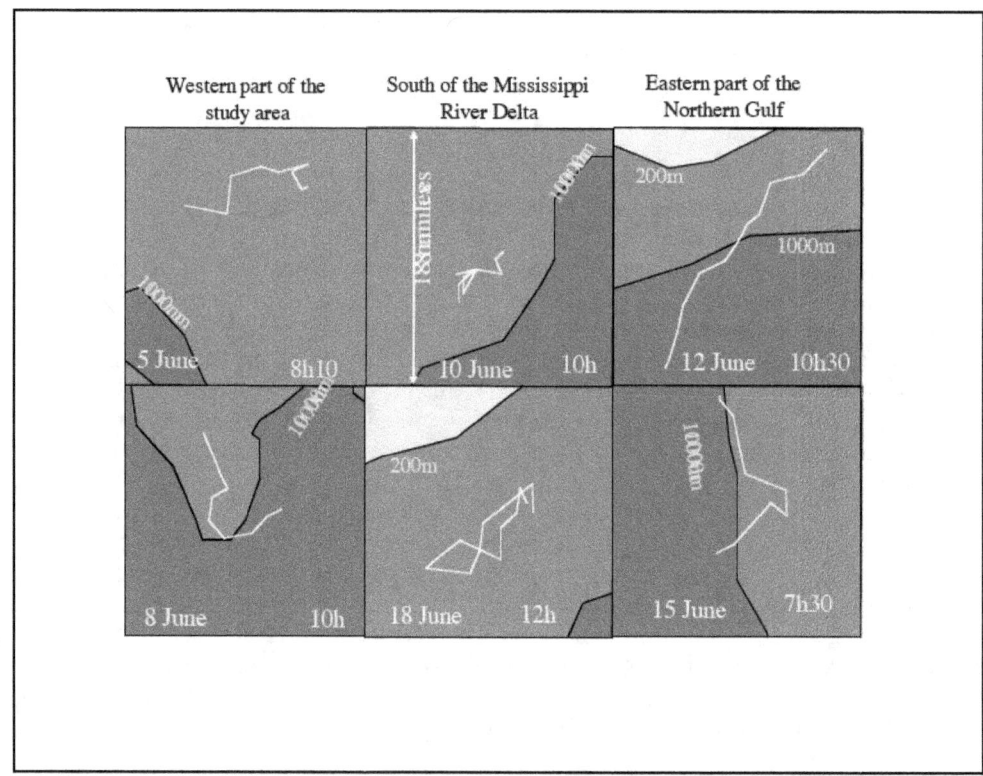

Figure 4.4.5. Small-scale movements of groups of sperm whales in different areas of the northern Gulf of Mexico. Positions were plotted every hour.

96

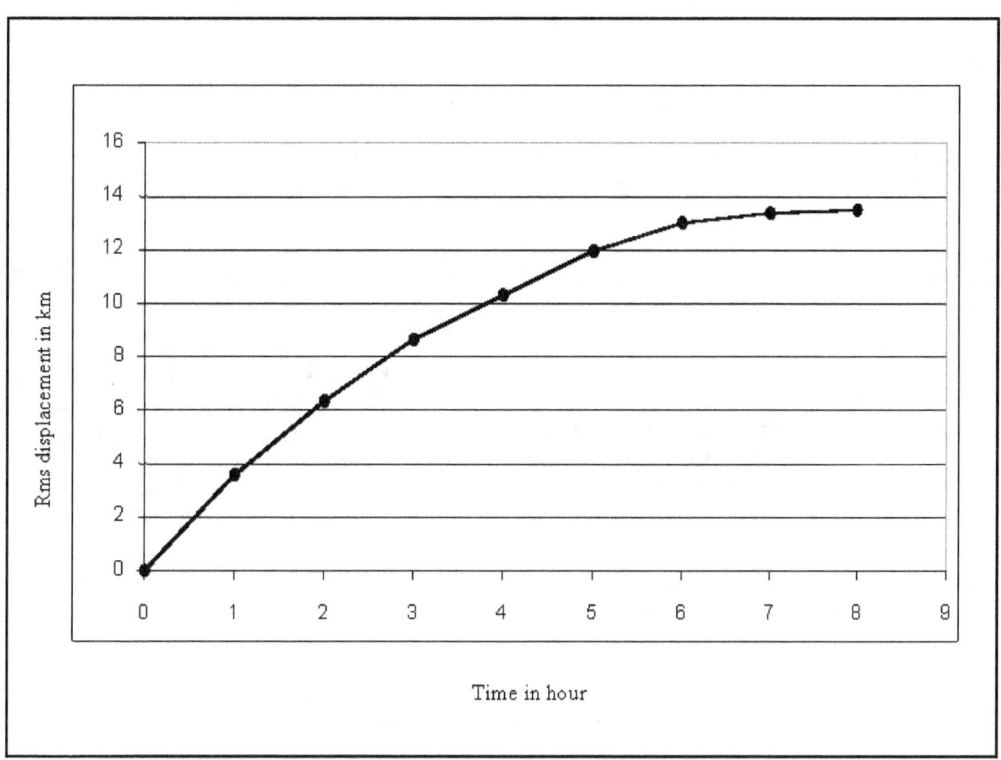

Figure 4.4.6. Root-mean square displacements for 8 groups that were followed for 8 to 12 hours.

12 individuals called units (Whitehead et al. 1991; Christal et al. 1998). These units usually associate with another unit for about one week to form what is commonly called the group or the nursery group (Whitehead et al. 1991; Christal et al. 1998).

Due to the significance of social organization in female sperm whales, it is important to investigate whether the population of the northern Gulf of Mexico follows a similar pattern of organization as that in other areas. To investigate sperm whale social organization in the northern Gulf, we used identification photographs collected during the SWSS project (2002 and 2003 field seasons, 109 individuals), as well as during the GulfCet project (1994 and 1996, 14 individuals). Furthermore, these 123 individuals were compared to the ~50 photo-identifications taken during the SWAMP project by NOAA Pascagoula in 2000 and 2001 (North Atlantic and Mediterranean Sperm Whale Catalogue). Although the maximum time span of the study was 9 years, most of the identifications came from the last SWSS field season, reducing the power of the data set for examining long term patterns of social organization. Furthermore, due to the difficulties of tracking a known sperm whale group at night using the R/V *Gyre*, sperm whales were never photographed on subsequent days, and thus the casual acquaintances (or group structure) could not be investigated. To determine the pattern of sperm whale social organization, we used the software SOCPROG (Whitehead 1999), especially developed for this purpose.

Our data showed that on four occasions, two individual sperm whales were sighted together and were then resighted together up to 9 years later. Similarly, on three occasions, three individuals were first sighted together and were resighted together again 4 years later. These results suggest that some individuals may have constant companions, which is consistent with the results from the SOCPROG program showing that our data best fit a model of constant companions and rapid disassociation. However these "snap-shot" images of time are not enough to describe details of social structure.

2. Group size

Estimating group size in the field is difficult, as foraging sperm whales are spread out over several nautical miles and as they spend about 75% of their time underwater. Therefore, group size is usually estimated using identification photographs and experience shows that, on average, two days are required for most individuals in a group to be identified (Whitehead 1999; pers. obs). In this study, group sizes will be slightly underestimated as groups were never followed on more than one day.

Figure 4.4.7 shows the results for 9 groups that were followed for 7 to 12 hours. Although group sizes were probably slightly underestimated, these results suggest that groups are smaller in the Gulf of Mexico than they are around the Galapagos Islands or Chile (Whitehead 2003). However, our results cannot discriminate whether these groups are formed of only one unit or of two small units, and thus additional data on groups followed on consecutive days are needed to answer this question of social affiliation.

Group size may influence the size of prey patch that can be efficiently exploited. The analysis of fine scale movements presented above is indicative of smaller prey patches.

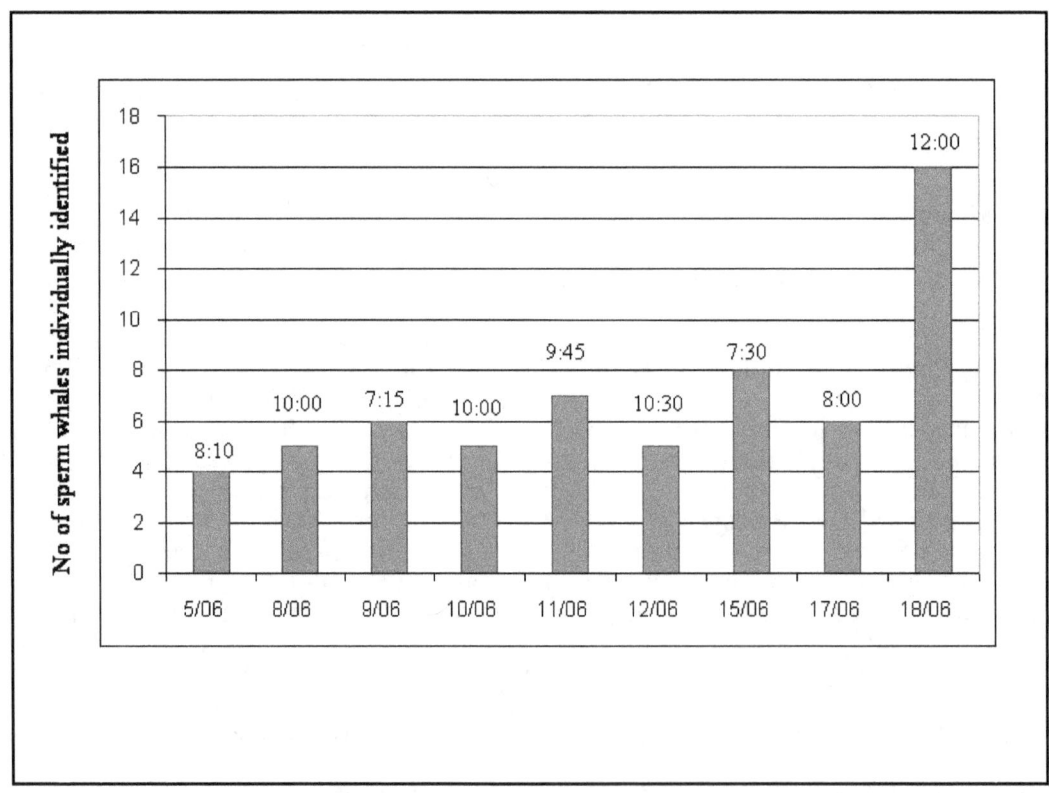

Figure 4.4.7. Estimated group sizes for groups that were followed >7 hours in June 2003. Numbers above bars represent times followed, in hr:min.

3. Occurrence of markings

In order to manage sperm whale populations, it is critical to have a good understanding of how their populations are structured within and between oceans (Whitehead 2003). During the 1970s and early 1980s, considerable efforts were put into defining within-oceans stocks (Donovan 1991), but success was very limited. Recent findings using genetic markers, occurrence of markings on flukes, and vocalizations have shown no consistent differences among whales of the same ocean (Whitehead et al. 1998; Dufault et al. 1999), and only small differences in mitochondrial DNA between different oceans (Lyrholm and Gyllensten 1998; Lyrholm et al. 1999). The near-absence of population structure on a geographical level explains the limited success of stock assessments within oceans (Whitehead 2003). However, no sample came from the northern Gulf of Mexico population, and investigation on whether this population is similar to other populations is being carried out using genetics research by SWSS scientist Dan Engelhaupt. Our data on acoustics and type and extent of markings also will feed into the population comparisons.

The degree of fluke marking on a sperm whale may vary between areas depending on factors such as predation levels (Gordon 1987) and thus may be an indicator of stock separation (Dufault and Whitehead 1998). The presence or absence of two types of marks, hole and missing portion (Figure 4.4.8) were used to assess the differences in marking between the three regions of the northern Gulf of Mexico, the Sea of Cortez, and the South East Pacific.

The results, given in Table 4.4.1, show that there is a significantly higher proportion of individuals with holes and/or missing tips in the Gulf of Mexico than in the Pacific Ocean (G-test:p<0.001). However, as expected, there were no significant differences between the two areas of the Pacific (G-test: p>0.5).

We plan to compare the markings of the northern Gulf of Mexico population to other areas in the Atlantic Ocean and particularly with the Caribbean, and to compare between areas within the Gulf of Mexico to investigate differences in markings from whales of other adjacent areas.

Figure 4.4.8. Example of 2 mark types (underlined) used to investigate differences in markings between regions.

Table 4.4.1

Percentage of Individuals Having Holes and/or Missing Portions in Their Flukes

	Northern Gulf of Mexico, n=105	Sea of Cortez (Pacific Ocean), n=565 (Jaquet unpublished data)	Galápagos/Ecuador (Pacific Ocean), n=289 (Dufault & Whitehead 1998)
Percent of individuals with holes	35	9	15
Percent of individuals with missing portions	43	25	21

4. Calving rates

Investigating whether a population of sperm whale is increasing, decreasing or stable is almost impossible to achieve by successively estimating abundance. It has been shown that for most populations of cetaceans that have been studied to date, the errors in estimating abundance are such that researchers would require decades to detect a trend in population abundance (Thompson et al. 2000). Usually, by the time a negative trend is detected, the population has already been considerably reduced. However, determination of demographic measures such as recruitment or calving rates allows investigation of how well a population is doing over smaller time scales of several years.

In both 2002 and 2003, the number of first-year calves, adult males, and other whales (adult females and immatures of both sexes) were counted in each group (after Kahn et al. 1993). First-year calves do not lift their flukes upon diving and thus cannot be identified individually; thus, following other researchers, only the minimum number of calves for each group was recorded. A group included two calves if two of them were observed simultaneously, or if after leaving one calf, the RHIB traveled in a straight line at a speed of over 10 km/h and another calf was sighted ahead of the vessel. To be consistent with other studies (Kahn et al. 1993) and allow comparisons between them, the relative abundance of mature males and first-year calves was calculated as the total number of different males identified, or minimum number of first-year calves divided by the number of other whales identified (adult females and immatures of both sexes).

The results, given in Table 4.4.2, indicate that a smaller proportion of first year calves and large mature males may have been encountered in the Gulf of Mexico in comparison to the Sea of Cortez. However, this difference was not significant (G-test: p=0.26 and p=0.053 respectively). A larger sample size is needed before conclusions can be drawn.

5. Length distribution

Investigating the length distribution of a population of sperm whales will provide crucial information on population structure such as age, sex, and maturity. As well as allow calculation of population parameters such as pregnancy rate and average age at maturity (Waters and Whitehead 1990). However, measuring sperm whales at sea is difficult as they spend most of their time underwater and as only part of their body can be seen while at the surface. In the past,

Table 4.4.2

Proportion of 1st Year Calves and Large Mature Males in the Northern Gulf of Mexico Versus the Sea of Cortez

	Northern Gulf of Mexico, n=104	Sea of Cortez, n=152 (Jaquet et al. 2003)
Proportion of 1st year calves	6.7%	11.2%
Proportion of large breeding males	0.96%	5.3%

two photographic techniques were used to measure sperm whales (Gordon 1990; Dawson et al. 1995); however, neither of them was suitable to use from the *Gyre*'s RHIBs. Therefore, in the past two years, we have been experimenting with another technique allowing us to measure identified individuals from the *Gyre*'s RHIBs.

This technique consists of taking an identification photograph with a calibrated digital camera and 300mm lens, and simultaneously measuring the distance to the fluke with a laser range finder. The fluke width then can be related to body length using a polynomial regression calculated from whaling and stranding data. The accuracy of this technique has been tested by repeatedly measuring known sperm whales off Kaikoura, New Zealand, and by comparing length distribution of Kaikoura whales and Sea of Cortez whales derived with this method to expected length distributions. These tests have shown that the technique gives reliable results and that the coefficient of variation due to the technique itself is low (CV=1.9%) (Jaquet and Gordon 2003).

Figure 4.4.9 shows the length distribution for groups of female and immature sperm whales (large breeding males were removed) for the northern Gulf of Mexico and the Sea of Cortez, respectively. In the Sea of Cortez, the modal group is between 10 and 10.2 meters, which is what is expected from whaling data (Clarke et al. 1980; Rice 1989; Kahn et al. 1993). However, in the Gulf of Mexico, the whales are smaller than would be expected and significantly smaller than the ones in the Sea of Cortez (comparisons of mean lengths, t-test: $p<0.001$).

Differences in length distribution can be due to a variety of factors, such as differences in whaling histories, how close the population is to carrying capacity, food resources, and feeding conditions in an area. More data and further analyses are needed before we can suggest possible reasons for the small size of whales in the northern Gulf of Mexico.

An acoustic method for measuring sperm whale body length involves measuring the time delay between the multiple sound pulses typically found within a sperm whale click: the so called inter pulse interval (IPI). Norris and Harvey (1972) first suggested that these pulses may form as sound was reflected between sound mirrors at the front and back of the sperm whale head and realized that this could form the basis of a method for measuring the length of live whales in the field. This was confirmed by Gordon (1991) who showed that the IPIs of whales were related to photographically derived body length in a way that was consistent with Norris and Harvey's hypothesis. Because many IPIs can be measured from a recording of a single whale, very precise measures of body length can be made. Pavan et al. (1998) were able to provide evidence for growth in a sperm whale from IPI analysis of recordings of the same whale made in two years.

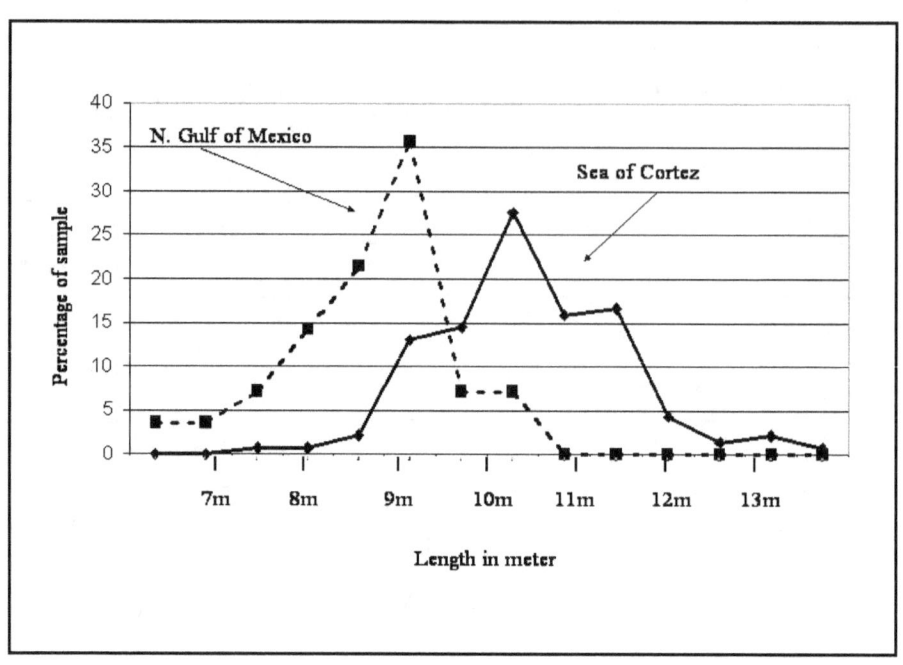

Figure 4.4.9. Length distribution for groups of female and immature sperm whales in the northern Gulf of Mexico and in the Sea of Cortez.

In applying this method during the current project we faced two challenges. The first was that recordings had to be made from small RHIBs in the open ocean. To overcome this, small-boat recording systems were assembled. These consisted of two HiTech HT01 hydrophones on 20m of cable and a hard disk recording system based on the Creative Labs Nomad recorder, which was housed in a waterproof case. The second problem was that it could be difficult to recognize the vocalizations of a known individual when, as was usually the case, recordings were being made in the middle of a large aggregation of foraging whales. However, we found that if recordings were made close to the fluke up position and immediately after the whales fluked, then the clicks of the whale that had fluked could usually be distinguished and followed for a minute or so. Analysis was restricted to these "identified" clicks. Recordings were analyzed using the IFAW *Rainbow Click* Program (Gillespie and Leaper 1996); this has a special module for measuring IPI using cross correlation to make accurate measurements of the time interval between pulses. In twelve cases, both photographic and acoustic length measurements were available for the same individual whale. These are plotted in Figure 4.4.10. Overall, the two length estimates were well correlated (Pearson's Coefficient 0.75, $p < 0.005$, n=12), providing further support for the validity of the photographic length-measuring approach used here. The agreement between these two measuring methods also gives us confidence that our body length results for the sperm whale population of the northern Gulf of Mexico are not biased.

6. Vocal repertoire
Genetic analysis can reveal genotypic differences between groups of animals from which differential patterns of breeding can be inferred, and in some cases, though rarely in sperm whales, more or less discrete breeding populations can be identified. Generally, very low levels of interbreeding need to exist for many generations for such patterns to emerge. Groups of animals can also differ from each other in non-genetically mediated ways too. For example,

102

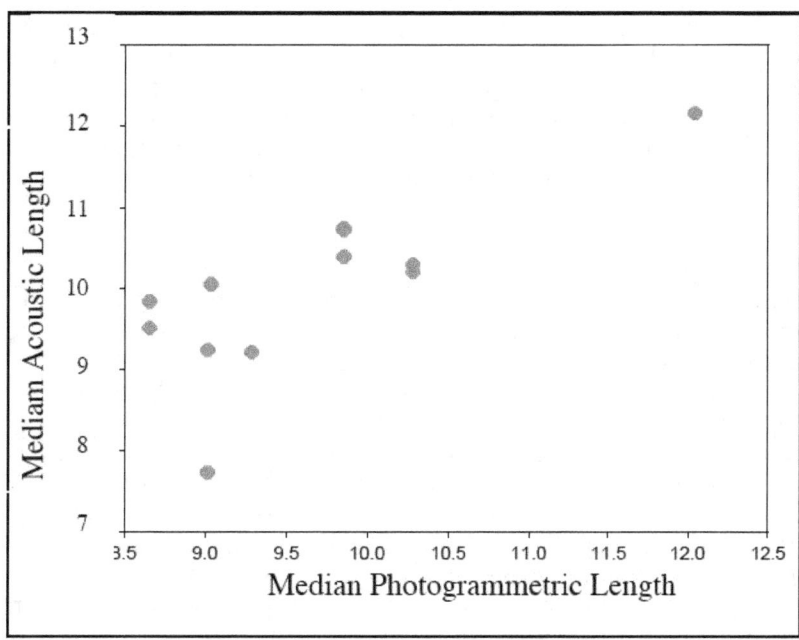

Figure 4.4.10. Plot of photographic and acoustic body length measurements of Gulf of Mexico sperm whales.

differences in experience and in the way that individuals interact can lead to differences in learned behavior. Such differences can become established very quickly, over time scales at which many human impacts occur, and they may well reflect factors that are significant to management. For example, animals may become either habituated or sensitized to human disturbance depending on their exposure to it. Such learned differences can be particularly informative in species in which there is cultural transmission of information.

In addition to the regular clicks and creaks that are associated with foraging, sperm whales make stereotyped patterns of clicks called "codas". These are typically heard when sperm whales come together at the surface in large tight groups to socialize. Recent work by Rendell and Whitehead (2003) suggests that codas are learned within "family" groups so that groups have characteristic repertoires of codas and coda types. These authors also provide evidence that codas reveal a hitherto undiscovered level of social organization in sperm whales. Each social unit belongs to a particular clan that can be distinguished on the basis of its coda repertoire. Units belonging to particular clans can be sympatric but social units associate preferentially with other units that belong to the same clan. Although clans can most easily be discriminated on the basis of coda vocalizations, there are indications that clan members share other behavioral, physical and genetic similarities.

Recordings containing codas from the Gulf of Mexico, the Azores and the Caribbean were analyzed using *Rainbow Click*, which has customized routines for coda analysis. The current dataset, which has been assembled over several years and to which a number of analysts have contributed, contains 3,194 Gulf of Mexico codas, 3,044 codas from the Azores and 1,927 codas from the Caribbean. Some 38 different codas were identified in this dataset using k-means cluster analysis. Further cluster analysis indicated the existence of three distinct acoustic clans. All units encountered in the Gulf of Mexico were members of a single, very distinct clan and

103

there were only three occasions on which units of this clan were encountered outside the Gulf, and then always in the Azores. The other two clans were not as geographically distinct as the "Gulf of Mexico" clan, although one tended to predominate in Caribbean encounters. These results are preliminary and will be refined as new data are analyzed, but they fit the pattern revealed by the photo-identification, genetic and satellite tag work also completed as part of SWSS which indicates that the population of sperm whales in the northern Gulf of Mexico that have been the subject of most of the SWSS and SWAMP studies are a discrete and relatively small population.

Conclusions and Future Work

On this cruise, we adapted and applied what must now be considered the "traditional" sperm whale research approach: using techniques of photo-identification, photogrammetry, observation, acoustic tracking, recording and analysis. Many of these methods will yield the best information when applied to long-term studies, but here they are already providing information on the basic biology of this population which expands on and complements the data being collected by other components of SWSS using exciting new techniques. It is encouraging to find that where the research topics overlap, the picture being provided by these different approaches is in good agreement. In particular, they are all pointing to the existence of a small population in the northern Gulf that is remarkably discrete and isolated when compared to other sperm whale populations, despite the fact that individuals can move great distances from the study area. Even within the study area, there is evidence of distinct habitat preferences and a strong tendency for certain individuals to show inter-annual fidelity to particular sites. There are also indications of some biological differences between the sperm whales encountered here and those that have been studied in other areas.

Acknowledgements

This research was conducted using software *Logger* 2000 and *Rainbow Click* developed by the International Fund for Animal Welfare (IFAW) to promote benign and non-invasive research.

4.5   Tracking Sperm Whale (*Physeter macrocephalus*) Dive Profiles Using a Towed Passive Acoustic Array

Dr. Aaron Thode[1]

[1]Marine Physical Laboratory, Scripps Institution of Oceanography, San Diego, CA 92093-0205

The Minerals Management Service (MMS) funded a research project to determine whether dive profiles of foraging sperm whales could be obtained using acoustic arrays towed behind a ship. The ability to non-invasively collect such data would permit the collection of information about dive descent rates, foraging depth, and possibly foraging time for a large number of animals over a large geographic area, under various noise conditions. In the long term, the ability to extract sperm whale range and depth information from towed arrays would be of great use in mitigation efforts by MMS and the oil industry in the Gulf of Mexico, because the sound field from an airgun array is highly directional, and knowledge of range and depth of a sperm whale is needed to accurately determine what sound levels foraging animals are receiving in the vicinity of an airgun array.

The work in 2002 and 2003 has shown that a passive acoustic method that uses two or three hydrophones deployed as either a vertical or large-aperture towed array can be used for tracking sperm whale dive profiles. The relative arrival times between the direct and surface-reflected acoustic paths are used to obtain the ranges and depths of animals with respect to the array, provided that the hydrophone depths are independently measured. Besides reducing the number of hydrophones required, exploiting the surface reflections simplifies automation of the data processing.

The 2002 deployment consisted of two short-aperture towed arrays separated by 170 m. In 2003, the configuration shown in Figure 4.5.1 was tested off the R/V *Ewing*, by attaching a rope to the end of a standard towed array, manufactured by SEAMAP, Inc. An autonomous acoustic flash-memory recorder (effectively an underwater Apple iPod) was attached to the rope so that the total array system was about 200 m long, sufficient to track animals out to 1000 m range. Ship noise was used to time-align the acoustic data. The recorder, manufactured by Greeneridge Sciences Inc., measures depth, temperature, and orientation as well. Future deployments will seek to get even wider separations to enable tracking to longer ranges.

Sperm whale ranges and depths can be measured because the sounds made from the whales ricochet off the ocean surface and bottom. By measuring when these "echos" arrive relative to the original sound, the position of the whale can be determined. Examples of echos are shown on a spectrogram in Figure 4.5.2. The theory of tracking is simple; the challenge is finding a way to extract this information automatically from the sound recordings. Note from the figure that three pieces of information can be obtained from each sound or 'click' an individual makes: the difference between the arrival times of the direct and surface-reflected paths on the forward and rear hydrophones, and the arrival time difference between the direct paths on both hydrophones.

In 2003, major progress was made in extracting the tracking information from the sound data. Figure 4.5.3 shows how one computer algorithm was able to extract the relative arrival times of the surface echoes relative to the direct paths (top two subplots) and the relative arrival times of the sounds on two different hydrophones (bottom subplot). Cepstral analysis was used to estimate times for the forward (top panel) and rear (middle panel) hydrophones, while a "rhythm analysis" that compared sets of 9 inter-click interval sequences between phones was used to derive the times in the lower panel. Note the presence of an additional "ghost" curve in the lower

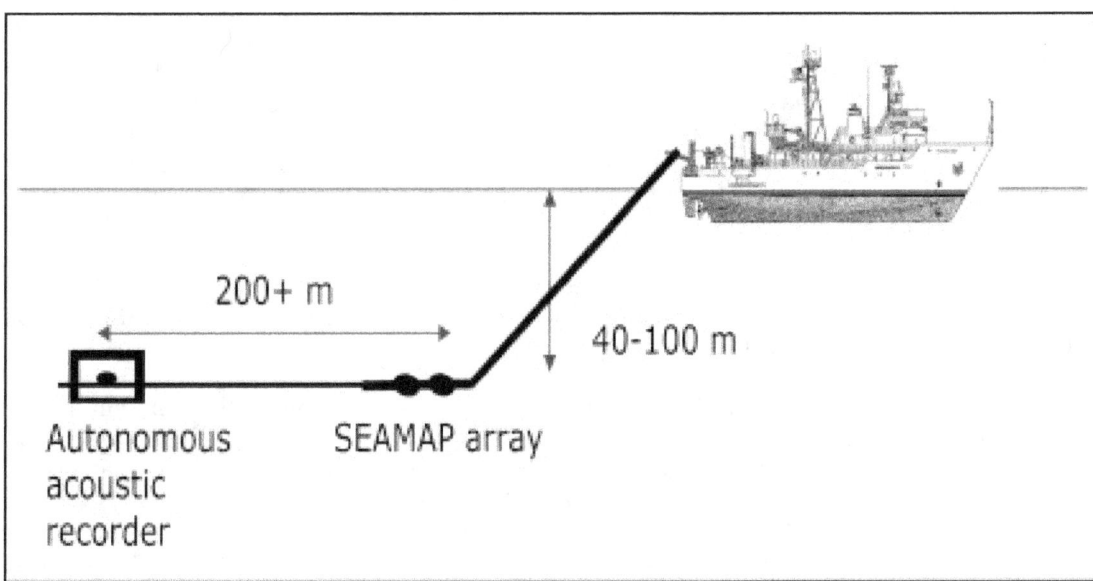

Figure 4.5.1. Deployment geometry of towed passive acoustic range-depth tracking system. This illustrates the acoustic propagation paths used in the 2003 tracking configuration. An autonomous acoustic recorder is attached to a 5/8" polypropylene rope, whose end is attached to a towed acoustic array manufactured by SEAMAP, Inc.

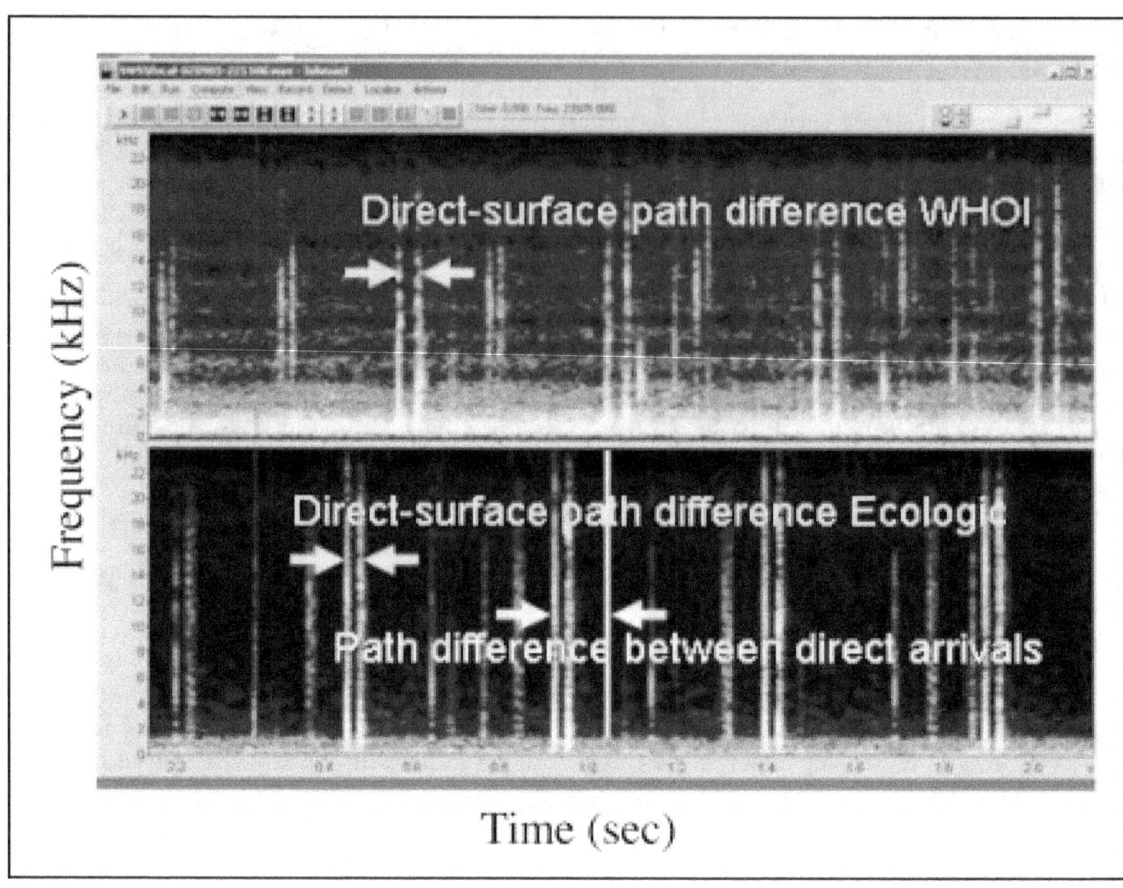

Figure 4.5.2. A spectrogram display illustrating the measurements required for range-depth tracking. It is taken from data collected during one nighttime test, 5 September 2002, using the Ishmael display software of David Mellinger. The top spectrogram display shows data from the forward, WHOI hydrophone, and the bottom display shows a simultaneous recording from the rear, Ecologic hydrophone.

panel. This represents the arrival time difference between the surface reflection on the rear phone and the direct path on the forward phone.

If the hydrophone depths and relative arrival times of the echos are found, the range and depth of the animal can be tracked. Figure 4.5.4 presents one result from 2003 that shows how the ship inadvertently passed almost directly over a whale foraging at 500 m depth. Standard tracking methods would have placed this animal 500 m to the side of the tracking vessel. This result thus demonstrates how a real-time range-depth tracking system might aid mitigation efforts during seismic surveys. A peer-reviewed publication on these methods has been submitted, and a more robust array deployment for 3-D tracking during 2004 is being planned.

106

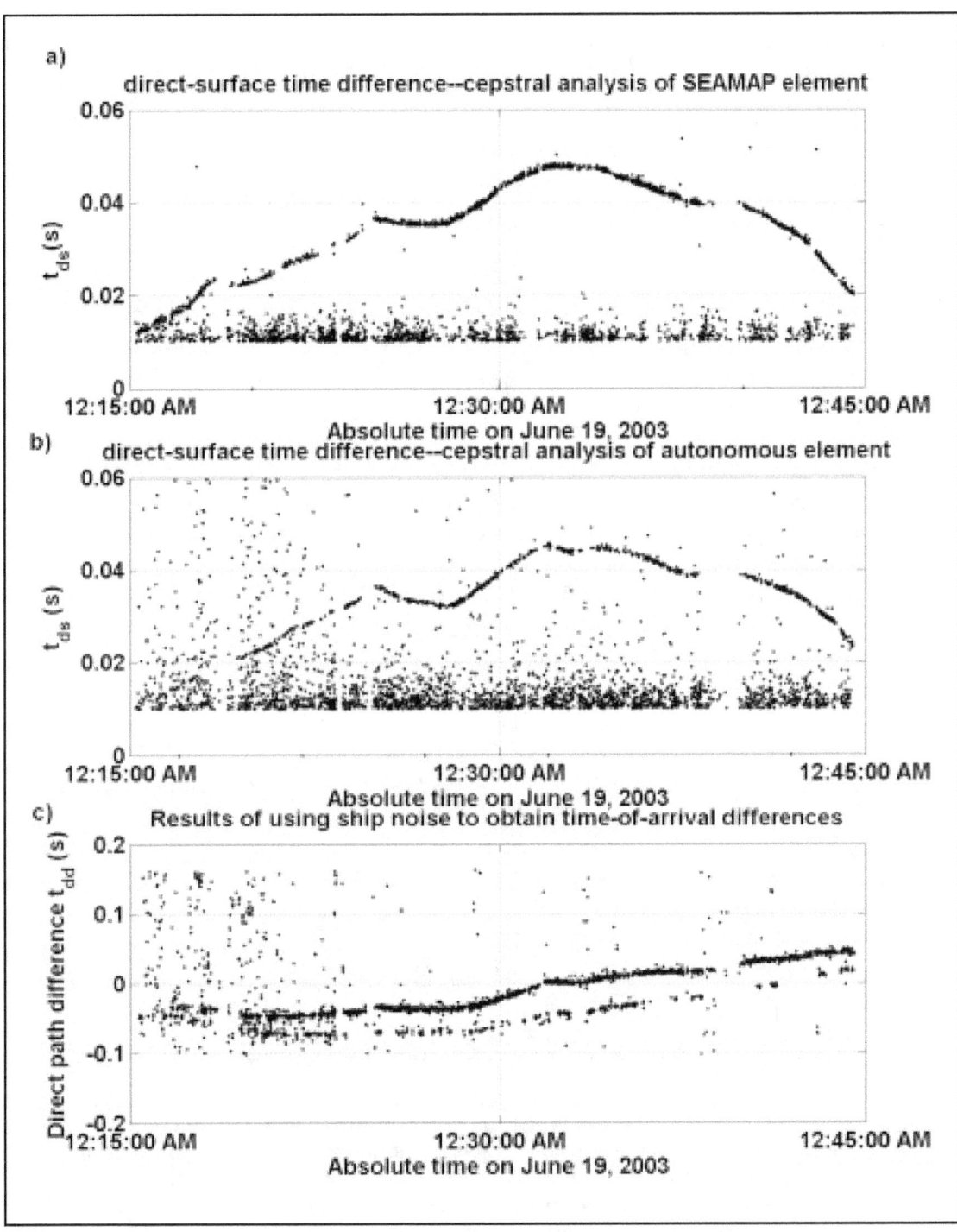

Figure 4.5.3. Example of automated estimates of relative arrival times of the surface echoes relative to the direct paths (top two subplots) and the relative arrival times of the sounds on two different hydrophones (bottom subplot) using data from 19 June 2003.

107

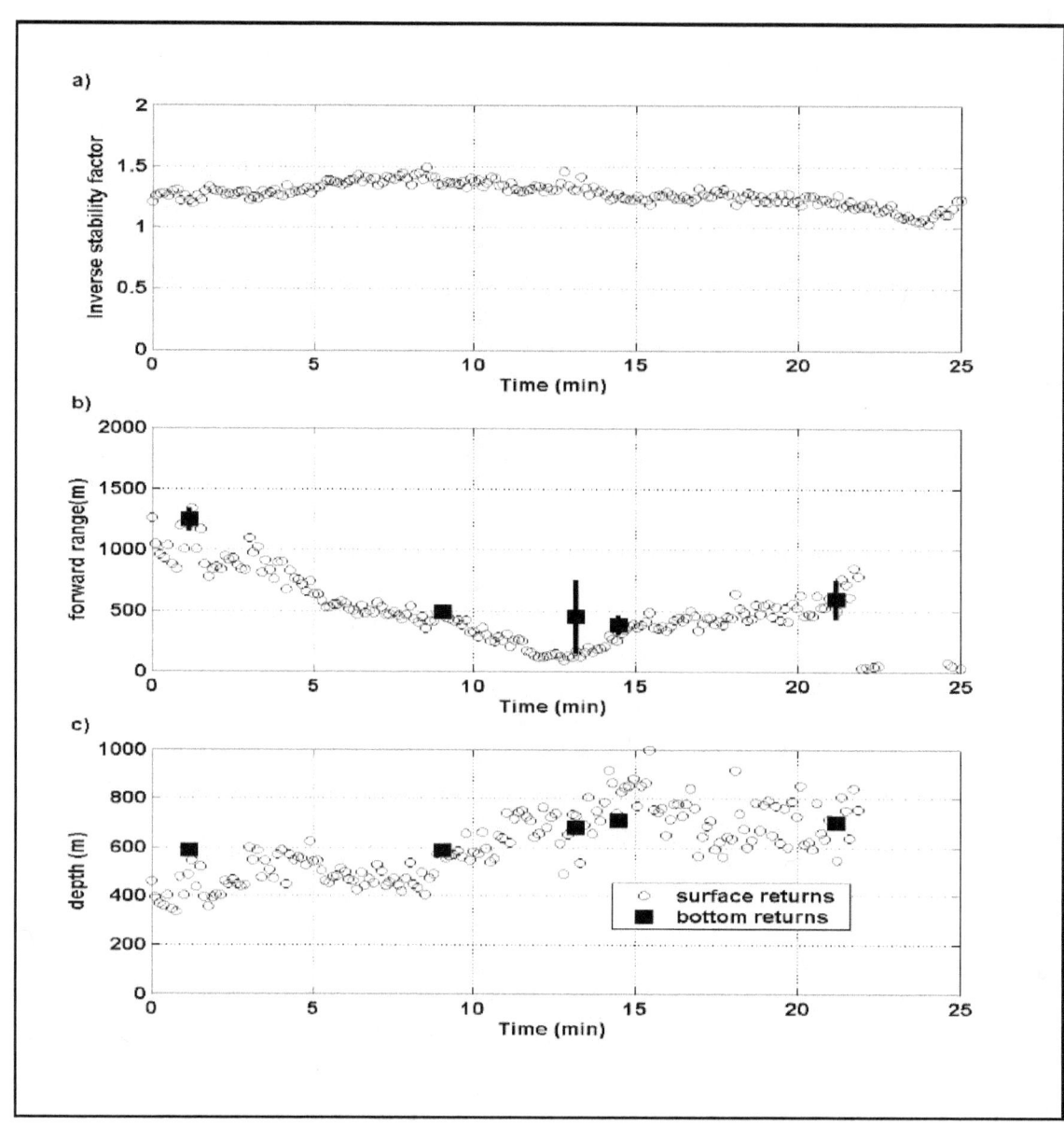

Figure 4.5.4. Example of range-depth tracking even in the presence of hydrophone clipping. The inverse stability factor versus time is given in the top panel. The range (m) of the whale from the vessel's forward hydrophone through time is shown in the middle panel. The depth (m) of the whale through time is shown in the lower panel. The ISP is a rough measure of a whale's azimuth. Values greater than one indicate the whale is forward of the array. The black squares mark independent localization estimates opportunistically obtained by exploiting bottom-reflected acoustic paths. Black bars on squares represent one standard deviation of the estimates derived from bottom returns over a 20 sec interval.

4.6 Habitat Characterization: Eddy Forced Variations in On-margin and Off-margin Summertime Circulation Along the 1000-m Isobath of the Northern Gulf of Mexico, 2002-2003

Douglas C. Biggs[1], Matthew K. Howard[1], Ann E. Jochens[1], Steven F. DiMarco[1],
Robert R. Leben[2], and Chuanmin Hu[3]

[1]Department of Oceanography, Texas A&M University, College Station TX 77843
[2]Colorado Center for Astrodynamics Research, University of Colorado, Boulder CO 80309
[3]College of Marine Science, University of South Florida, St Petersburg FL 33701

Areas along the 1000-m isobath where sperm whales were encountered in summer 2003 are not the same as those where sperm whales were found in summer 2002. Post-cruise reports from R/V *Gyre* cruises in summers 2002 and 2003 and from R/V *Ewing* for summer 2003 summarize where sperm whales were (and show where they were not) found after searching along the 1000-m isobath with combined BigEye and hydrophone surveys. However, since each post-cruise report is focused on a specific 3-4 week time period, these cruise reports alone do not convey the magnitude of circulation differences along the 1000-m isobath between summer 2003 and summer 2002. Our purpose in this short summary is to provide a synopsis of how eddy-forced variations in on-margin and off-margin flow apparently drove these between-summer differences.

In preparing this summary, we merged hydrographic data collected from the oceanographic ships with remote sensing of sea surface height (SSH) mapped by satellite altimeters and with ocean color mapped by the SeaWiFS satellite. The list of co-authors who contributed to this summary is a lengthy one, since our synopsis is based on cooperative work among three institutions. Texas A&M University oceanographers are responsible for collection and analysis of hydrographic data from the oceanographic ships and for the overall program management that is in place among the universities cooperating for the Sperm Whale Seismic Study (SWSS). Our co-authors from the Colorado Center for Astrodynamic Research (CCAR) at the University of Colorado (CU) and from the Institute for Marine Remote Sensing (IMaRS) at the University of South Florida (USF) provided altimetry and ocean color data, respectively. By the time of the SWSS workshop in Houston, TX, in November 2003, CCAR had reprocessed the 2002 and enough of the 2003 near-real-time altimetry data to allow us to animate a 21-month hindcast of the basin-wide SSH field. This covered the period from 1 January 2002 through 30 September 2003 with a one-day time step. We showed this analysis product at the November 2003 workshop. IMaRS collects and processes SeaWiFS data with a focus on the eastern Gulf of Mexico (east of 91°W). They generate analysis products, including composites every week and composites every month. By the time of the November 2003 workshop, this IMaRS hindcast included the 22 month period January 2002 through October 2003.

Loop Current Dynamics and Slope Eddies in 2002
The SSH analysis product shows that a gradient of increasing SSH from north to south (i.e., from shelf to slope) existed over most of the north central Gulf of Mexico for most of the first four months of 2002. This is evident in animations of the hindcast data as a temporally persistent although spatially variable region of negative-to-positive sea surface height anomaly. In the negative SSH part of this gradient, which usually includes the 800-1000 m isobaths, doming of nutrient-rich midwater close to the surface likely favors enhanced planktonic new production along this continental margin (Wiseman and Sturges 1999; Biggs and Ressler 2001). Such conditions, we believe, jump start biological production throughout the food chain, and likely result in more potential prey for sperm whales and other apex predators.

Early in 2002, the Loop Current (LC) shed a Loop Current Eddy (LCE), named "Quick Eddy". In March-April 2002, Quick Eddy cleaved into two pieces: a western QE1 and a central QE2. In the first half of May 2002, QE2 shed a warm filament that extended north into the DeSoto Canyon (Figure 4.6.1). During the second half of May and the first half of June 2002, this warm filament consolidated into a warm slope eddy (WSE), the inshore edge of which reached the Mississippi Canyon region south of the Mississippi River delta (see the middle and end-of-month summary figures in the left column of Figures 4.6.2 and 4.6.3). A composite of SeaWiFS ocean color imagery for the month of June 2002 shows that the anticyclonic circulation around this WSE pulled green water offshore into the eastern part of the SWSS field area (Figure 4.6.4, top panel). A property-property plot of ship-measured chlorophyll fluorescence (a proxy for chlorophyll standing stock) versus surface salinity is a generally straight-line relationship (Figure 4.6.5). Such a straight-line relationship denotes the entrainment process is largely conservative. Thus, the high chlorophyll concentration off-margin arises from seaward transport of phytoplankton coming in from river or estuarine sources. Chlorophyll concentrations change (decrease) off-margin primarily due to mixing with adjacent, low-chlorophyll surface water, although some of the scatterplot data (the green-color points that lie above the straight line in Figure 4.6.5) suggest there was some local phytoplankton growth from "new" nutrients as well.

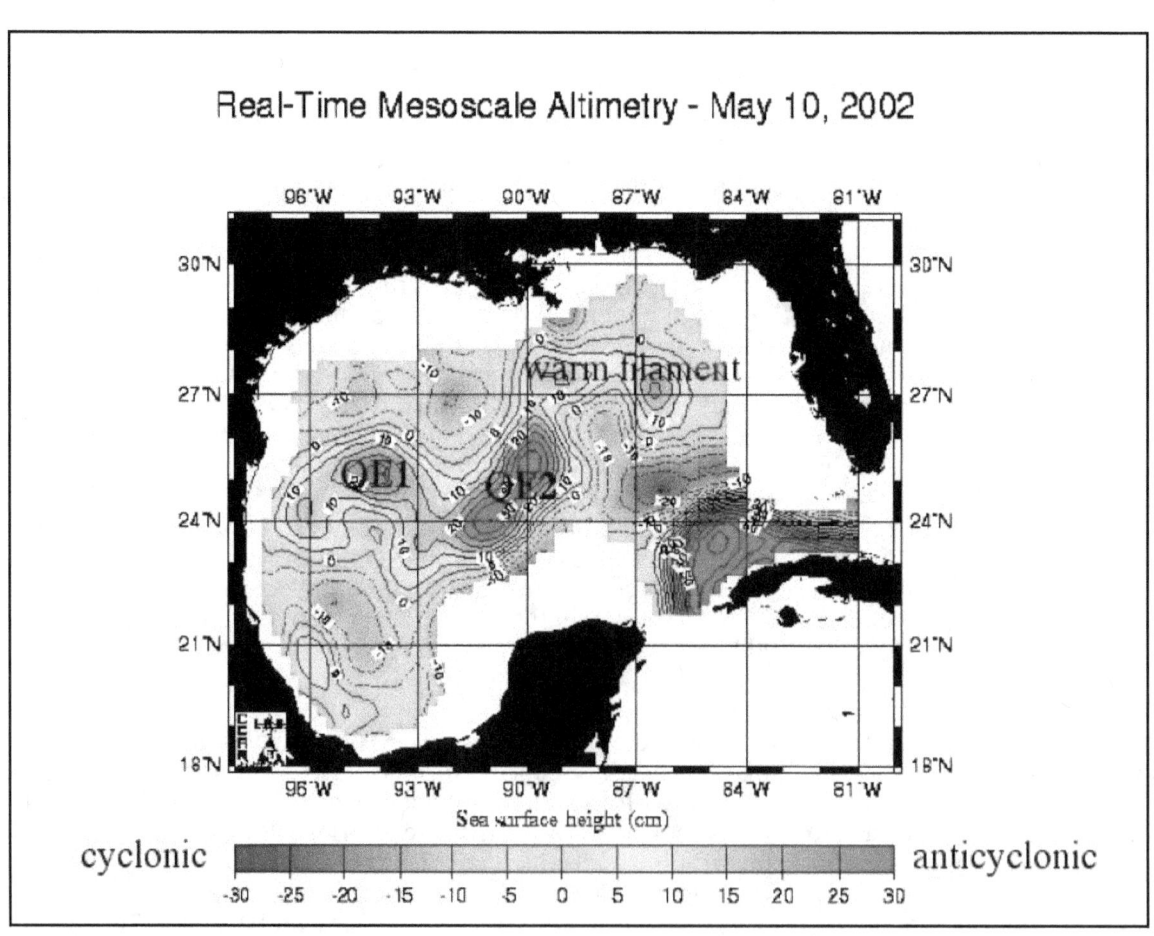

Figure 4.6.1. SSH field for 10 May 2002. This field illustrates the warm filament extending on margin from the northern periphery of Loop Current Eddy QE2.

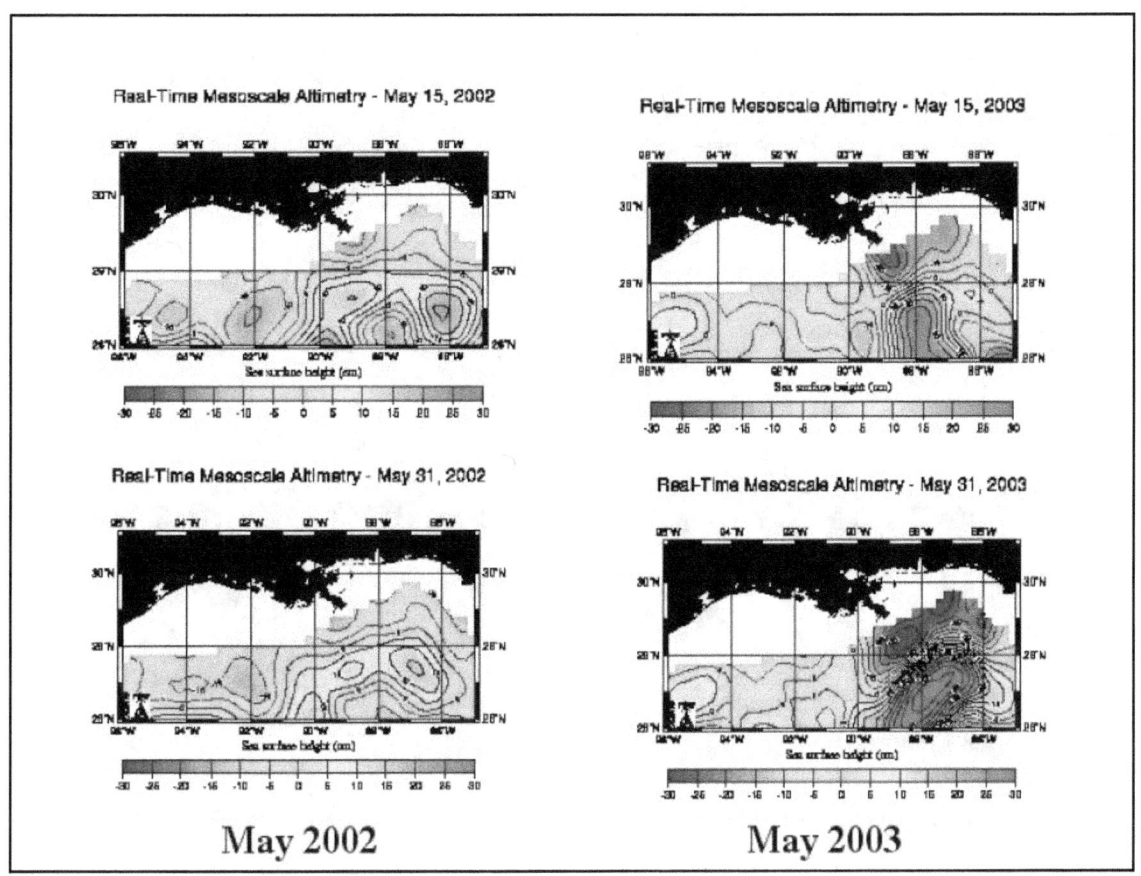

Figure 4.6.2. Comparison of SSH conditions along the northern margin of the Gulf of Mexico in May 2002 and May 2003.

In mid-June 2002, the gradient of increasing SSH over the slope between 94°W and 88°W indicated there was west to east flow along most of the 1000-m isobath, but off-margin flow west of 94°W and east of 88°W (Figure 4.6.3, top left panel). Hydrographic data (XBT, CTD, and ADCP data) from the SWSS 2002 S-tag cruise confirm that off-margin flow was present in both of these areas. This off-margin flow of "green water" was best developed east of 88°W. It was strongest during June and July 2002 while the anticyclonic WSE remained in DeSoto Canyon (Figure 4.6.6, top panels). In October 2002, by which time the WSE was no longer visible as a local SSH high in the DeSoto Canyon, the off-margin transport of "green water" was much reduced (Figure 4.6.6, bottom panels).

Animation of the SSH altimetry maps makes it easy to see that between early July and mid August 2002 what during the 2002 S-tag cruise was a large-scale anticyclonic circulation in the deepwater south of 27°N had broken up into several much smaller anticyclonic eddies. By mid-August, when the SWSS 2002 D-tag cruise sailed for sea, these minor eddies were distributed pretty much all along the continental margin of the north central Gulf. By combining altimetry with ocean color, it can be seen that a pair of WSEs south of Mississippi Canyon and in DeSoto Canyon were entraining green water from the shelf and transporting this off margin in July and August 2002 (Figure 4.6.7). Hydrographic data from the SWSS 2002 D-tag cruise confirm that

111

off-margin flow of low salinity green water was present in most of the region from 90°W to 88°W. A property-property plot of chlorophyll fluorescence versus salinity indicates there was "new" production as well (Figure 4.6.8). The 2002 D-tag cruise also documented locally high chlorophyll in a "bulls-eye" of high ocean color visible in the August 2002 monthly composite of SeaWiFS imagery in deepwater southeast of Mississippi Canyon (Figure 4.6.7, lower right). The SSH data show this high-color feature was a mesoscale cyclonic circulation (Figure 4.6.7, lower left). Several groups of sperm whales were encountered in and around this feature during the 2002 D-tag cruise and to the northeast in the DeSoto Canyon.

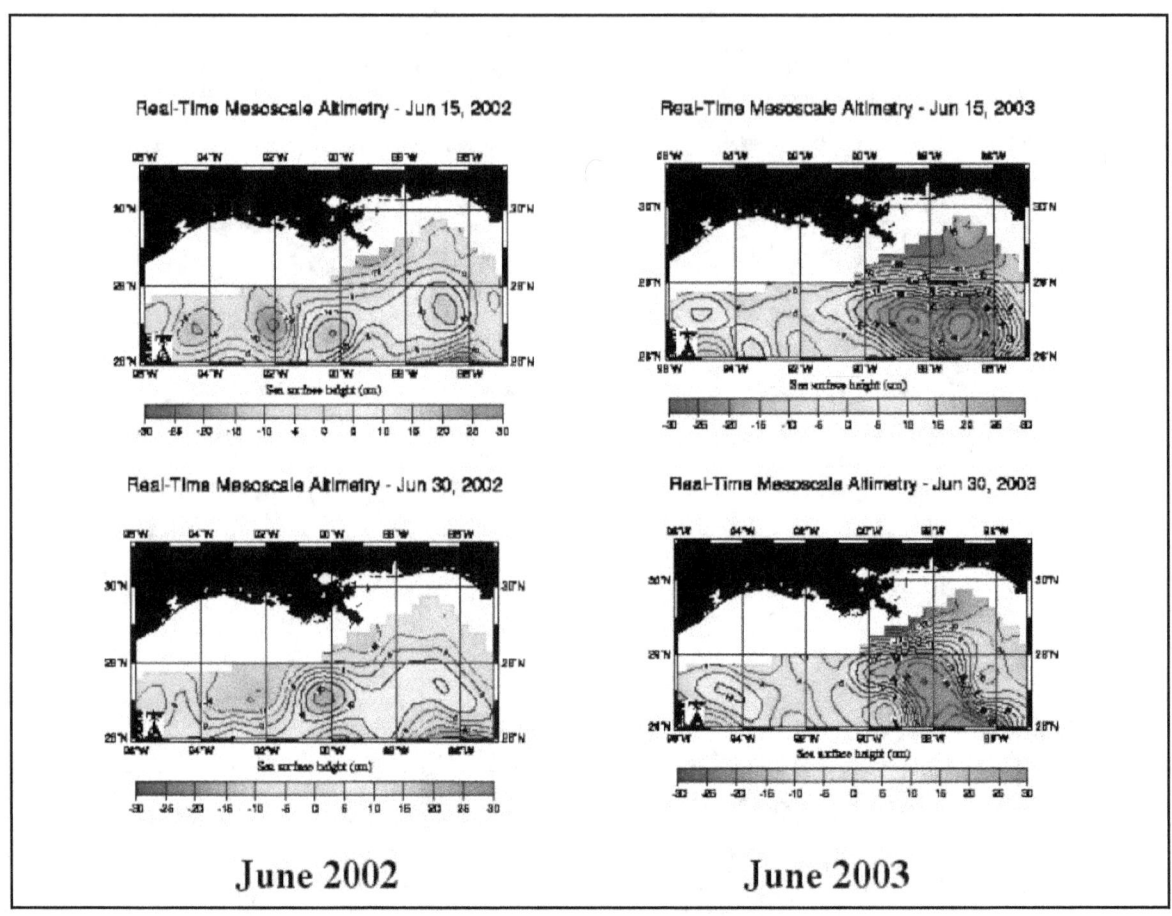

Figure 4.6.3. Comparison of SSH conditions along the northern margin of the Gulf of Mexico in June 2002 and June 2003.

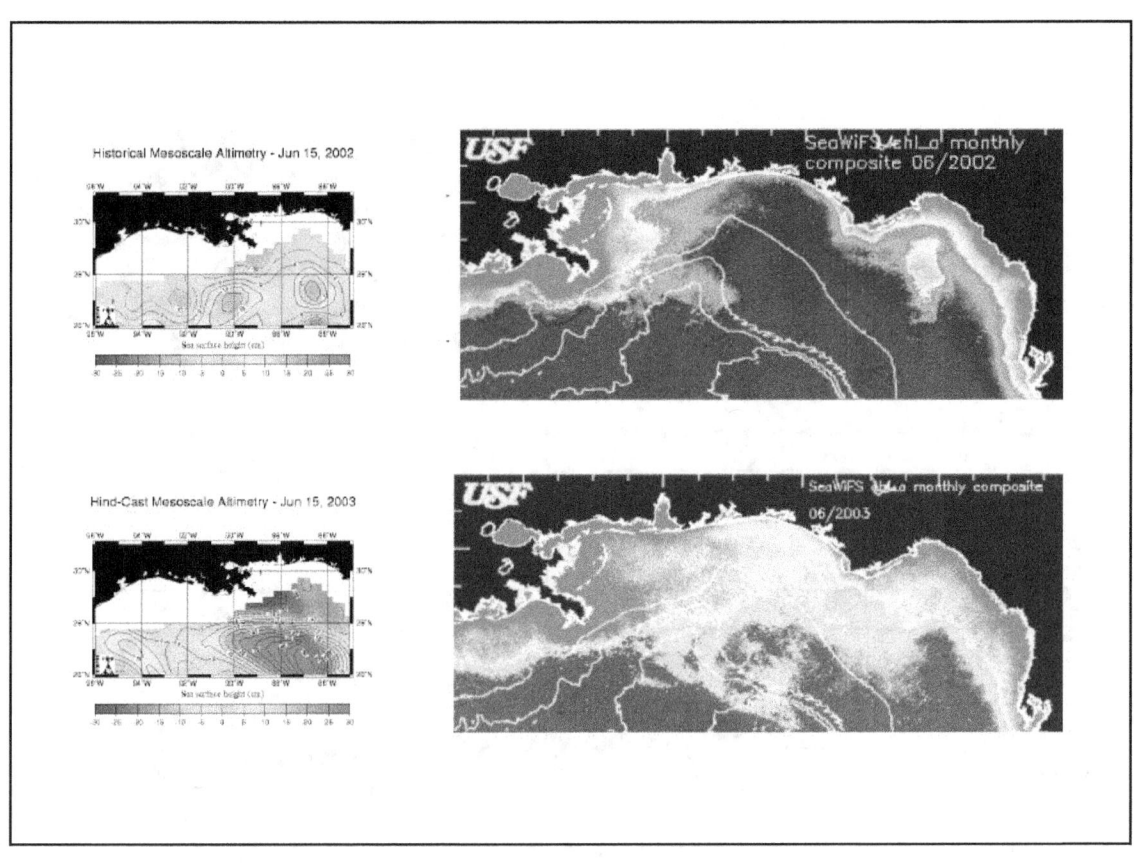

Figure 4.6.4. Comparison of monthly composite SeaWiFS imagery and SSH conditions for June 2002 and June 2003.

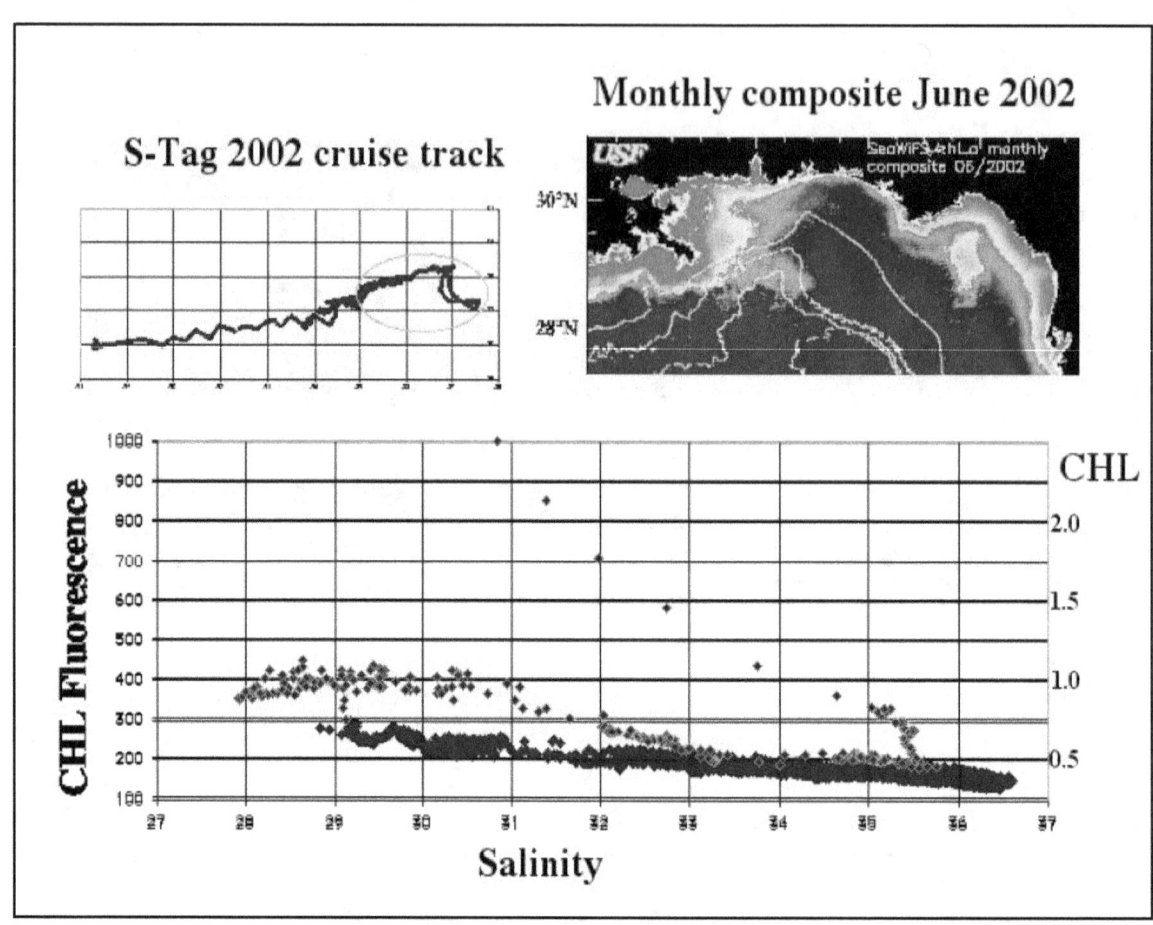

Figure 4.6.5. Chlorophyll fluorescence versus salinity for June 2002 S-tag cruise on *Gyre*. This plot illustrates the generally conservative (straight-line) mixing of low salinity "green water" with high salinity "blue water". Green-colored data denote measurements in the high-shear edge of the green water entrainment region.

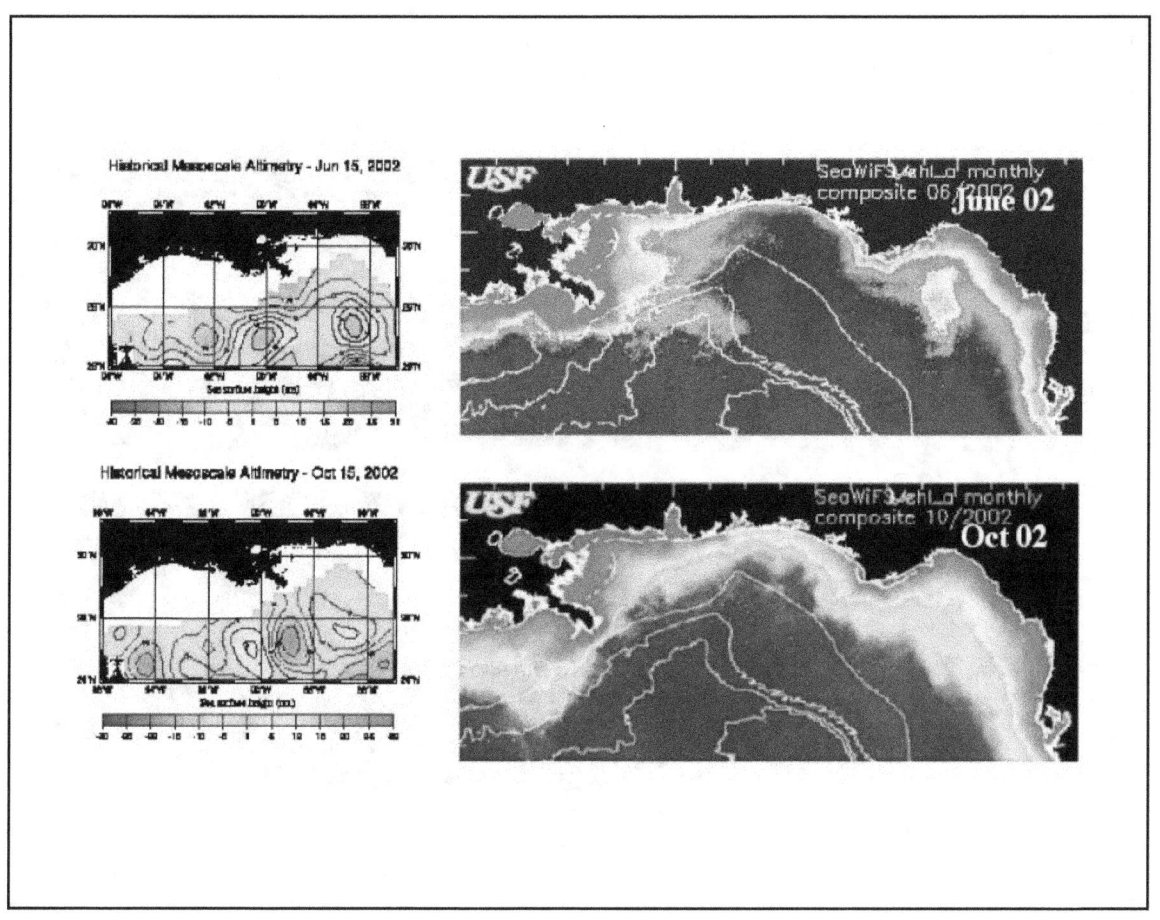

Figure 4.6.6. Comparison of monthly composite SeaWiFS imagery and SSH conditions for June 2002 and October 2002.

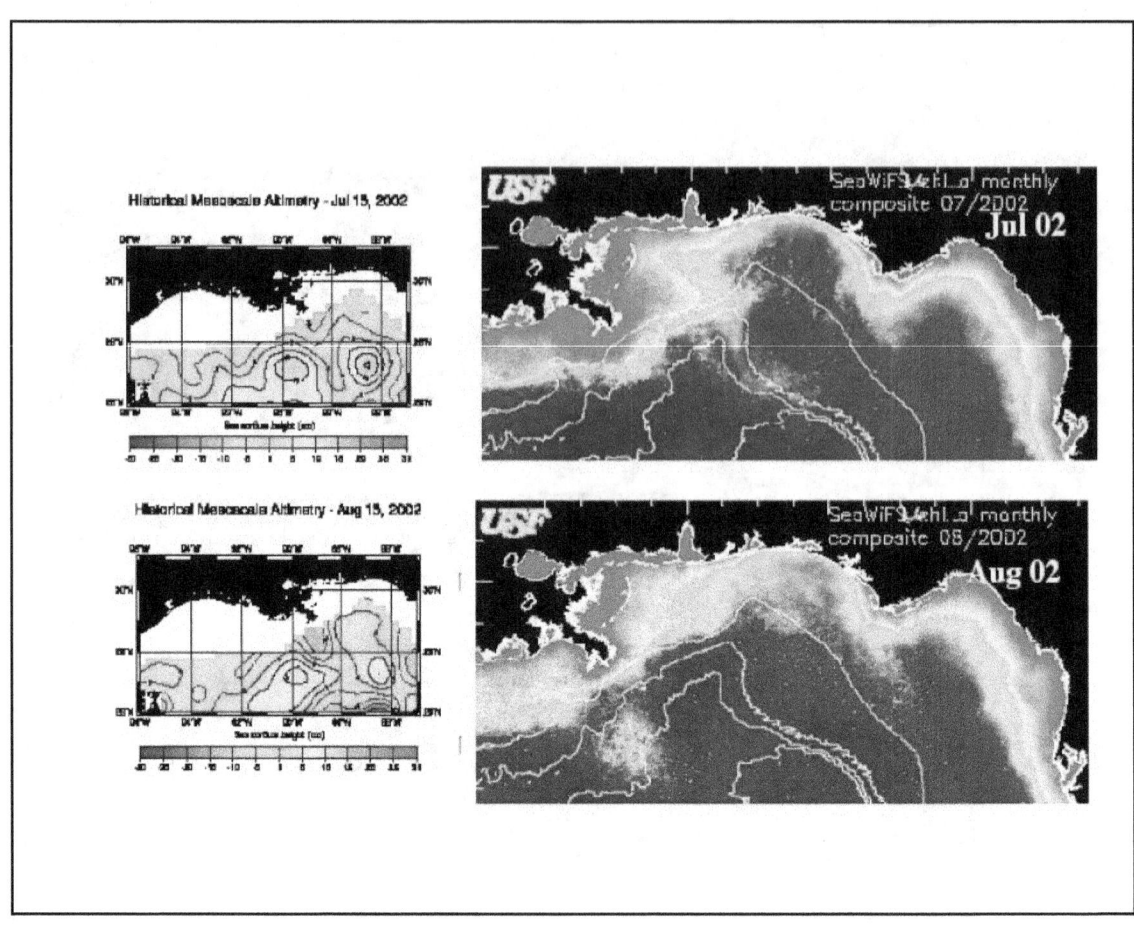

Figure 4.6.7. Comparison of monthly composite SeaWiFS imagery and SSH conditions for July 2002 and August 2002.

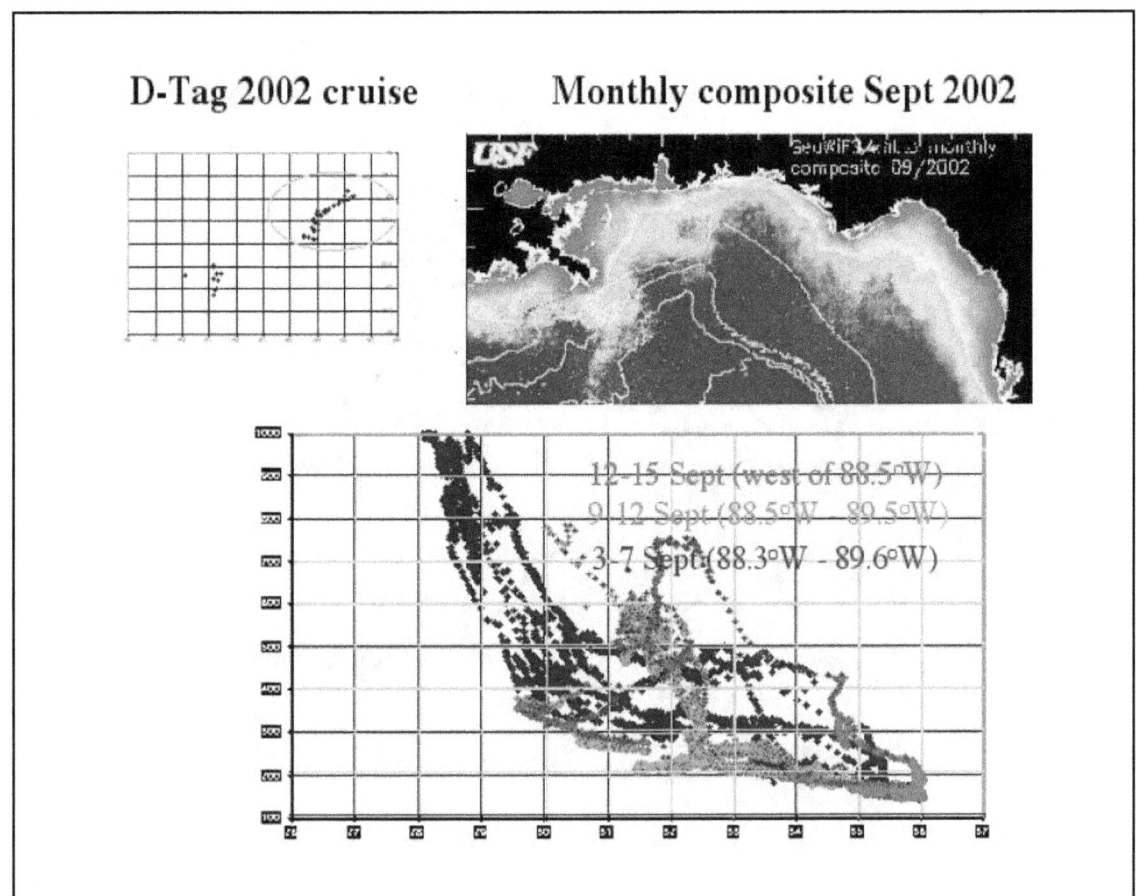

Figure 4.6.8. Chlorophyll fluorescence versus salinity for September 2002 D-tag cruise on *Gyre*. This plot illustrates that non-conservative (non-straight-line) relationships now prevail. "New" production is indicated when fluorescence values do not follow straight lines.

Loop Current Dynamics and Slope Eddies in 2003

Animation of the SSH altimetry maps shows that during the first four months of 2003, as in January-April 2002, circulation was generally cyclonic along the 1000-m isobath in the NE Gulf, including Mississippi Canyon and DeSoto Canyon. The LC surged north of 27°N during this four-month period. In late February 2003 it appeared as if an LCE would separate. However, this anticyclonic circulation feature re-attached to (was recaptured by) the LC. The next LCE separated from the LC during the first two weeks of May 2003. This separation produced a large and energetic LCE, which Horizon Marine named "Eddy Sargassum" (Figure 4.6.9). SeaWiFS imagery confirms the mid-May 2003 separation. A 7-day composite for 18-24 May (Figure 4.6.10) shows high-chlorophyll "green water" being drawn off margin near 86°W and entrained south to about 26°N and then west of about 90°W in the high-velocity periphery of this new, super-size LCE.

117

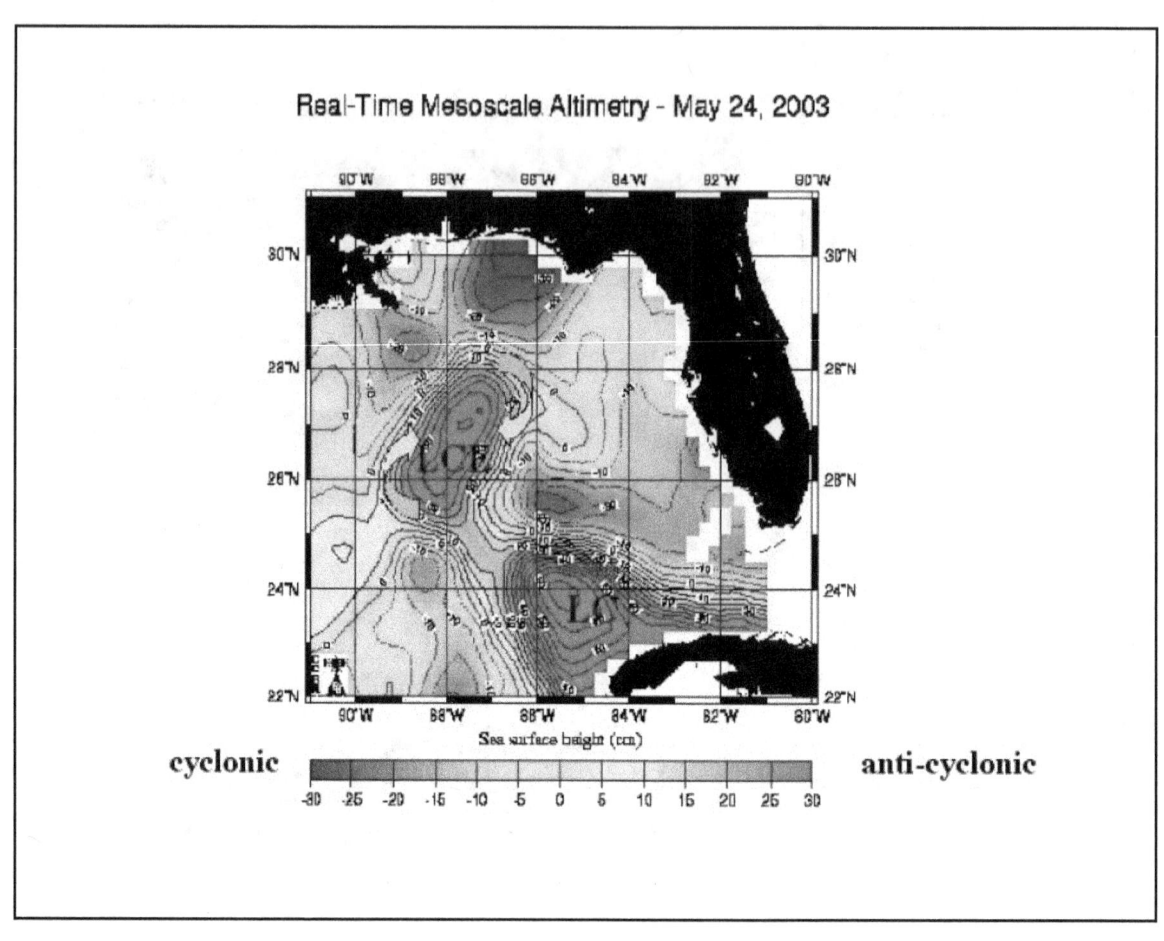

Figure 4.6.9. SSH conditions in May 2003, showing separation of LC Eddy "Sargassum."

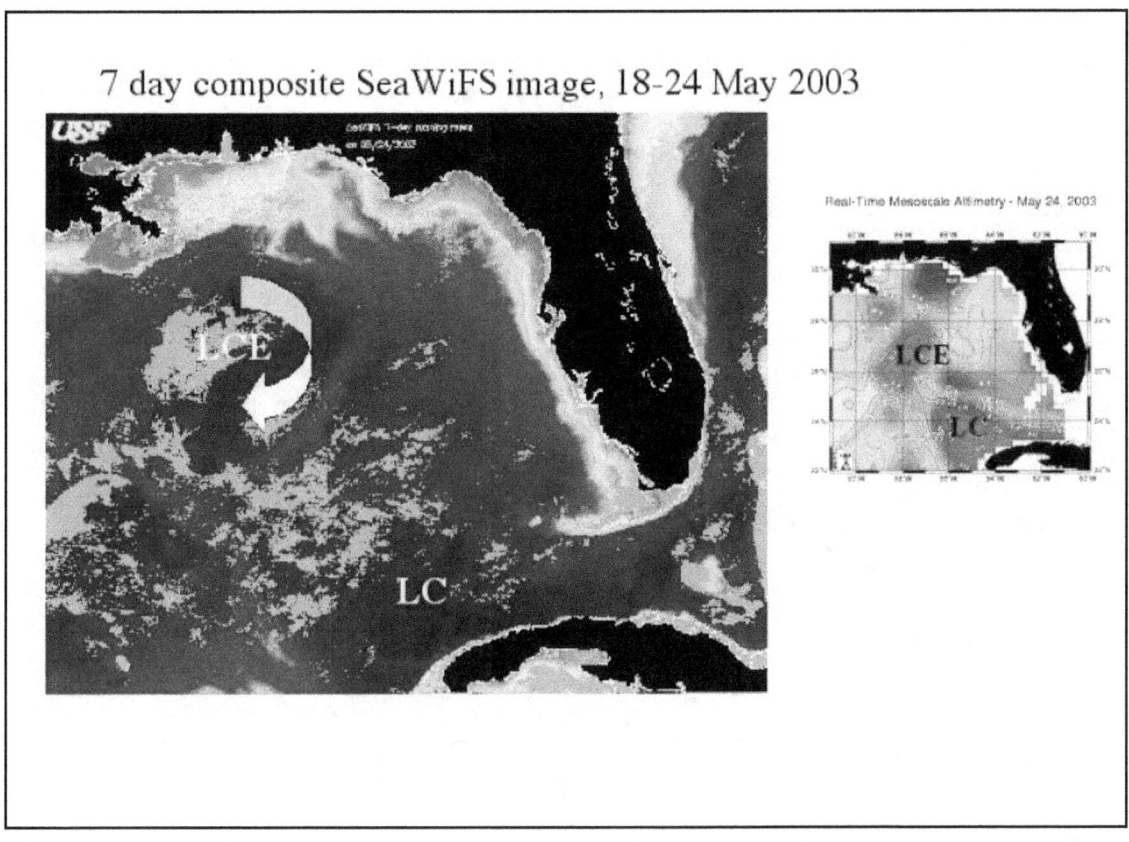

Figure 4.6.10. SeaWiFS composite for 18-24 May 2003, confirming separation of LC Eddy "Sargassum."

The SSH animation shows that after separation from the LC, Eddy Sargassum pushed northward (on-margin) and that the long axis, which initially was oriented N-S, rotated clockwise (Figure 4.6.2, right-hand panels). By the middle of June 2003, the long axis was oriented W-E and its northern periphery extended almost to the shelf-slope break (Figure 4.6.3, right-hand panels). CTD 5, taken from *Gyre* on 11 June 2003, confirms the presence of Subtropical Underwater (salinity > 36.7) in the upper 200 m (Figure 4.6.11). This CTD and the XBTs dropped 9-11 June and again 17-20 June show that the 15°C depth along the northern margin was deeper than 250 m (Figures 4.6.12 through 4.6.14). XBTs dropped from *Ewing* while this vessel searched for sperm whales in Mississippi Canyon during 11-17 June 2003 also show 15°C depths greater than 250 m (Figure 4.6.13). These hydrographic data collected from both oceanographic vessels confirm that, in mid-June 2003, Mississippi Canyon was full of Caribbean water that had advected north with the LC (Figure 4.6.15).

Sperm whales were not encountered by either ship in the area of 89.3-90.5°W where and when LCE Sargassum was interacting with the 1000-m isobath (Figures 3.1.2 and 3.1.6; Tables 3.2.7 and 3.2.8). Rather, groups of whales were found west of 90.5°W and east of 89.3°W, where 15°C depths and the SSH maps indicate these areas were outside the core of Eddy Sargassum (Figures 4.6.14, 4.6.15, and 4.6.16). Data from *Gyre* confirmed there was a very sharp surface front at the northern periphery of Eddy Sargassum. On the morning of 16 June 2003, *Gyre* documented the presence of a sharp boundary between low-chlorophyll "blue water" and higher-chlorophyll

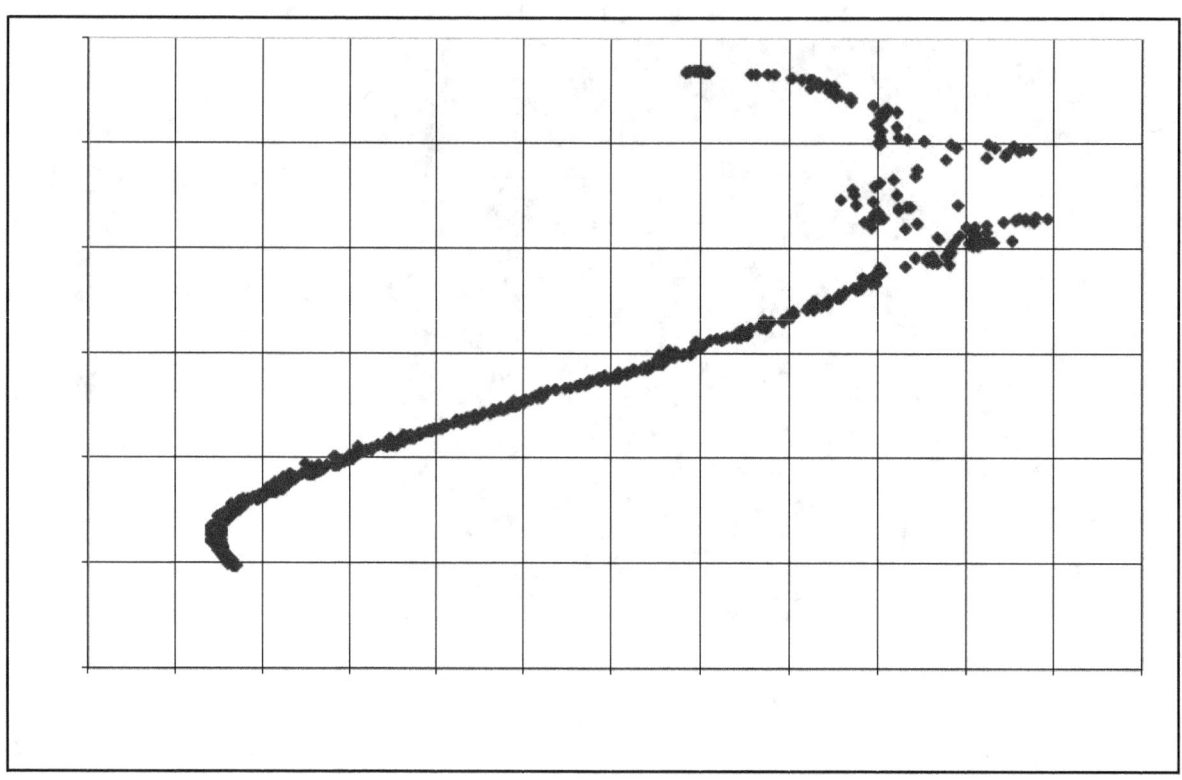

Figure 4.6.11. CTD profile from 11 June 2003 shows subsurface evidence for Subtropical Underwater.

"green water" near 28.87°N, 88.33°W (Figure 4.6.17). From 16 to 18 June 2003, *Gyre* followed several groups of sperm whales in the green water northeast of this front. In contrast, none were found inside the blue water front marking the northern periphery of the LCE. This was not unexpected, since the GulfCet 2 program also found sperm whales to be uncommon in the interior of LCEs (Biggs et al. 2000).

In June 2003, along the boundary between blue and green water just northeast of Mississippi Canyon, we documented a "hot spot" of locally high chlorophyll fluorescence. A property-property plot of chlorophyll fluorescence versus salinity (Figure 4.6.18) suggests this resulted from turbulent mixing that brought "new" nutrients to the surface. When *Gyre* returned to this area during the SWSS 2003 S-tag cruise, however, the hot spot had relaxed and mixing of green water with blue water was generally conservative (Figure 4.6.19). During the two weeks that passed between the time this area was visited by the SWSS 2003 WSHC cruise and the 2003 S-tag cruise, the SSH time series shows that Eddy Sargassum had moved away from (rebounded seaward from) the 1000-m isobath. In confirmation of this change in geometry, CTDs taken and XBTs dropped during the 2003 S-tag cruise show no evidence for Subtropical Underwater, and 15°C depths were < 255 m (Figure 4.6.20). Thus, hydrographic conditions along the 1000-m isobath appear to have returned to "normal" by mid-July 2003, and on the 2003 S-tag cruise sperm whales were again encountered between 89-91°W, as well as to the northeast of Mississippi Canyon (Figures 3.3.7 and 3.3.10).

The comparison of SeaWiFS monthly composites for June 2002 and June 2003 (Figure 4.6.4) shows more green water was entrained and moved farther offshore in summer 2002 than summer 2003. A similar comparison of April 2003 (before LCE separation) with June 2003 (LCE close off-margin) is convincing evidence that this entrainment was forced by the presence of LCE Sargassum close off-margin (Figure 4.6.21). Recall that a comparison of SeaWiFS monthly composites for June 2002, with a WSE present on the 1000-m isobath, and October 2002, with no WSE present, showed that WSEs also can entrain shelf water and move it off margin (Figure 4.6.6), although the magnitude of the entrainment and transport off-margin was not as great as during summer 2003 when a full-blown LCE is present.

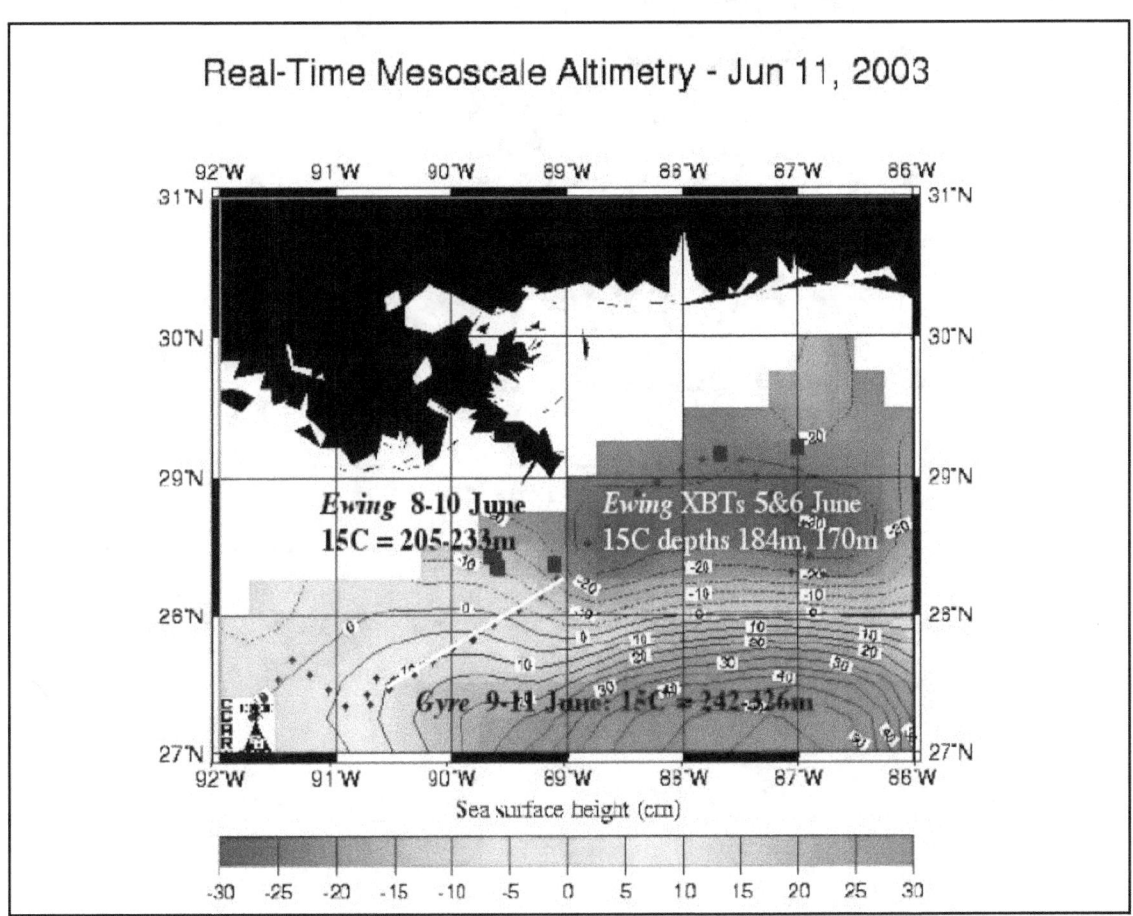

Figure 4.6.12. Relation of SSH to 15°C depths from XBT drops in early June 2003. XBT stations from *Gyre* are diamonds and from *Ewing* are squares. Reported are the 15°C depths for three areas. The white line denotes the XBTs from *Gyre* for which the range of depths are given.

121

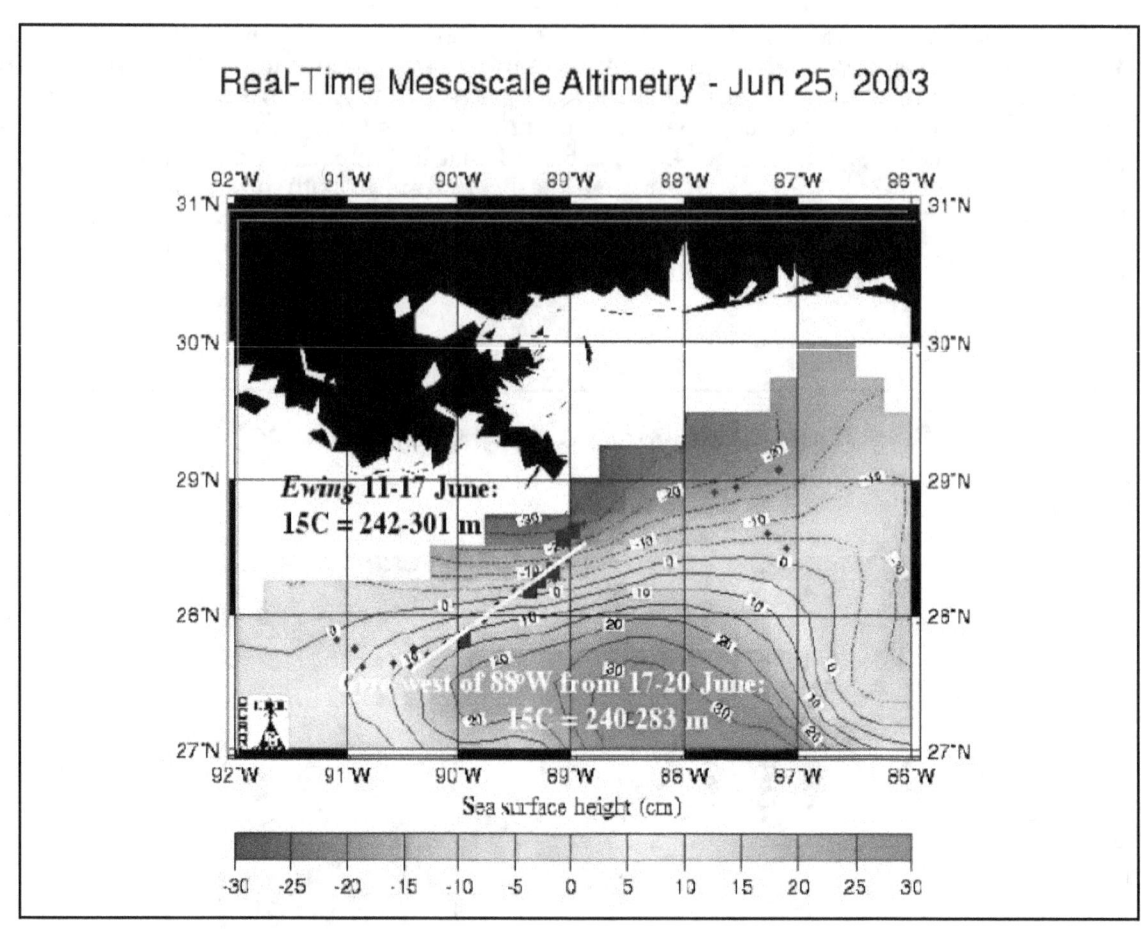

Figure 4.6.13. Relation of SSH to 15°C depths from XBT drops in mid-June 2003. XBT stations from *Gyre* are diamonds and from *Ewing* are squares. Reported are the 15°C depths for two areas. The white line denotes the XBTs from *Gyre* for which the range of depths are given.

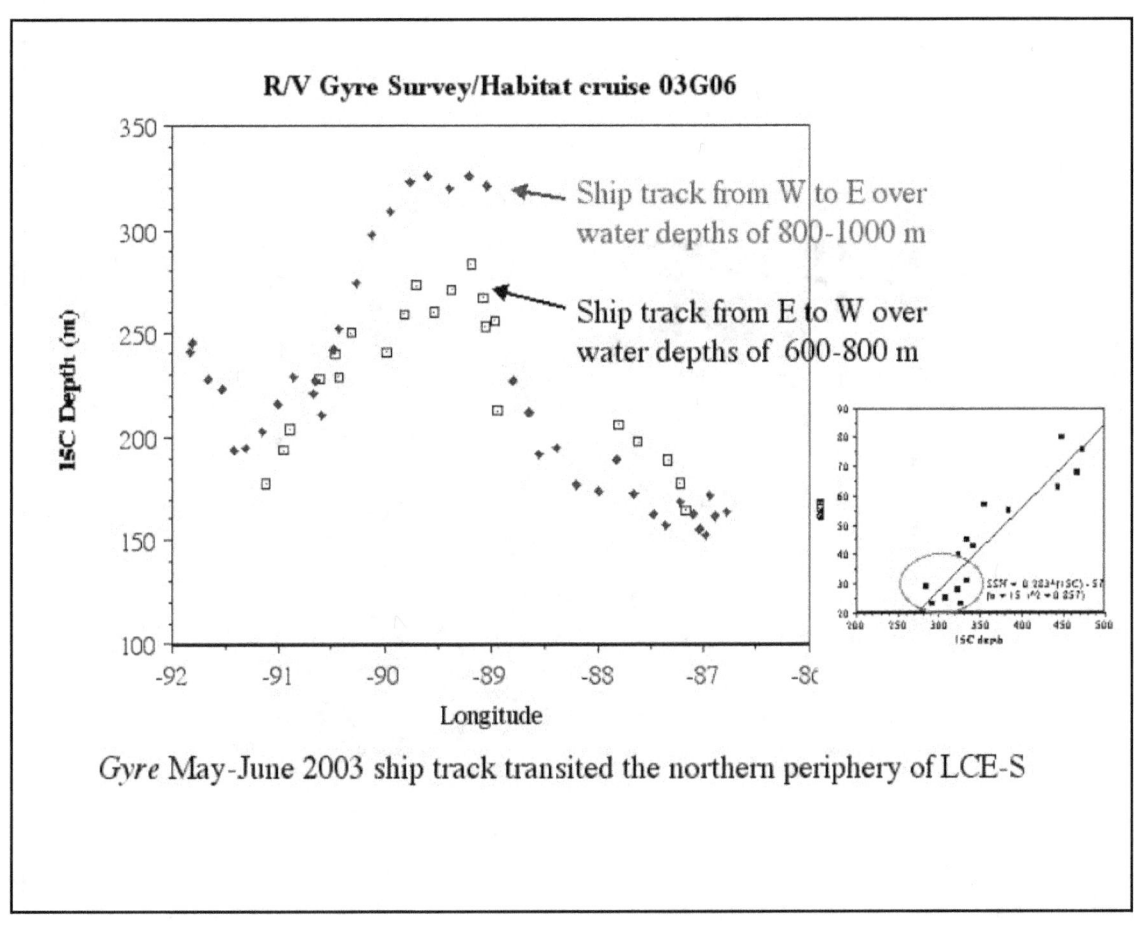

Figure 4.6.14.   Synopsis of 15°C depths, determined during SWSS 2003 WSHC cruise on *Gyre*, plotted versus longitude. Compare this with Figures 4.6.12 and 4.6.13 and with the following Figure 4.6.15 to see locations in relation to SSH. Inset shows that the 15°C depth is a proxy for SSH.

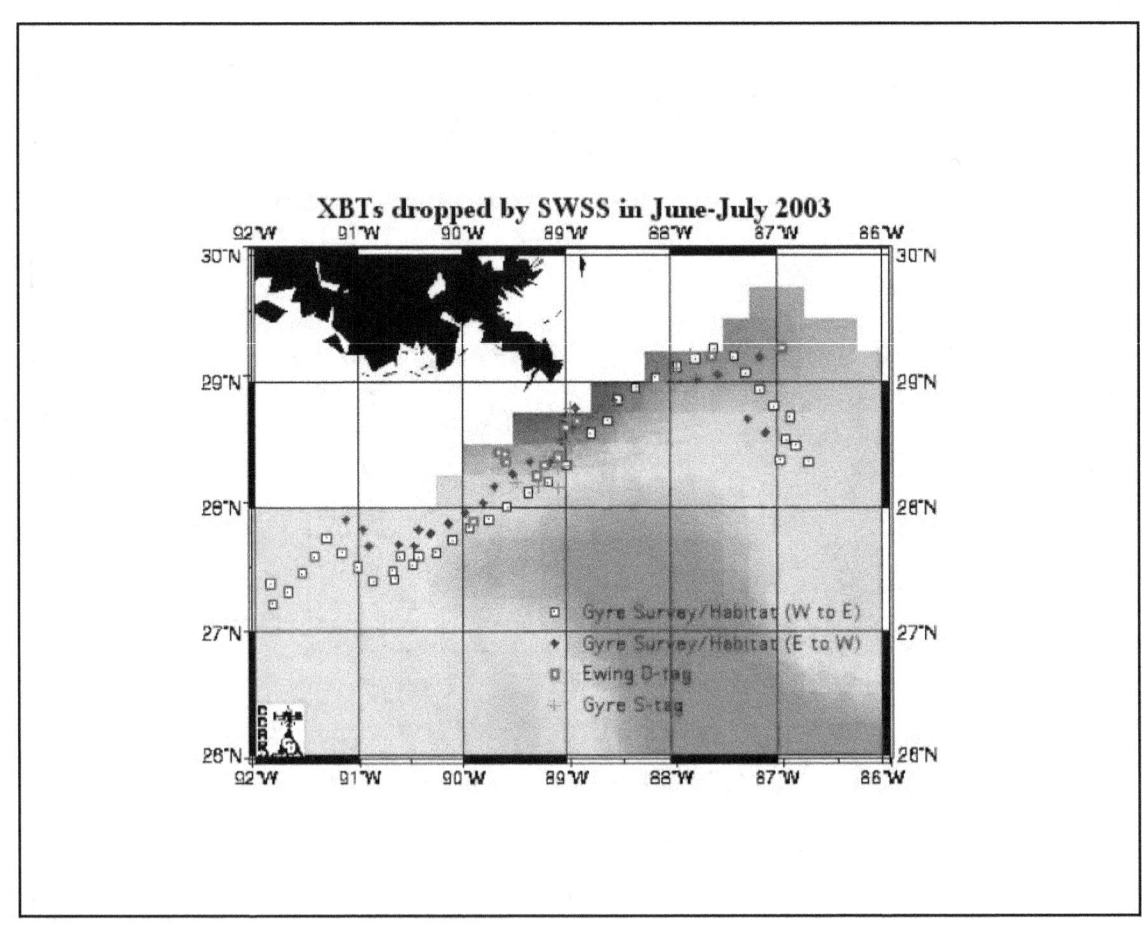

Figure 4.6.15. Summary plot of location of XBT stations occupied by R/V *Gyre* and R/V *Ewing* in June and July 2003, superimposed on SSH conditions for mid-June 2003.

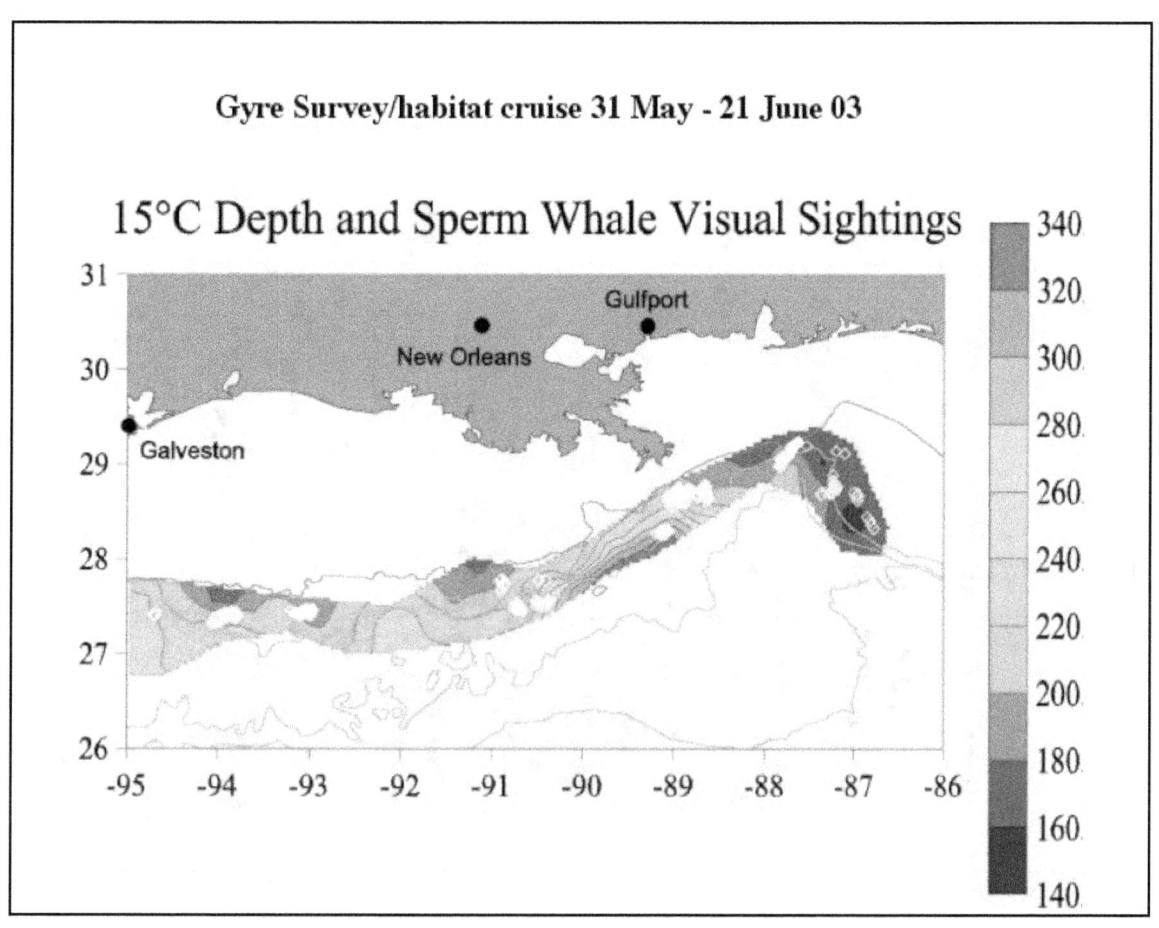

Figure 4.6.16. Sperm whale sightings superimposed on 15°C depth during SWSS 2003 WSHC cruise on *Gyre*.

Figure 4.6.17. At the northern edge of LCE "Sargassum," the SWSS 2003 WSHC cruise encountered a sharp surface front on 16 June 2003.

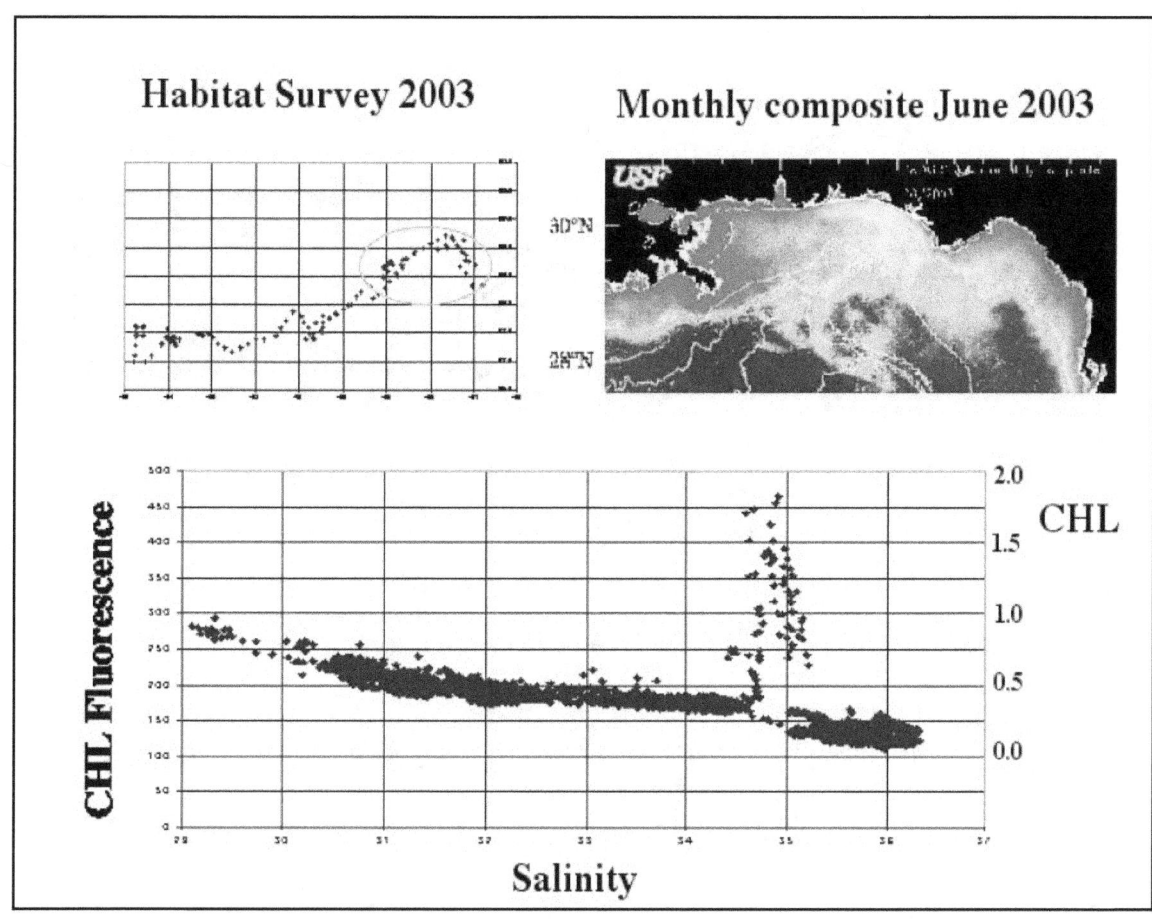

Figure 4.6.18. Chlorophyll fluorescence versus salinity on SWSS 2003 WSHC cruise on *Gyre*. Plot shows the "hot spot" of locally high chlorophyll fluorescence at the boundary between blue water and green water during the cruise.

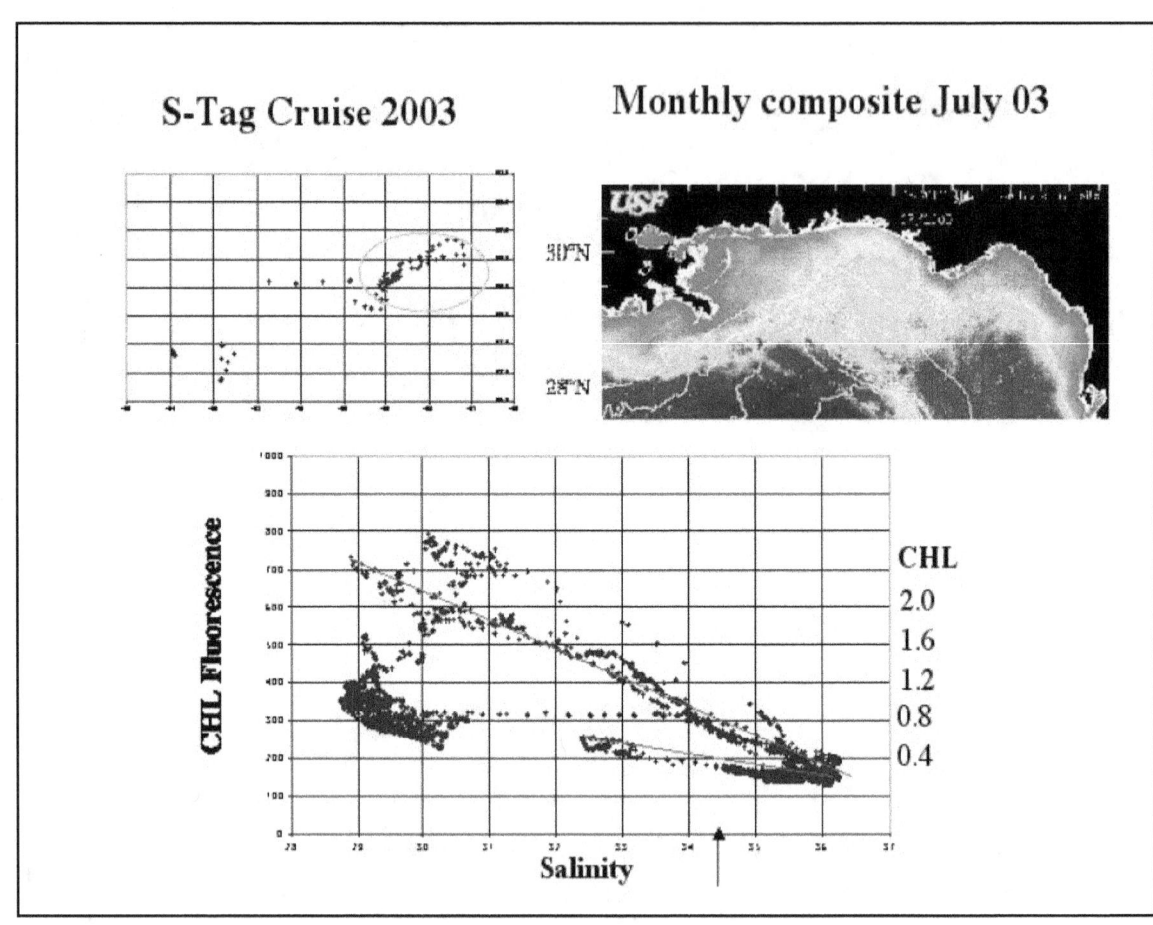

Figure 4.6.19. Chlorophyll fluorescence versus salinity on SWSS 2003 S-tag cruise on *Gyre*. In contrast to the 2003 WSHC cruise, mixing was generally conservative (simple dilution of green water with blue water) during the 2003 S-tag cruise.

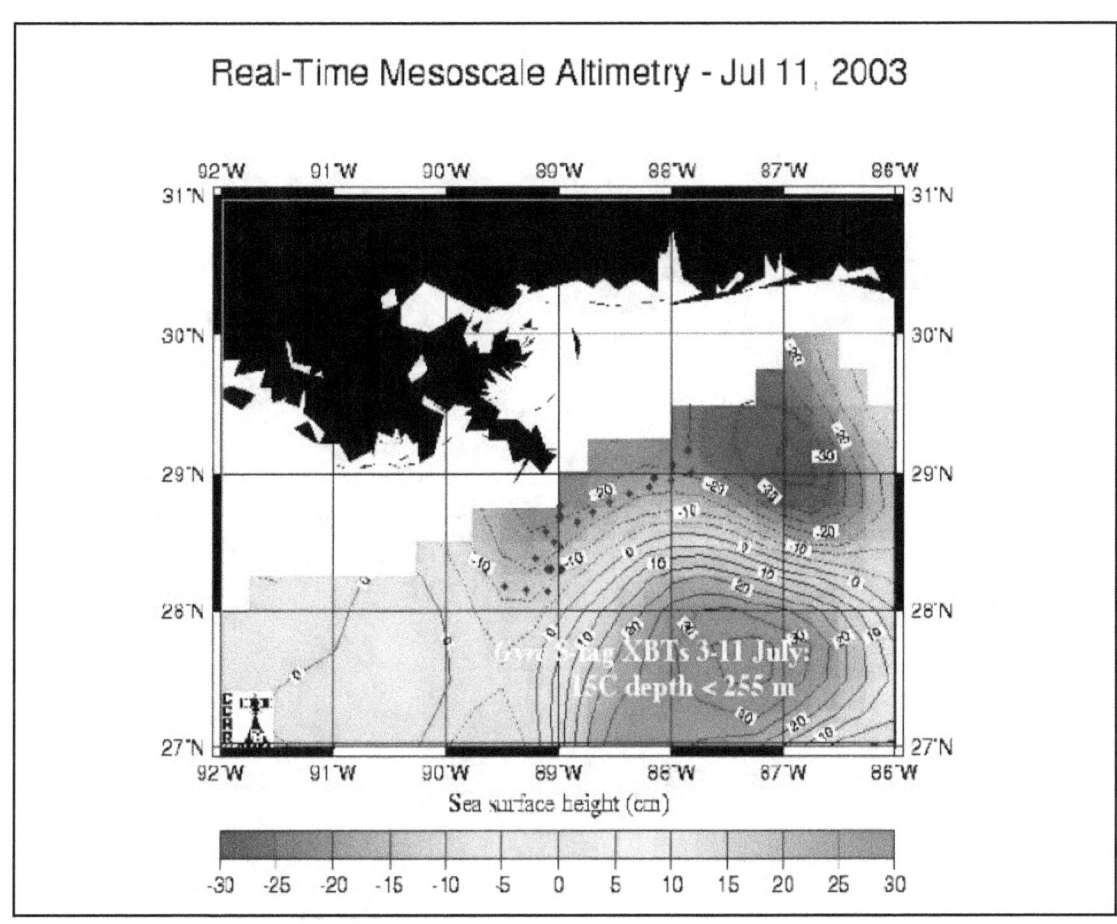

Figure 4.6.20. Relation of SSH to 15°C depths from XBT drops made on the July 2003 S-tag cruise on *Gyre*. XBT stations are diamonds.

Summary

Loop Current Eddies and slope eddies contribute biological and physical heterogeneity along the continental margin of the northern Gulf of Mexico. Temporal and spatial variations in the geometry of the eddy field along the 800-1200 m isobaths determine whether low salinity green water flows off margin, or if high salinity blue water flows on margin. Green water is biologically rich and we hypothesize it supports more prey for the squid upon which whales prey. Locally high chlorophyll can develop at the periphery of eddies, when or where high velocity currents (> 2 knots) create vertical shear and thus upwelling of nutrients from midwater. Moreover, locally high chlorophyll also can develop when or where nutrient-rich water domes upward in cyclonic eddies. Cyclonic eddies and other nutrient-rich features that persist for 3-4 months in time may be important feeding grounds for sperm whales along the continental slope of the Gulf of Mexico. LCEs, in contrast, appear to generate the opposite effect.

There is hydrographic evidence (e.g., deep 15°C depths) that, when the large, energetic LCE Sargassum interacted with the 1000-m isobath in early June 2003, it displaced the upper 1000 m or so of usual water in the Mississippi Canyon area with low-nutrient, low-chlorophyll "ocean

129

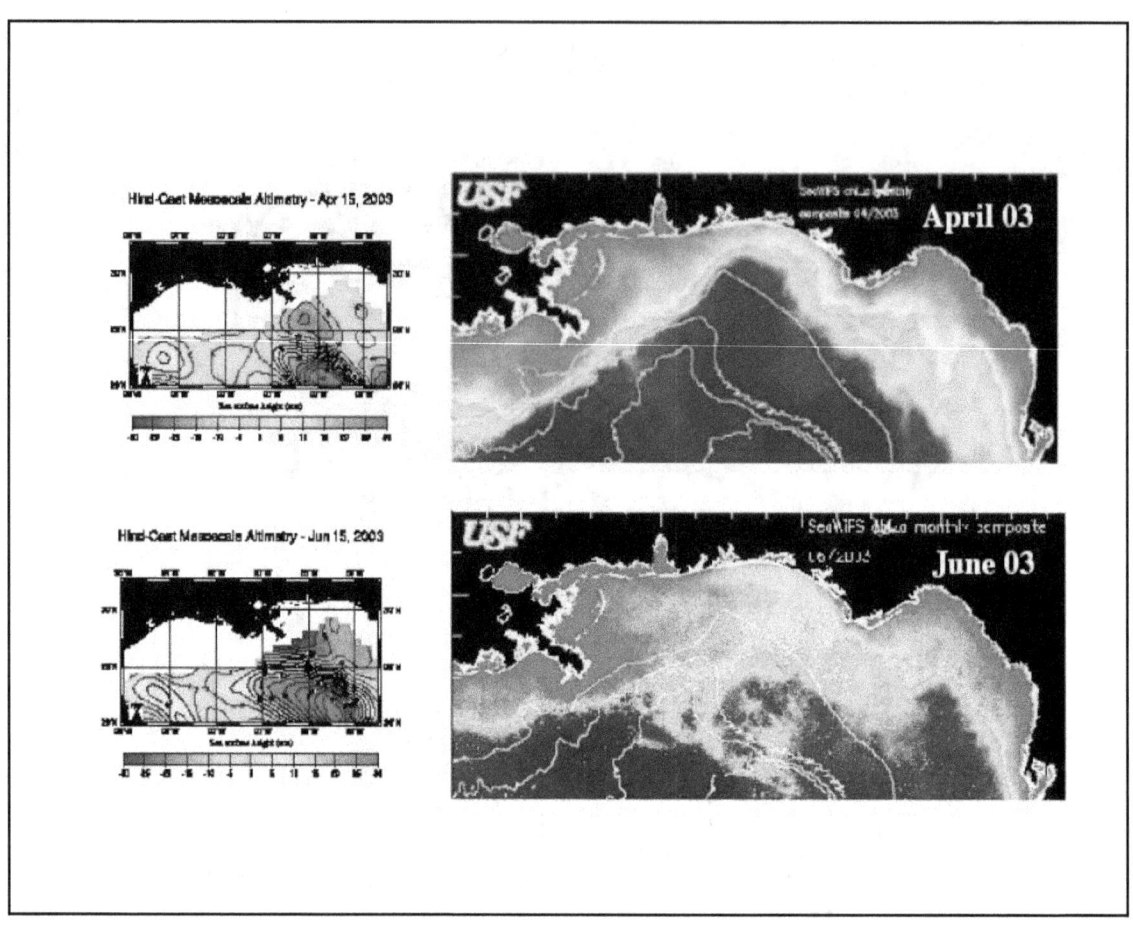

Figure 4.6.21. Comparison of monthly composite SeaWiFS imagery and SSH conditions for June 2003 and April 2003.

desert" water of Caribbean origin. We hypothesize that sperm whales usually seen in this area (i.e., summer 2002) moved west and/or east out of this area during early June through late June when this LCE reached farthest north along the margin. Whales were in greater abundance in summer 2003 west of 92°W and east 88.5°W than in the region 89.3-90.5°W where the LCE reached its shallowest point along margin. We presume the whales left when their deep-living squid prey was also displaced by this bolus of northward-moving Caribbean water. Return to normal conditions of hydrography (and squid prey?) appears to have occurred after this LCE moved back (rebounded) into deeper water, since by early July 2003 the 15°C depth had returned to normal levels, and whales were again encountered in Mississippi Canyon.

Acknowledgments
TAMU and CCAR support came from MMS-TAMRF cooperative agreement 1435-01-02-CA-85186. USF support came from NASA contracts NAS5-97128 and NAG5-10738. SeaWiFS data are the property of Orbimage Corporation and data use here is in accordance with the SeaWiFS Research Data Use Terms and Conditions Agreement of the SeaWiFS project.

130

4.7   Habitat Characterization: Upper-Ocean Current Observations During Summer: 2002 and 2003 Central Slopes of the Northern Gulf of Mexico

Dr. Steven F. DiMarco[1], Ann E. Jochens[1], and Matthew K. Howard[1]

[1]Department of Oceanography, Texas A&M University, College Station, TX 77843-3146

Ship-mounted acoustic Doppler current profiler (ADCP) observations were recorded during each leg of SWSS cruises during the summers of 2002 and 2003. Shipboard ADCPs provide profiles of current speed along the ship track. Up to two ADCPs of different operating frequencies were used: a 150-kHz narrowband model and a 38-kHz phased-array Ocean Surveyor Model. Only 150-kHz ADCP data were collected in 2002; both instruments were available in 2003. The nominal vertical range of the 150-kHz ADCP is about 200 m; the 38-kHz is about 800 m. The ADCP data were collected in five-minute intervals, which translate to 2-3 km horizontal spatial resolution when the ship is traveling at 8 knots (4 m/s). Vertical resolution was set to 4 m bins for the 150-kHz and 16-m bins for the 38-kHz ADCP. Position and pitch, roll, and yaw (navigation) data were recorded at 1-second intervals using an Ashtech 3DF GPS antennae array. Differential GPS fixes were used as available. The navigation data were merged with the raw ADCP data during post-cruise processing. Jochens and Biggs (2003) give a description of the standard ADCP processing protocol and quality control procedures used (see also Jochens and Nowlin 1999).

It is critical when processing shipboard ADCP data to obtain accurate estimates for ship velocity. This is because the downward looking transducers of the ADCP are providing estimates of fluid movement past the transducer head. The fluid movement is the vector sum of the ship velocity and the ocean current velocity. The ship speed therefore must be subtracted from the transducer speed to yield the current velocity. Complicating this calculation is the fact that the ship speed is typically much larger than the current velocity (order 20-30:1) so ship speed must be estimated with high precision. Further, an elaborate scheme to correct the ADCP output for an offset with respect to the ship's beam must also be used (Murphy et al. 1992) using a regression of the GPS determined ship velocity and the ADCP-determined ship bottom track velocity.

Several quality control indicators, which aid in the interpretation and analysis of horizontal velocity estimates, are built into the ADCP estimates. These include vertical and error velocities, which provide an indication of homogeneity of the fluid flow; percent good, which reports the percentage of usable or "good" pings used to create the five-minute average ensemble; correlation, which quantifies the correlation of the outgoing acoustic pulse with the received scattered pulse; and echo intensity, which is a measure of received signal strength.

Nowlin et al. (2001) summarized the basic features of currents in the deepwater Gulf of Mexico. These are briefly described. The energetic motions associated with the Loop Current, Loop Current Eddies, and other smaller and weaker anticyclonic and cyclonic features usually dominate the surface circulation of the deep Gulf of Mexico. Except for the occasional hurricane, wind driving is usually weaker than the mesoscale eddy forcing. Tidal forcing is dominated by the M2, K1 and O1 tidal constituents and is also weak (2-3 cm/s in the deep Gulf). Freshwater forcing is also weak except in the coastal currents of the continental shelf.

Sea surface height (SSH) estimates from altimeter data (courtesy of R. Leben, CCAR) reveal that the summers of 2002 and 2003 were typical in terms of the physical features of the circulation of the northern Gulf of Mexico.

During the summer of 2002, the Loop Current was south of the northern slopes of the Gulf of Mexico and not directly influence the circulation there. Several small-scale (50 km) circulation features were present on the northern Gulf slopes. The cruise track roughly followed the 1000-m isobath. Currents along the 1000-m isobath generally followed contours of SSH height indicating mostly geostrophic flow. However, there were departures from this. This can be expected as SSH imagery is based on a 10-day blend of altimeter data. Therefore, the movement of circulation features during this period and features smaller than about 30 km are generally not reflected well in the altimeter data but can often be seen in the ADCP data.

The mean vertical profile of current speed during the summer 2002 S-tag cruise shows speed decreasing with depth from about 30 cm/s at the surface to about 10 cm/s at 200 m. The standard deviation of current shows a similar pattern with slightly less amplitudes of 25 cm/s to 10 cm/s. The maximum speed profile during the cruise also decreased with depth from 70 cm/s at the surface to 40 cm/s at 200 m. Current speeds seen during the September 2002, D-tag cruise were less than during the June cruise. Mean speeds ranged from 20 cm/s at the surface to 10 cm/s at 200 m; maximum speeds ranged from 60 cm/s to 30 cm/s.

A newly detached Loop Current Eddy, Eddy Sargassum, dominated the circulation of the northern Gulf of Mexico during the summer of 2003. The center of this eddy was roughly located at 27°N, 87°W on 11 June 2003 (Figure 4.6.1). Currents were generally quiescent in the western regions of the cruise track, i.e., west of 91°W. However, east of 91°W the currents were intense on the outer northern limb of the Eddy. Mean currents exceeded 40 cm/s near surface and decreased to less than 5 cm/s at 800 m. Current standard deviation. Maximum currents exceeded 120 cm/s near surface and near the Eddy and decreased to 50 cm/s at about 300 m and 30 cm/s at 800 m.

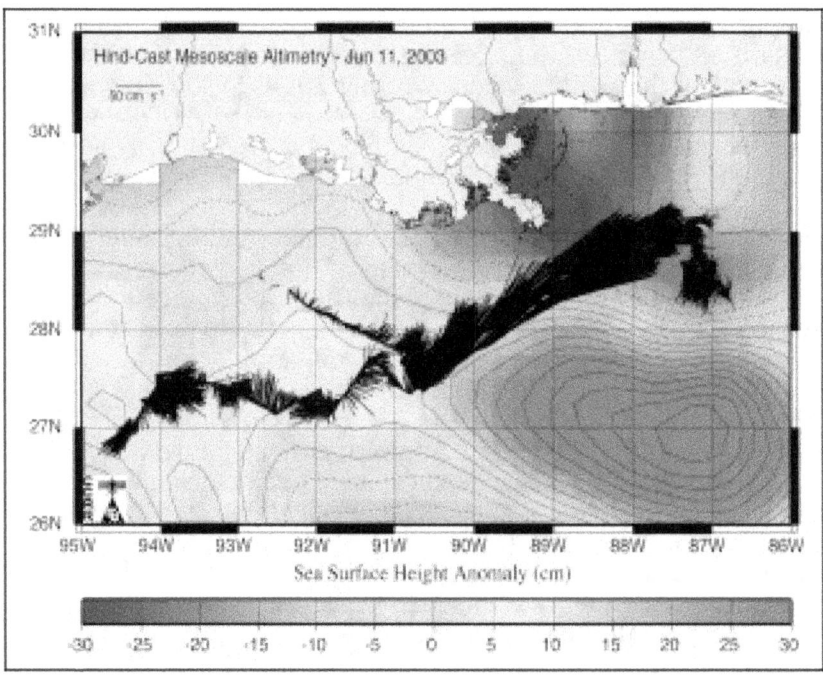

Figure 4.7.1. Sea surface height anomaly field for 11 June 2003 with currents at 41 m from the 38-kHz ADCP superimposed. Loop Current Eddy Sargassum (red) generated large surface currents (> 50 cm s^{-1}) and dominated the circulation of the northern Gulf of Mexico during the summer of 2003.

132

4.8   Habitat Characterization: Midwater Trawling Program

Dr. John Wormuth

Department of Oceanography, Texas A&M University, College Station, TX 77843-3146

The objectives of the midwater trawling were to sample the potential prey fields at depths where sperm whales are known to feed and to sample areas where whales are actively feeding as well as areas where they are not observed to be feeding. In order to achieve these objectives, we used a 14.8 m^2 Isaacs-Kidd midwater trawl with an inner liner mesh of 4 mm terminating in a 0.333 mm mesh plankton net. The fishing intervals chosen were 0-400 m, 400-600 m and 600-800 m. The two deeper intervals were selected to partition the feeding depths of whales recorded in the previous field year. The 0-400 m interval was chosen to look at those components the trawl would sample on its way down to the deeper intervals. Depth and temperature were recorded with a Sea Bird TDR Model 39. Volume filtered was measured with a General Oceanics flow meter.

Tows were taken at night following the day's completion of over-the-side operations. This limited our ability to sample in "non-whale" areas, but reduced time lost to reacquiring whales prior to dawn. A total of 24 successful trawls were completed in cyclonic, anticyclonic, and other regions. Samples were sorted into fish, crustaceans and cephalopods. Displacement volumes were measured for each component. Temperature profiles for each of the three categories were plotted and showed remarkable uniformity with each category.

The first hypothesis tested, using an ANOVA was: there is no difference in component displacement volumes for tows to different maximum depths. The only statistically significant results showed that fish biomass in the 0-400 m tows was greater than for tows from 400-600 m and for tows from 600-800 m.

The second hypothesis tested, using a significance test of correlation coefficients was: there is no difference in displacement volumes in different environments. Table 4.8.1 shows the results of these comparisons. Fish and crustaceans displacement volumes showed the highest significant positive correlation coefficient.

A predictable relationship was established between meters of wire out and depth of the trawl (Fig. 4.8.1). This allowed us to reliably fish in the targeted depth intervals and minimize the volume filtered in the non-targeted intervals by paying out wire quickly going through layers not of interest and slowing wire speed in layers of interest. We were able to average 50% of the total volume filtered in the targeted layer (Fig. 4.8.2).

The largest squid collected was a *Histioteuthis arcturi* of 30 cm total length (7.8 cm mantle length) that was caught in Trawl #5 in the westernmost series of trawls fished mostly in the 600-800 m interval. This family of squid is often found in the stomachs of sperm whales and can grow to mantle lengths of 20 cm or more. The most common family in the trawl collections was Enoploteuthidae. These species do not grow large enough to be in the diet of sperm whales. No identifiable giant squid (*Architeuthidae*) juveniles were collected. The squid eggs dip netted are presently being examined at the Smithsonian for comparison to other collections.

Dominant fish groups collected are: Gonostomidae, Stomiatidae (the bristlemouth Cyclothone); Sternoptychidae (hatchet fishes), and Myctophidae (lantern fishes). At present, the cephalopods and hatched fishes have all been identified to the lowest possible taxonomic level. Unidentified specimens are juveniles. The myctophids are presently being worked up as are the crustaceans. Dominant crustaceans to date are: Penaeidae (*Sergestes* and *Gennadas*), Euphausiidae (*Euphausia, Nematobrachion* and *Thysanopoda*), and Caridea (*Systellaspsis* and *Acanthephyra*).

Table 4.8.1

Results of Z Tests of All Combinations of Displacement Volumes (DV) for All Trawls

	Correlation coefficient	Degree of freedom	Z-Value	Probability level (p)
FISH DV, CRUSTACEA DV	0.69	23	3.81	0.0001***
FISH DV, SQUID DV	0.21	23	0.95	0.341
FISH DV, > 2MM DV	0.48	23	2.27	0.023*
FISH DV, < 2MM DV	0.44	23	2.08	0.038*
CRUSTACEA DV, SQUID DV	0.14	23	0.61	0.542
CRUSTACEA DV, > 2MM DV	0.29	23	1.25	0.211
CRUSTACEA DV, < 2MM DV	0.12	23	0.52	0.602
SQUID DV, > 2MM DV	0.45	23	2.08	0.038*
SQUID DV, < 2MM DV	0.09	23	-0.38	0.702
> 2MM DV, < 2MM DV	0.57	23	2.84	0.005**

* $p < 0.05$
** $p < 0.01$
*** $p < 0.001$

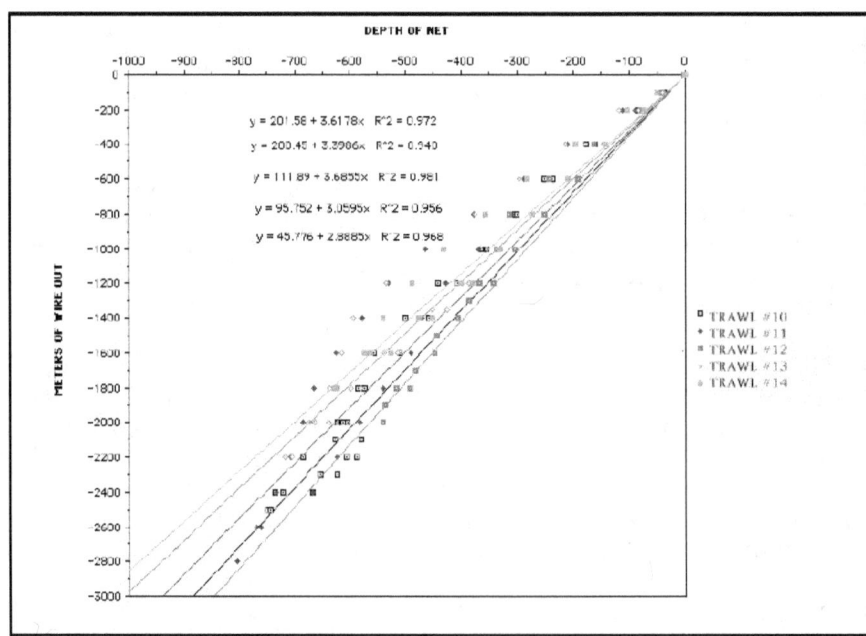

Figure 4.8.1. The relationship between meters of wire out and depth of the trawl for five tows representing different wind and current conditions.

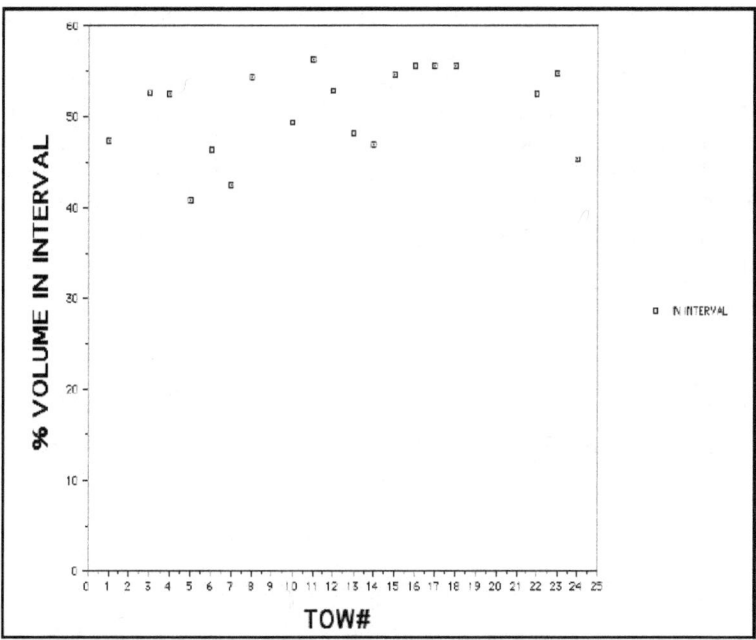

Figure 4.8.2.   The volume filtered in the targeted depth interval as a percentage of the total volume filtered for each trawl.

4.9   Habitat Characterization: 38-kHz ADCP Investigation of Deep Scattering Layers

Amanda M. Olson[1], D. C. Biggs[1], and S. F. DiMarco[1]

[1]Department of Oceanography, Texas A&M University, College Station, TX 77843-3146

A hull-mounted 38-kHz phased-array ADCP was used to acoustically survey the continental margin of the northern Gulf of Mexico during four SWSS cruises and two cruises of the MMS-supported Deep Gulf of Mexico Benthic study (DGoMB) in 2002-2003. ADCPs have been used since the 1980's to measure the acoustic volume backscatter return from plankton in the water column as a proxy for the standing stock of zooplankton and small-size micronekton, but in practice these previous studies have generally been limited to the upper 200 meters due to the relatively high frequency of operation (150-300 kHz). Although raw data from the 38-kHz ADCP have not been corrected for signal losses from spherical spreading, the backscatter data from this phased-array ADCP provides relative backscatter counts that are nonetheless useful metrics to compare biological scattering layers. The daytime depth of the main deep scattering layer (DSL) at 400 to 500 meters was resolved, and locally high backscatter intensity can be seen down to 800 meters. Vertical migration rates between 2-12 cm/sec were calculated. Our main objective was to image scattering layers of prey species below the main deep scattering layer from 600 to 800 meters below the surface where, from the D-tag data shared by our colleagues from Woods Hole Oceanographic Institution, we knew that Gulf of Mexico sperm whales were diving during nighttime as well as daytime.

When relative backscatter from the mid-slope region of the northern Gulf of Mexico was compared to the backscatter from the deep basin, we noticed more frequent and more intense patches and layers of deep scattering below the main DSL from 500 to 800 meters over the mid-

135

slope (Figure 4.9.1). Patches and scattering layers below the main DSL were very infrequent in the deep basin (Table 4.9.1). Although some vertically migrating animals descend down to 800 meters during the daytime, these patches appear to be independent of the vertical migrating layer since they are present both daytime and nighttime and give a much higher intensity signal. From the acoustic return alone, we are not able to tell what species are represented by these patches, however we know that at 38-kHz the ADCP receives signal from scatterers from about 1 cm up to 10 cm. So based on their size, these organisms are likely small fish and squid and their prey. Because deep scattering was common over the slope and almost never observed in the deep basin, these patches may represent important sperm whale prey species and could be correlated with the location of sperm whales.

Table 4.9.1

Occurrence of Scattering Below the Main DSL (> 650 m) Out of the Number of Possible Days in Water Less Than or Greater Than 1000 Meters for Each Cruise While Over the Slope and Deep Basin

Cruise Name	Occurrences in < 1000 Meters (800-1000)	Occurrences in > 1000 Meters
SWSS 2002 S-tag	5/9	0/1
DGoMB August 2002	0/0	1/5
SWSS 2003 WSHC	9/15	1/2
SWSS 2003 S-tag	7/10	0/3
TOTAL	**21/34**	**2/11**

Eddy circulation features can have a large impact on the biology as well as the physics in the Gulf of Mexico. Cold-core, cyclonic eddies are associated with nutrient enrichment and increased biological productivity. Whales and other predators are attracted especially to the boundaries of these eddies where prey are accumulated (Griffin 1999; Biggs et al. 2000).

During the SWSS 2003 WSHC cruise in May/June 2003, the ship track went from the western Gulf of Mexico toward the east. At the time of the cruise, the western region had no strong eddy features, but there was a large anticyclonic eddy in close proximity to a strong cyclonic eddy in the eastern region. The ADCP backscatter signal showed differences between the eastern and western regions. The backscatter signal at 100 meters had a higher nighttime average in the eastern region with eddies (days 9-20) than that in the western region without eddies (days 1-8). Daytime backscatter, represented as the lowest daily signal when migratory animals are in the DSL, was greatest on days 8-10 of the cruise (Figure 4.9.2).

Scattering layers below the main DSL were observed about 1/4 of the time in the anticyclone region and about 1/2 of the time in all other regions including that of the cyclonic eddy, the confluence region between the two eddies, and in the western region with no eddies (Table 4.9.2). Eddy features seemed to have an influence on the main DSL and also on deeper scattering layers. However, the strongest hydrographic influences on scattering layers were observed as the

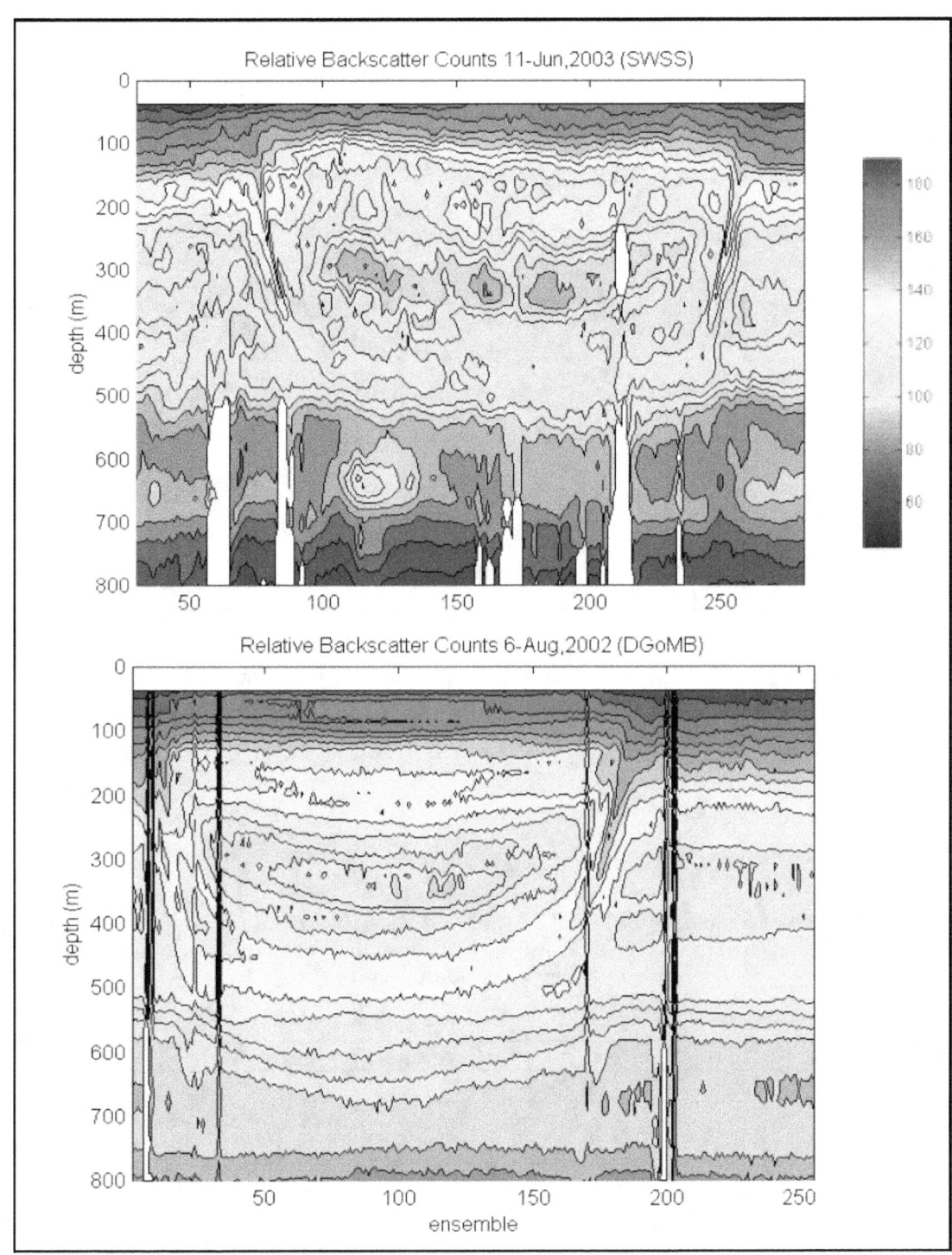

Figure 4.9.1. Relative backscatter counts shown for Gulf of Mexico slope region (top) and for the deep basin region (bottom). The horizontal axis represents time, where each ensemble is a 5 minute average.

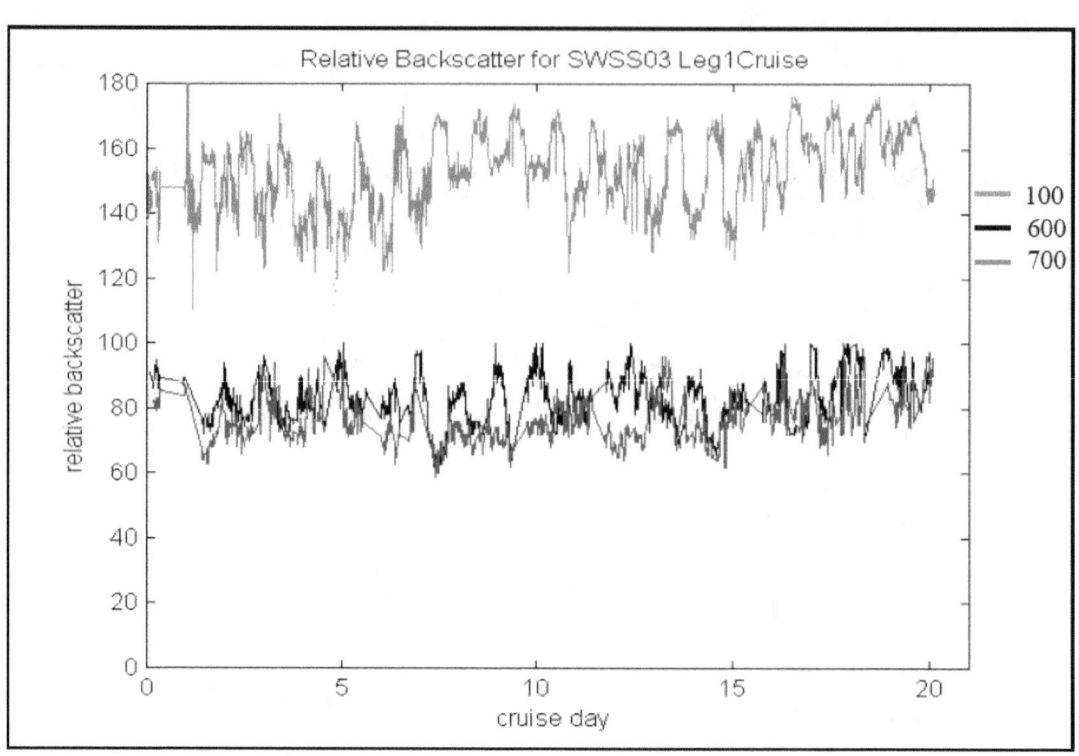

Figure 4.9.2. Relative backscatter counts recorded by the 38-kHz ADCP for the 100, 600, and 700 m depth bins for the SWSS 2003 WSHC cruise.

Table 4.9.2

Occurrence of Scattering Below the Main DSL (> 650 m) Out of the Number of Possible Days When in Cyclonic, Anticyclonic, Boundary, or No Feature in the Four Hydrographic Regions

Cruise	Cyclone	Anticyclone	Confluence	Other
SWSS 2002 S-tag	0/1	0/1		3/8
SWSS 2003 WSHC	2/2	1/3	1/1	4/5
SWSS 2003 S-tag	0/3		2/7	0/3
TOTAL	**2/6**	**1/4**	**3/8**	**7/16**

ship crossed the Mississippi River plume on 12 June 2003. There was a sudden change from the blue water of the anticyclone to surface green water entrapped on top of the cyclone. Moving into this surface green water coincided with the daytime DSL shoaling to about 250 meters, or more than 200 meters more shallow than its daytime depth of 450 to 500 meters in the adjacent blue water. The shoaling to 250 m presumably was caused by increased extinction of light penetration to deeper waters, caused by an increase in phytoplankton and sediment loads in the surface green water. At 250 meters in the river plume, the vertically migrating organisms were at a daytime light levels comparable to 500 meters in the blue water. This light level effect might also be an explanation for why we see relatively lower backscatter at deeper depth bins when there is high intensity at shallower bins. The rapid extinction of downwelling irradiance by phytoplankton and other small particles in the low salinity, green surface water apparently causes the deep living organisms to prefer shallower depths.

5 LITERATURE CITED

Arnbom, T. 1987. Individual identification of sperm whales. Reports of the International Whaling Commission 37: 201-204.

Biggs, D.C., and P.H. Ressler. 2001. Distribution and abundance of phytoplankton, zooplankton, ichthyoplankton, and micronekton in the deepwater Gulf of Mexico. Gulf of Mexico Science 19: 7-35.

Biggs, D.C., R.R. Leben, and J.G. Ortega-Ortiz. 2000. Ship and satellite studies of mesoscale circulation and sperm whale habitats in the northeast Gulf of Mexico during GulfCetII. Gulf of Mexico Science 18: 15-22.

Caldwell, K.D., Caldwell M.C., and D.W. Rice. 1966. Behavior of the sperm whale, *Physeter catodon*. In: Norris, K.S. ed. Whales, dolphins and porpoises. University of California Press, Berkeley. Pp. 677-717.

Christal, J., H. Whitehead, and E. Lettevall. 1998. Sperm whale social units: variation and change. Canadian Journal of Zoology 76: 1431-1440.

Clarke, R., O. Paliza, and L. Aguayo. 1980. Some parameters and an estimate of the exploited stock of sperm whales in the southeast Pacific between 1959 and 1961. Reports of the International Whaling Commission 30: 289-305.

Clarke, M.R. 1985. Cephalopod biomass-estimation from predation. In: Boyle, P.R., ed., Cephalopod life cycles. Academic Press, New York, NY. Pp. 221-237.

Davis, R.W., W.E. Evans, and B. Würsig. 2000. Cetaceans, sea turtles and seabirds in the northern Gulf of Mexico: distribution, abundance and habitat associations. U.S. Dept. of the Interior, Minerals Management Service, New Orleans, LA. OCS Study MMS 2000-003.

Dawson, S.M., C.J. Chessum, P.J. Hunt, and E. Slooten. 1995. An inexpensive, stereophotographic technique to measure sperm whales from small boats. Reports of the International Whaling Commission 45: 431-436.

Donovan, G.P. 1991. A review of IWC stock boundaries. Reports of the International Whaling Commission, Special Issue 13: 39-68.

Dufault, S. and H. Whitehead. 1998. Regional and group-level differences in fluke markings and notches of sperm whales. Journal of Mammalogy 79: 514-520.

Dufault, S., H. Whitehead, and M. Dillon. 1999. An examination of the current knowledge on the stock structure of sperm whales (*Physeter macrocephalus*) worldwide. Journal of Cetacean Research and Management 1: 1-10.

Gillespie, D. and R. Leaper. 1996. Detection of sperm whale (*Physeter macrocephalus*) clicks, and discrimination of individual vocalisations. In: Evans, P.G.H., ed., European Research on Cetaceans, Lisbon. Pp. 87-89.

Gordon, J.C. 1987. The behaviour and ecology of sperm whales off Sri Lanka. Doctor of Philosophy Thesis. Darwin College, Cambridge, MA.

Gordon, J.C.D. 1990. A simple photographic technique for measuring the length of whales from boats at sea. Reports of the International Whaling Commission 40: 581-588.

Gordon, J.C.D. 1991. Evaluation of a method for determining the length of sperm whales (*Physeter catodon*) from their vocalizations. Journal of Zoology 224: 301-314.

Griffin, R.B. 1999. Sperm whale distributions and community ecology associated with a warm-core ring off Georges Bank. Marine Mammal Science 15: 33-51.

Jaquet, N., and H. Whitehead. 1999. Movements, distribution and feeding success of sperm whales in the Pacific Ocean, over scales of days and tens of kilometers. Aquatic Mammals 25: 1-13.

Jaquet, N., D. Gendron, and A. Coakes. 2003. Sperm whales in the Gulf of California: residency, movements, behavior, and the possible influence of variation in food supply. Marine Mammal Science 19: 545-562.

Jaquet, N., and J.C.D. Gordon. 2003. Size differences between two populations of sperm whales: Application of a simple technique to measure sperm whales at sea. Abstract of the 15th Biennial Conference on the Biology of Marine Mammals, Greensborough, NC, December 2003.

Jochens, A.E., and W.D. Nowlin, Jr., eds. 1999. Northeastern Gulf of Mexico Chemical Oceanography and Hydrography Study: Year 2 - Annual Report. U.S. Dept. of the Interior, Minerals Management Service, Gulf of Mexico OCS Region, New Orleans, LA. OCS Study MMS 99-0054. 123 pp.

Jochens, A.E., and D.C. Biggs, eds. 2003. Sperm whale seismic study in the Gulf of Mexico; Annual Report: Year 1. U.S. Dept. of the Interior, Minerals Management Service, Gulf of Mexico OCS Region, New Orleans, LA. OCS Study MMS 2003-069. 139 pp.

Kahn, B., H.Whitehead, and M. Dillon. 1993. Indications of density dependent effects from comparisons of sperm whale populations. Marine Ecology Progress Series 93: 1-7.

Kawakami, T. 1980. A review of sperm whale food. Scientific Reports of the Whales Research Institute 32: 199-218.

Lyrholm T., and U. Gyllensten. 1998. Global matrilineal population structure in sperm whales as indicated by mitochondrial DNA sequences. Proceedings of the Royal Society of London Series B: Biological Sciences 265: 1679-1684.

Lyrholm, T., O. Leimar, B. Johanneson, and U. Gyllensten. 1999. Sex-biased dispersal in sperm whales: contrasting mitochondrial and nuclear genetic structure of global populations. The Royal Society of London Series B: Biological Sciences 266(1417): 347-354.

Murphy, D.J., D.C. Biggs, and M.L. Cooke. 1992. Mounting and calibrating an Acoustic Doppler Current Profiler. Marine Technology Society Journal 26(3): 34-38.

Norris, K.S., and G.W. Harvey. 1972. A theory for the function of the spermaceti organ of the sperm whale (*Physeter catodon*). In: Galler, S.R., K. Schmidt-Koenig, G.J. Jacobs, and R.E. Belleville eds., Animal Orientation and Navigation. NASA Special Publication. Pp. 397-417.

Nowlin, W.D., Jr., A.E. Jochens, S.F. DiMarco, R.O. Reid, and M.K. Howard. 2001. Deepwater physical oceanography reanalysis and synthesis of historical data: synthesis report. U.S. Dept. of the Interior, Minerals Management Service, Gulf of Mexico OCS Region, New Orleans, LA. OCS Study MMS 2001-064. 528 pp.

Pavan, G., C. Fossati, M. Manghi, and M. Priano. 1998. Acoustic measure of body growth in a photo-identified sperm whale. The World Marine Mammals Science Conference, Monaco. 105 pp.

Rendell, L., and H. Whitehead. 2003. Vocal clans in sperm whales (*Physeter macrocephalus*). Proceedings of the Royal Society of London Series B: Biological Sciences 270: 225-231.

Rice, D.W. 1989. Sperm whales (*Physeter macrocephalus*). In: Ridgway, S.H., and R. Harrison eds., Handbook of Marine Mammals, Academic Press, London. Pp. 177-123.

142

Thomas, L., J.L. Laake, J.F. Derry, S.T. Buckland, D.L. Borchers, D.R. Anderson, K.P. Burnham, S. Strindberg, S.L. Hedley, M.L. Burt, F.F.C. Marques, J.H. Pollard, and R.M. Fewster. 1998. Distance 3.5. Release 6. Research Unit for Wildlife Population Assessment, University of St. Andrews, UK. Available: http://www.ruwpa.st-and.ac.uk/distance/

Thompson, P.M., B. Wilson, K. Grellier, and P.S. Hammond. 2000. Combining power analysis and population viability analysis to compare traditional and precautionary approaches to the conservation of coastal cetaceans. Conservation Biology 14: 1253-1263.

Waters, S., and H. Whitehead. 1990. Population and growth parameters of Galápagos sperm whales estimated from length distributions. Reports of the International Whaling Commission 40: 225-235.

Whitehead, H., and T. Arnbom. 1987. Social organization of sperm whales off the Galápagos Islands, February-April 1985. Canadian Journal of Zoology 65: 913-919.

Whitehead, H. 1989. Formations of foraging sperm whales, *Physeter macrocephalus*, off the Galápagos Islands. Canadian Journal of Zoology 67: 2131-2139.

Whitehead, H. 1990. Mark-recapture estimates with emmigration and re-immigration. Biometrics 46: 473-479.

Whitehead, H., S. Waters, and T. Lyrholm. 1991. Social organization of female sperm whales and their offspring: constant companions and casual acquaintances. Behavioral Ecology and Sociobiology 29: 385-389.

Whitehead, H. 1996. Variation in the feeding success of sperm whales: temporal scale, spatial scale and relationship to migrations. Journal of Animal Ecology 65: 429-438.

Whitehead, H. 1998. Cultural selection and genetic diversity in matrilineal whales. Science 282: 1708-1711.

Whitehead, H., M.C. Dillon, S. Dufault, L. Weilgart, and J. Wright. 1998. Non-geographically based population structure of South Pacific sperm whales: dialects, fluke-markings and genetics. Journal of Animal Ecology 67: 253-262.

Whitehead, H. 1999. Variation in the visually observable behavior of groups of Galápagos sperm whales. Marine Mammal Science 15: 1181-1197.

Whitehead, H. 2003. Sperm whales: social evolution in the ocean. The University of Chicago Press, Chicago, IL.

Wiseman, W.J., Jr., and W. Sturges. 1999. Physical oceanography of the Gulf of Mexico: Processes that regulate its biology. In: Kumpf, H., K. Steidinger, and K. Sherman, eds. The Gulf of Mexico Large Marine Ecosystem. Blackwell Science, Inc., Malden, MA. Pp. 77-92.

Würsig, B., T.A. Jefferson, and D.J. Schmidly. 2000. The marine mammals of the Gulf of Mexico. Texas A&M University Press, College Station, TX.

APPENDIX: D-tag/CEE Mitigation Protocol

On 3 June 2003, NOAA Fisheries issued permit #981-1707 to Dr. Peter Tyack of Woods Hole Oceanographic Institution. This permit authorized the controlled exposure experiments that would be conducted on the D-tag/CEE cruise, as well as the tagging activities themselves. To assure compliance with the permit requirements, Dr. Tyack and his science team developed a protocol for mitigation and monitoring during the seismic playbacks that were to be conducted as part of the D-tag/CEE cruise. On 4 June 2003 prior to the departure of the cruise, this protocol was sent to the scientists who would be in charge of science operations on board both the participating vessels, R/V *Maurice Ewing* and M/V *Kondor Explorer*. The protocol is given below in its entirety.

Protocol for mitigation and monitoring during seismic playbacks on board the MV Kondor during the DTAG-SW03 WHOI experiment in the Gulf of Mexico

Peter Tyack, PI, Permit Holder
Douglas Nowacek, Mitigation Coordinator, Co-investigator

SAFETY RADIUS

The aim of this protocol is to minimize the possibility that any marine mammal or sea turtle will be exposed to received sound levels exceeding 180 dB re 1 μPa rms during the emission of seismic pulses for playback experiments in the Gulf of Mexico. This 180 dB criterion is consistent with guidelines listed for cetaceans by NMFS (2000) and the specifications issued by NMFS for the Tyack permit 981-1707-00. A safety radius will be conservatively defined for the space around an active seismic source that takes into account the possible variability and complexities in sound transmission caused by refraction, bottom echoes, etc. The area within this radius should be clear of all cetaceans and sea turtles. Different configurations of seismic arrays during ramp-up and variation in oceanographic conditions will lead to different radii for the 180 dB zone. The 180 dB zone is estimated to be about 950 m for the full array to be used. This zone will be fine tuned on the basis of the calibrations made during the engineering test to be conducted well away from cetacean concentrations before the first playback experiment. In order to maintain a conservative safety radius in the face of uncertainty and variability of the sound field, the safety radius will be maintained at 1.5 times the expected 180 dB radius. Therefore, for the full array, the safety radius will be 1.5 x 950 = 1425 m. We are primarily sighting animals at the surface, and sound energy is directed downwards, so think of this safety radius as a cylinder with a top circle radius of the safety radius centered on the airgun array, and with the cylinder extending down to the seafloor directly below the ship.

PROCEDURE

Engineering Test:
The engineering test will require the Kondor as the source vessel (SV) and the Ewing for making calibrated acoustic measurements. Both ships should rendezvous at a site decided based upon the preliminary mitigation procedure below. The engineering test should follow these protocols:

Preliminary mitigation: avoid areas where beaked whales or *Kogia* have been sighted

The preliminary mitigation procedure involves selecting a site for calibration in an area with low numbers of cetaceans expected based upon historical sighintgs, and that is far from historical sightings of beaked whales and *Kogia*. These species are difficult to sight; their vocalizations are difficult to detect and identify, and their sensitivity to sound is particularly poorly understood.

145

This calibration site should be selected using the GIS plots created by Valeria Teloni using sightings data collated by Joel Ortega, and measuring distances from possible calibration sites to the nearest sighting of these species in the database. Ewing and SV should consult together on choice of site based upon the sighting data and operational logistics.

Phase I: one hour prior to the ramp-up.
The engineering test should only take place in daylight with good sighting conditions. Acoustic and visual monitoring for turtles and cetaceans will start as soon as the SV gets within an hour of the suggested start position, in order to ensure that the startup location is free of whales, and that the monitoring teams are operating smoothly by the time of transmission. It may be useful to run a track around the planned location for onset of sound transmissions, to help ensure that the area is clear of marine mammals and sea turtles. However, the ship track must be compatible with operational requirements of preparation of the sound sources.

There will be three or more visual observers scanning with naked eye and Fujinon 7x50 reticle binoculars at all times from one hour before until one hour after sound transmissions. If there is any concern about observer fatigue, and if there are not enough skilled observers to alternate two teams, there should be a temporary pause in transmissions until the observers are back to par. The observers will work from a high vantage point. At least one observer must have a clear view aft towards the airgun array, and one must have a clear view forward. Together, the observers must be able to cover 360 degrees around the ship. Sighting conditions must be appropriate for sighting out to the safety radius. The initial safety radius will be taken to be 1425m, centered on the airgun array. This should be conservative, since it is taken from a 20 gun array that has a larger total displacement than the Kondor array. The mitigation coordinator (MC) will confirm this with the airgun operators and with acoustic modelers on board the OV prior to the engineering test. No sound transmissions should take place if the observers do not believe the sighting conditions are appropriate.

At least one additional person will monitor underwater sound from a towed array of hydrophones at all times from one hour before until one hour after sound transmissions. This acoustic monitor will also visually monitor spectrograms and waveforms of these signals. A continuous recording will be made of this acoustic record at all times from one hour before until one hour after sound transmissions. The visual and acoustic monitoring teams will be in constant contact with the MC, who will be informed of all turtle and cetacean detections in real time, with data on range and bearing to the animals when available. The MC can also play the role of observer or monitor at the same time.

The position of the animals will be logged in order to minimize the chances that the ramp-up or subsequent transmissions will occur in areas with marine mammals close enough to trigger mitigation. If any cetacean or turtle is detected, the MC will work out any changes needed in the planned location of the SV for startup. Acoustic and visual monitoring for cetaceans will continue and ramp-up will not start until after an hour of visual and acoustic monitoring around the SV. Because of the potential sensitivity of beaked whales or *Kogia*, if any of these species are detected during that time, even outside of the security radius, the SV will relocate at least 30 km to find a new area for the calibrations well away from these species.

Phase II: Ramp-up to full array.

The safety radius for sound transmission will be set by the configuration of airguns firing, adjusted by modeling of propagation based upon the conditions for each playback. Once the engineering test is completed, these calibrated measurements will be used to fine-tune the 180 dB radius and safety zone for each phase of ramp-up and for the full array.

146

Detections of beaked whales or *Kogia* sp.

The seismic transmissions will be stopped if any beaked whales or *Kogia* are detected by visual or acoustic methods <u>at any distance</u> during sound transmission. If there is a positive detection of one of these species, the playback experiment will be halted. A new playback will not be started until the Ewing has moved at least 30 km from the location of the sighting.

Detections of sea turtles, baleen whales, sperm whales or delphinids.

Course alteration
If a marine mammal or sea turtle is detected outside the safety radius and, based on its position and the relative motion, is likely to enter the safety radius, alternative ship tracks will be plotted against anticipated mammal or turtle locations. If practical, the vessel's course and/or speed will be changed in a manner that avoids the marine mammal or sea turtle approaching within the safety radius while also minimizing the effect to the planned science objectives. The marine mammal activities and movements relative to the seismic vessel will be closely monitored to ensure that the marine mammal does not approach within the safety radius. If the mammal or sea turtle appears likely to enter the safety radius, further mitigative actions will be taken, i.e., either further course alterations or shutdown of the airguns. If the monitors lose track of a mammal or sea turtle that might, because of its position and swim direction, have come near the safety radius, the MC will follow conservative procedures to ensure that the animal would not be exposed within this radius.

Shutdown procedures
Vessel-based observers using visual aids and acoustical arrays will monitor marine mammals and sea turtles near the seismic vessel for 60 min prior to start up, during all airgun operations, and for 60 min after cessation of airgun operations. No airguns will be operated during periods of darkness or in conditions where visual observers cannot effectively monitor out to the range of the safety radius. Visual observers will always keep a pair of Fujinon 7x50 reticle binoculars handy and will always know what reticle indicates the safety zone. The range of any sighting anywhere near the safety radius will immediately be checked using the reticles.

Airgun operations will be suspended immediately when marine mammals are observed or otherwise detected within, or about to enter, designated safety zones based on the 180 dB rms criterion specified by NMFS. The MC will also call for a shutdown if the monitors lose track of an animal that could come within the safety zone. The shutdown procedure should be accomplished within a "one shot" period of the determination that a marine mammal is within or about to enter the safety zone. This means that the observers and acoustic monitor must be in constant contact with the MC, who must also have the ability to immediately contact the airgun operators. The observers, monitors, MC and airgun operators should conduct dry run tests of the procedure to assure that it meets these demanding timing specifications. There should be fall-back communication methods available.

Airgun operations will not resume until the marine mammal(s) or sea turtle(s) is/are outside the safety radius. Once the safety zone is clear of marine mammals or sea turtles, the observers will advise that seismic surveys can re-commence. The restart decision will be made by the MC. If the source has shutdown, the following "ramp-up" procedure will be followed.

Ramp-up procedure
A "ramp-up" procedure will be followed when the airgun arrays begin operating after a specified-duration period without airgun operations. If the MC determines that conditions are appropriate for restarting transmissions within 5 minutes of the shutdown, the ramp-up will start at 6 dB lower source level than just before shutdown. If the "no shooting" period lasts more than 5 minutes , ramp-up will begin with the smallest gun in the array that is being used. Guns will be

added in a sequence such that the source level of the array will increase in steps not exceeding 6 dB per 5-minute period over a total duration of approximately 20-25 min (4-5 iterations for 9-16 gun arrays 1-2-4-8-16). MC will work out details of this ramp up plan, and will communicate them to Ewing and Tyack for evaluation one day before the engineering test. Engineering test should confirm that the planned order of addition of airguns leads to the planned increase in source level before the first CEE.

Phase III: Post exposure observations
Visual observers and acoustic monitors will make every effort to continue to monitor for marine mammals for one hour after exposure. These data will facilitate evaluation of potential responses to the sound transmissions, especially if the ship turns back to recover part of the area covered during sound transmission.

Protocol for Controlled Exposure Experiments to be conducted after a sperm whale is tagged.

Phase I: Between "tag on" and one hour prior to the ramp-up.

Radio contact will be kept between the observation vessel the R/V Ewing (OV), and the seismic source vessel the M/V Kondor (SV). The playback coordinator (PC) on the OV will communicate to the MC on the SV when the tag is on, and direct the vessel towards a suitable position at the required distance from the tagged animal. The goal for this advance location of the SV will be to position it so that the tagged whale(s) are likely to be the closest whales, at a distance so that the initial RL at the whale is below the goal maximum RL, which will be reached as the SV approaches the tagged whale(s). The PC and MC during this time should work out a plan for the SV to pass by the tagged whales being followed by the OV to a closest point of approach (CPA) specified by the goal maximum received level at the tagged whales.

Acoustic and visual monitoring for turtles and cetaceans will start as soon as the SV gets near the suggested start position, in order to find a "no whale" area for startup. There will be at least two visual observers scanning with naked eye and Fujinon 7x50 reticle binoculars at all times from phase 1 until one hour after sound transmissions. The observers will work from a high vantage point. At least one observer must have a clear view aft towards the airgun array, and the other must have a clear view forward. Together, they must be able to cover 360 degrees around the ship. **Sighting conditions must be appropriate for sighting out to the safety radius**. At least one person will monitor underwater sound from a towed array of hydrophones at all times from phase 1 until one hour after sound transmissions. The acoustic monitor will also visually monitor spectrograms and waveforms of these signals. A continuous recording will be made of this acoustic record at all times from phase 1 until one hour after sound transmissions. The visual and acoustic monitoring teams will be in radio contact with the MC, who will be informed of all turtles and cetacean detections in real time, with data on range and bearing to the animals when available. The MC can also play the role of observer or monitor at the same time.

If any cetacean or turtle is detected, the MC will communicate to the PC to work out any changes needed in the planned location of the SV for startup. This change will aim to both avoid proximity to any non-focal animals and to keep the required distance to the focal whales. The position of the animals will be logged in order to plan the starting of the ramp-up in areas with no detections.

Phase II: One hour prior to the ramp-up.

The MC will receive advance notice from the PC at least one hour before the playback is to commence. Acoustic and visual monitoring for cetaceans will continue and ramp-up will not

148

start until after an hour of visual and acoustic monitoring around the SV. It may be useful to run a track around the planned location for onset of sound transmissions, to help ensure that the area is clear of marine mammals and sea turtles. Because of the potential sensitivity of beaked whales or Kogia, if any of these species are detected during that time, even outside of the security radius, the SV will relocate at least 10 km to find a new area for CEE well away from these species. This distance differs from the Engineering Test in order to keep open the possibility for a large scale SV relocation that still allows for a CEE to a tagged whale. If there is any concern about exposure of *Kogia* or beaked whales, the OV will continue tracking the tagged whales, and use the follow as a control follow or coda playback. Avoiding by maneuver of the vessel should only occur with species at lower uncertainty about risk of impacts beyond level B harassment and which we can continue to track, species such as dolphins or baleen whales (visual) or sperm whales (acoustic).

Phase III: Ramp-up to full array playback.

The safety radius for sound transmission will be set by the configuration of airguns firing, adjusted by calibration tests and modeling of propagation based upon the conditions for each playback.

Detections of beaked whales or *Kogia* sp.

The seismic transmissions will be stopped if any of this species are detected by visual or acoustic methods at any distance. If there is a positive detection of one of these species, the playback experiment will be halted. A new playback will not be started until the SV has navigated at least 10 km from the location of the sighting.

Detections of sea turtles, baleen whales, sperm whales or delphinids.

Course alteration
If a marine mammal is detected outside the safety radius and, based on its position and the relative motion, is likely to enter the safety radius, alternative ship tracks will be plotted against anticipated mammal locations. If practical, the vessel's course and/or speed will be changed in a manner that avoids the marine mammal approaching within the safety radius while also minimizing the effect to the planned science objectives. The marine mammal activities and movements relative to the seismic vessel will be closely monitored to ensure that the marine mammal does not approach within the safety radius. If the mammal appears likely to enter the safey radius, further mitigative actions will be taken, i.e., either further course alterations or shutdown of the airguns.

Shutdown procedures
Vessel-based observers using visual aids and acoustical arrays will monitor marine mammals near the seismic vessel for 60 min prior to start up, during all airgun operations, and for 60 min after cessation of airgun operations. No airguns will be operated during periods of darkness or in conditions where visual observers cannot effectively monitor out to the range of the safety radius. Visual observers will always keep a pair of Fujinon 7x50 reticle binoculars and will always know what reticle indicates the safety zone. The range of any sighting anywhere near this radius will immediately be checked using the reticles. Airgun operations will be suspended immediately when marine mammals are observed or otherwise detected within, or about to enter, designated safety zones based on the 180 dB criterion specified by NMFS in its permit for scientific research issued to Tyack. If any marine mammal or sea turtle are sighted within the safety zone, detailed data must be collected about the incident and Tyack should be contacted as soon as possible, preferably immediately. The shutdown procedure should be accomplished within a "one shot" period of the determination that a marine mammal is within or about to enter

the safety zone. The observers and airgun operators should conduct dry run tests of the procedure to assure that it meets these demanding timing specifications.

Airgun operations will not resume until the marine mammal(s) is/are outside the safety radius. Once the safety zone is clear of marine mammals, the observers will advise that seismic surveys can re-commence. The restart decision will be made by the MC If the source has shutdown, the following "ramp-up" procedure will be followed.

Ramp-up procedure
A "ramp-up" procedure will be followed when the airgun arrays begin operating after a specified-duration period without airgun operations. If the MC determines that conditions are appropriate for restarting transmissions within 5 minutes of the shutdown, the ramp-up will start at 6 dB lower source level than just before shutdown. If the "no shooting" period lasts more than 5 minutes , ramp-up will begin with the smallest gun in the array that is being used. Guns will be added in a sequence such that the source level of the array will increase in steps not exceeding 6 dB per 5-minute period over a total duration of approximately 20-25 min (4-5 iterations for 9-16 gun arrays 1-2-4-8-16).

Improving estimates of range to acoustic detections of marine mammals:

Efforts will be made throughout the cruise to determine the detectable range of vocalizing marine mammals, to relate received levels on the Seamap array to visually-measured ranges, and to determine range to acoustic contacts using target-motion analysis. Because there will always be some uncertainty in the range to an acoustically-tracked animal, the MC will apply conservative estimates of range, and react appropriately (continue, avoid, or shut-down) as above.

Representative case scenarios for mitigation

       Note 1: all scenarios assume that if any animal is detected within the 180 dB range, shutdown will occur immediately
       Note 2: Scenarios assume seismic playback is already underway, see below for pre-exposure conditions

Delphinids, sperm and baleen whales, and sea turtles

1. Sightings or acoustic detections dead ahead
   a. If range can be determined
      i. If range is sufficient, use course correction to safely avoid safety zone.
      ii. If animals are being tracked, but there is temporary uncertainty as to range when movement of ship and/or animals would bring them within safety zone within 5-10 min, either shut down or maintain option to ramp down to half power if that is sufficient to resolve concerns about animals coming within safety zone.
   b. If range cannot be determined, probably because of acoustic detection (likely to be within 3 km or so)
      i. Assign additional visual observer to watch for surfacings
      ii. If no confirmation of range but bearing is still ahead after 5 min, change course if a new heading can be confidently chosen until range and bearing are determined
      iii. If still no confirmation of range but still ahead after 10 min, then full shut down until ship passes by animal to the point where the animal is certain to be outside of the safety radius.
2. Sightings or acoustic detections off forward quarters, i.e., 10 - 90^0 to port or starboard of bow

150

a. If animal(s)' direction of movement is parallel to ship, alter path if necessary to maintain exposure outside of safety zone, monitor location and continue experiment

b. If direction of movement is away from ship's path, monitor and continue

c. If direction of movement is directly towards or on an intersecting path, monitor and prepare for shutdown

    i. Alter ship track accordingly to avoid 180 dB exposure

    ii. If visual/acoustic contact is lost for ≥5 min, and observers believe animal was still on a course from a position where maneuvering is not enough to eliminate risk of animal coming within safety zone, shutdown until ship has moved outside of area of risk.

3. Sightings or acoustic detections off stern quarters or astern

    a. Monitor locations and continue experiment unless direction of animal(s) movement is towards the ship; if so, follow 2c.

4. For these species, all rampup to follow protocol above.

Beaked and Kogiid whales – if any confirmed detections, cease all seismic activity and move to a location ≥10 km away. If it is possible, attempt to restart experiment with pre-exposure protocol and full ramp-up. Otherwise conduct coda playback or control observations.

Pre-Exposure

    If any delphinids, sperm or baleen whales or sea turtles are detected during pre-exposure observations, i.e., the hour before ramp-up, alter ship's course to avoid their expected locations at time of ramp-up. No ramp-up will begin if any of these species are within the safety radius, set to 1.5 times the range for the 180 dB zone.

    If any beaked whales, or *Kogia* are sighted during the pre-exposure, travel ≥10 km before starting and adjust start time/location of CEE accordingly.

The Department of the Interior Mission

As the Nation's principal conservation agency, the Department of the Interior has responsibility for most of our nationally owned public lands and natural resources. This includes fostering sound use of our land and water resources; protecting our fish, wildlife, and biological diversity; preserving the environmental and cultural values of our national parks and historical places; and providing for the enjoyment of life through outdoor recreation. The Department assesses our energy and mineral resources and works to ensure that their development is in the best interests of all our people by encouraging stewardship and citizen participation in their care. The Department also has a major responsibility for American Indian reservation communities and for people who live in island territories under U.S. administration.

The Minerals Management Service Mission

As a bureau of the Department of the Interior, the Minerals Management Service's (MMS) primary responsibilities are to manage the mineral resources located on the Nation's Outer Continental Shelf (OCS), collect revenue from the Federal OCS and onshore Federal and Indian lands, and distribute those revenues.

Moreover, in working to meet its responsibilities, the **Offshore Minerals Management Program** administers the OCS competitive leasing program and oversees the safe and environmentally sound exploration and production of our Nation's offshore natural gas, oil and other mineral resources. The MMS **Minerals Revenue Management** meets its responsibilities by ensuring the efficient, timely and accurate collection and disbursement of revenue from mineral leasing and production due to Indian tribes and allottees, States and the U.S. Treasury.

The MMS strives to fulfill its responsibilities through the general guiding principles of: (1) being responsive to the public's concerns and interests by maintaining a dialogue with all potentially affected parties and (2) carrying out its programs with an emphasis on working to enhance the quality of life for all Americans by lending MMS assistance and expertise to economic development and environmental protection.